791.5309 HAY
Shadow woman : the
extraordinary career of
Pauline Benton
Hayter-Menzies, Grant, 1964
-, author.

D1601132

SHADOW WOMAN

GRANT HAYTER-MENZIES

SHADOW WOMAN

The Extraordinary Career
of Pauline Benton

McGill-Queen's University Press

Montreal & Kingston · London · Ithaca

© McGill-Queen's University Press 2013
ISBN 978-0-7735-4201-3 (cloth)
ISBN 978-0-7735-8909-4 (ePDF)
ISBN 978-0-7735-8910-0 (ePUB)

Legal deposit third quarter 2013
Bibliothèque nationale du Québec

Printed in Canada on acid-free paper that is 100% ancient forest
free (100% post-consumer recycled), processed chlorine free

McGill-Queen's University Press acknowledges the support of the
Canada Council for the Arts for our publishing program. We also
acknowledge the financial support of the Government of Canada
through the Canada Book Fund for our publishing activities.

Library and Archives Canada Cataloguing in Publication

Hayter-Menzies, Grant, 1964–, author
Shadow woman : the extraordinary career of Pauline Benton
/ Grant Hayter-Menzies.

Includes bibliographical references and index.
Issued in print and electronic formats.
ISBN 978-0-7735-4201-3 (bound).
ISBN 978-0-7735-8909-4 (ePDF).
ISBN 978-0-7735-8910-0 (ePUB)

1. Benton, Pauline. 2. Puppeteers – United States – Biography.
3. Performance artists – United States – Biography. 4. Shadow
shows – United States – History–20th century. 5. Puppet theater –
United States – History – 20th century. 6. Shadow puppets –
United States – History – 20th century. 7. Performance art – United
States – History – 20th century. I. Title.

PN1982.B45H39 2013   791.5'3092   C2013-903276-2
C2013-903277-0

This book was designed and typeset by studio oneonone

When you go to a Chinese theatre, approach it
as you would the Edge of the World. Let the scales
fall from your eyes and you will behold a Wonderland.
The Hosts of Heaven will ride upon the wind.
Emperors pavilioned in splendor will sit before you.
Glittering barbarians will flash past in a glowing
pageant. As in Homeric days gods and men will
fight together. The sea will reveal its depths, and
you will glimpse the marvels of the Western Heaven.
  B.S. Allen, *Chinese Theatres Handbook*

Those who love the Shadows, it seems,
love also the glorious past.
  Li Tuochen

To
Wan-go Weng
and
Stephen Kaplin and Kuang-Yu Fong
with gratitude

To
Les and Freddie
with love

To the memory of
Cui Yongping

CONTENTS

ILLUSTRATIONS

PREFACE BY JIANG YUXIANG

The name Pauline Benton is by no means strange to me. I first came to know about Miss Benton from Jo Humphrey's book, *Monkey King: A Celestial Heritage* (New York, 1980). Based on material from Jo's book, I wrote an introduction entitled "Pauline Benton and the Red Gate Shadow Players," which was included in my book *Chinese Shadow Theatre and Folklore* (Taipei, 1999) under the chapter "Chinese Shadow Theatre Going Global."

Dr Berthold Laufer, the famous German American orientalist, was the first man to bring Chinese shadow puppets to the United States. Equally important, Pauline Benton was the first person to plant the seeds of Chinese shadow skills in America. During her lifetime, Miss Benton devoted more than fifty years to researching and spreading Chinese shadow theatre. Pauline and her Red Gate Shadow Players gave touring shows for many years, making it possible for the American people to enjoy such a wonderful Chinese art. After she retired, she spent most of her time training apprentices while also giving performances of traditional Chinese tales using those traditional shadow puppets. Miss Benton was undoubtedly a pioneering envoy for grassroots cultural exchanges between Chinese and Americans.

Culture is created within national boundaries, but it can be spread beyond national borders. Chinese shadow theatre is not only a valued intangible cultural heritage of the Chinese people, but it is commonly shared and appreciated around the globe. We are living at a time when traditional Chinese shadow theatre is on the verge of being devoured by surging waves of modernization. Presently, both the United Nations and the Chinese government have called for the rescue and preservation of intangible cultural heritage, including Chinese shadow theatre.

We spare no effort to devote ourselves to this demanding preservation work. It is right in these days that we remember more than ever those researchers and artists who have made great contributions to shadow theatre, both in China and America.

Pauline Benton is an outstanding representative of them.

Prof. Jiang Yuxiang (江玉祥)
Sichuan University
President, Folklore Society of Sichuan Province
21 February 2012
Translated by Wang Qing (王清)

FOREWORD

It is unlikely that a tourist walking into the Carmel Mineral Art Shop in early 1960s Carmel-by-the-Sea, California, would have noticed anything special about the older lady who sat at the counter, an array of sparkling amethyst, calcite, quartz, and fools' gold on shelves behind her.

She was short, stocky, with silver hair that most of her life looked permanently windblown and which, as she aged, made her seem increasingly eccentric. Some may have noted her eyes. In her broad, aging face, they were the bright blue more appropriate to a child than to a woman on the brink of old age. Yet for all her childlike appearance, and long before she clerked in a seaside rock shop, Pauline Benton was an artist of profound gifts. This would not have been easy to detect in the quotidian anonymity of her day job, but some thirty years earlier she had been heralded as the only woman shadow master in the world, practitioner of a performance art at least a thousand years old when she first encountered it in 1920s Beijing.[1]

Had you followed Pauline to the cottage she shared with a friendly ginger cat just down the street from the shop, through narrow lanes not unlike the *hutong*, or alleys, of the Beijing of her youth forty years earlier, you would have found the rich jumble of an eclectic life. The many *objets d'art* crowding the walls and floors of her pine-panelled home – blackwood tables, porcelains, tapestries – all spoke of Asia. But what you would have been struck by most was the presence of shadow figures, hundreds of them – the *dramatis personae* of the ancient art of shadow theatre – which Pauline had brought from China years earlier. Beings from legend and history, lovers and warriors, and a zoo's worth of animals were there to "greet you, colorful and distinc-

xvi
FOREWORD

tive," wrote a visitor to Pauline's in the early 1970s, an "esoteric cast of characters, two-dimensional and of delicate parchment," all of which "live in traveling cases, carefully labeled 'Demons,' 'Ladies,' 'Entertainers,' 'Emperors' and other diversified categories such as 'Clouds.'" These flat, articulated figures, twelve to fourteen inches tall, made of carved and painted translucent donkey parchment, were manipulated against a cloth or paper screen illuminated from behind, thus appearing as coloured shadows – dancing, commanding, fighting, praying – in plays called *piyingxi*, or "leather shadow shows." Many of these plays had the same plots as Beijing Opera but were considerably older. Since at least the Song dynasty, shadow figures had performed in temples and palace gardens to instrumental and vocal accompaniment in dramas and comedies based on fables, legends, and historical events. In country villages they were seen as something more than diversionary entertainment: they were the shades of departed heroes or ancestors or the manifestations of wonder-working gods, their performances propitiations to please not an audience of fellow mortals but the deities of the harvest themselves.[2]

To Pauline Benton, this cast of characters, often erroneously referred to as "puppets," was known by a far simpler and warmer term; for her, they were "actors." But so was the animator who helped them take the stage. They were a safe form of projection for a woman who was shy, nervous, and rather ordinary in front of an audience, but who behind her shadow stage breathed such life into delicate maidens, lovelorn heroes, and triumphant warriors, her voice a "fine and supple" instrument, that it was easy to imagine her as being to the footlights born.[3]

As old as shadow theatre was, with an ancestry said to date from a magician's effort to brighten the mood of a depressed Han dynasty ruler (a legend that Pauline, though knowing better, exploited to the full), it offered one element of the modern, foreshadowing a seminal piece of Western culture. "Little did the Chinese realize in 121 BC when an historian first mentioned shadow plays," a journalist would later write of Benton's performances, "that they were the forerunner of the present day Technicolor cartoons made famous by Walt Disney."[4] It was not such a far-fetched notion, Mickey Mouse and Chinese shadow theatre. In his 1932 book *With Love and Irony*, Chinese author Lin Yutang, who believed that screening Disney cartoons at international conferences could help avert war, included a sketch of a Confucian-robed Mickey facing down a bearded emperor from Beijing Opera. Just as Mickey Mouse's mishaps and triumphs spoke to eternal riddles of the human condition, so did Pauline's White Snake Lady or Monkey King, those forerunners of Disney cartoons.[5]

Uniquely Chinese though they were, *piyingxi* characters seemed to transcend Chinese history even as they epitomized it, communicating common truths that could be understood regardless of the background or language of the audience. Yet they were not modern enough for the China of Chairman Mao Zedong. Denounced during the Cultural Revolution as relics of the "four olds" – Old Customs, Old Culture, Old Habits, and Old Ideas – shadow figures were buried or burned, troupes disbanded, the art form judged a product of China's feudal past and consigned to the dustbin of history. Shadow theatre's little and big actors joined an exclusive group of the culturally condemned, along with Confucius, the "feudal romantic" poetry of Li Bai, and anything that did not glorify the slim joys of a robotic proletariat.

Pauline tried to update her version of *piyingxi*, devising similar animal plays enacted by plastic and highly coloured figures in an ironic echo of the changes exacted of shadow players under the Communists, when gods and emperors were replaced with politically correct and non-suspect cartoon animals. But it was beyond her, this particular Great Leap. Pauline belonged not in the neutered plastic world of Disney any more than she did the ideological tyranny of the Cultural Revolution, but in the lamp-lit glamour of the Qing empire, when Manchu noblewomen sighed over the tragic romance of *The White Snake* in the privacy of walled gardens and when illiterate farmers enacted sacred dramas with incense and firecrackers. Like the Monkey King, Sun Wukong, who changed his shape to suit all situations, Pauline knew that in shadow theatre she had been given an opportunity for adventures as colourful as those celebrated in the Ming dynasty novel from which Monkey came. Like his, hers was also a strange destiny: that she, a middle-class American woman, was meant to become not just a shadow master herself – a bizarre aspiration in China, where the art was restricted to men and never open to foreigners – but that she was also meant to save *piyingxi* from dying out, even if this meant transplanting it outside the nation where it had driven down such deep roots. Those deep roots mattered to Pauline. To her, shadow theatre was not just a by-product of Chinese history: it *was* Chinese history. And unlike foreigners who collected Chinese objects to place them in the cold safety of museums, Pauline collected shadows to give them another chance to live, even as she also knew that catching the Monkey King was beyond the powers of even the most puissant generals of heaven.

❊

I first learned about Pauline Benton while looking for a subject to write about that would take in the changing world of Beijing in the 1920s and 1930s, as seen through the eyes of a foreigner.

Thanks to my friend and colleague David Hogge of the Smithsonian Institution, I was put on the path of Benjamin March, the American-born Chinese art expert who, I discovered, had seen and written about Chinese shadow theatre in the ancient Chinese capital. I then found that March was not the only American in Beijing with an interest in what was, even then, seemingly becoming a lost art. Twenty-five-year-old Pauline Benton saw her first shadow plays in her aunt's garden in 1923, and she found her whole life changed. From knowing nothing about shadow theatre, Benton became an expert, through her own studies, through working with one of the last imperial-era shadow masters and receiving help from sympathetic Chinese experts, and from observing performances in remote villages in northern China. She went even further. The only woman shadow master of her day, Pauline made a name for herself at a time when the world of Depression-era America craved for the exotic, adding another chapter to the catalogue of stereotypes that Americans devised about the Chinese: a timeless, unchanging culture to gaze back on with longing in the disruptive years between the Great Depression and the Second World War.

Born in Kansas in 1898, a daughter of educator Dr Guy Potter Benton, Pauline spent most of her childhood, teen years, and young womanhood on the campuses of universities where her father served as president. His nomination as head of the University of the Philippines brought Pauline, her sister Helen, and their mother Mary to Manila in 1921. Through her maternal aunt, Dr Emma Konantz, a mathematics professor at Beijing's Yenching University, Pauline encountered and studied shadow theatre, an art form restricted to Chinese males and becoming harder to find with each passing year. Concluding that it was dying out, Pauline made it her goal to preserve it by taking it back to the United States. Founding her own company, the Red Gate Shadow Players, in New York in 1932, Pauline took a gamble that paid off.

Lauded by critics and the leading lights of Chinese culture in America, Red Gate made it to the White House of President Franklin Delano Roosevelt, riding a tide of sympathy for the Chinese, who were suffering Japanese threats and finally invasion in 1937. Throughout the Sino-Japanese War and into the years of the Second World War, Pauline and Red Gate offered benefit performances to aid the Chinese. When civil war between Nationalists and Communists was followed by Communist takeover, the subsequent Korean War and the Cultural Revolution strained relations between China and the United States, and traditional art forms like shadow theatre were imperilled in China and suspect in a newly distrustful America. Pauline went into retirement, but throughout the fractious 1950s and 1960s she never stopped learning or sharing her knowledge. And in the last few years of her life she gave one more glowing performance, which showed how ardent her love for shadow theatre still was.

Not only did I want to explore and celebrate the life of this most unusual woman, who as a person remained – and remains – more mysterious even as her fame as a shadow master grew, but also to explore and celebrate the shadow theatre whose survival she made her number-one mission in life. I also wanted to find out if there were any people today who, like Pauline, saw not just a past but a future in Chinese shadow theatre. Most gratifyingly, I did find many: Stephen Kaplin and Kuang-Yu Fong of Chinese Theatre Works, Jo Humphrey of Yueh Lung Shadow Theatre, Cui Yongping and Wang Shuqin of the Cui Shadow Puppet Museum (*pi ying yi shu bo wu guan*) in Beijing, Professor Jiang Yuxiang in Sichuan Province, and Annie Katsura Rollins, a modern-day Pauline Benton if there ever was one. And this, happily, is to name only a few. Shadow theatre may never be as popular as it was over a century ago, in or out of China, but with these artists on its side it will never disappear.[6]

✳

This is not meant to be a technical or academic book. It leans heavily on the research and findings of devoted scholars of Chinese shadow theatre. Pauline Benton's life story could not be told without explaining the art form to which she dedicated her life or the circumstances that allowed her form of shadow theatre to flourish as entertainment in North America, and this has been my primary aim in exploring and sharing her story.

I have rendered all Chinese romanization in pinyin except for examples used in quoted material. Because it was her choice, and because I want to leave her words as she offered them, I have intentionally left intact the Wade-Giles orthography that Pauline used in her translation of *The White Snake* shadow-play script, which forms the appendix to this volume. Where there are typos or errors, I make every effort to clarify and explain her intentions. Any errors in the telling of her story are entirely mine.

SHADOW WOMAN

Chapter 1

CULTURAL GEOGRAPHIES

In spring 1921, three American women – Mary Benton and her daughters, twenty-six-year old Helen and Pauline, aged twenty-four – stood on the deck of their passenger ship as its white hull sliced through the jade waters of Manila Bay.[1] None of them had ever been this far away from the familiar trappings of home, though the Manila they approached did not look especially Asian. Spain, which had ruled the Philippines for centuries before the United States laid claim to the scattered islands, had left tangible proofs of occupation. Manila was a place of low-slung structures, thickly walled, with portcullises and gates dating from early in the Spanish colonial era. It was defensive, heavy-looking, in which even the churches dared scarcely a spire, huddled against the earthquakes and typhoons that were as regular a part of Manila's calendar as religious festivals. Yet these dull walls concealed a colourful, violent, loud, and passionate world in which East and West, Asia and Europe mingled, inextricably entangled. It was an atmosphere that would exercise a profound influence on all three women.[2]

Mary Benton, along with Helen and Pauline, had lived the peripatetic yet cloistered life of many university administrators' families. Mary's husband, Dr Guy Potter Benton, had served as president of several Midwestern colleges, most notably Miami University in Oxford, Ohio. A vigorous and good-humoured man, descended from hardy Connecticut settlers, Dr Benton had modern ideas regarding women's rights and in 1902 had helped found Miami's first sorority, Delta Zeta. He was known for his love of ceremony and his ability to bond with his students, and for his YMCA educational work in Europe during and after the First World War he had been awarded the Army Distinguished

Service Medal. In 1921 he had accepted the presidency of the University of the Philippines, which is why his wife and daughters were standing on the deck of a ship watching Manila shimmer in the tropical heat.

The Bentons had been abroad once before. They had spent a year in Europe in 1909–10, enjoying that last act of the *belle époque* before war swept out nineteenth-century niceties for good. While children were dragged through museums, then as now, and most of them would rather have been somewhere else, Pauline's interests were precocious for her eleven years. Her small leather travel diary covers only October 1909 to February 1910, but each day shows how much she enjoyed spending hours in the most renowned galleries and historic spots of Belgium, Holland, and Germany. She also experienced a marked delight at seeing the colourful costumery of power in a Europe still ruled by kings, queens, and archbishops, exclaiming over a pair of "swell footmen." And she could live for days off the pleasure of being smiled at by the hefty yet maternal German empress, even as she easily imagined the ghosts of lords and ladies posturing about the ramparts of every castle she visited. But if much was expected of the Benton children in developing their interior worlds, not much acquaintance with the realities of ordinary life was afforded them. If Pauline's mother Mary had led a relatively sheltered life since her marriage, her daughters were even less worldly than she, a fact that seems to have shaped what they did with their lives. Helen did not marry until her late twenties – in an era when most eligible young women were already settled matrons with children and social responsibilities well before then. And Pauline never married.[3]

Mary's sister, Dr Emma Konantz, who had arrived in Beijing just after the end of the First World War, had become a passionate collector of Chinese artifacts, and after landing in Manila, Mary Benton also discovered and began purchasing Chinese antiques, especially embroidered textiles. She found that her timing and opportunities to learn could not have been better than they were in the early 1920s. The fall of the Qing dynasty and the political chaos of China in the warlord mayhem that followed ensured that all manner of luxury items soon flooded the markets in Asia and abroad, at bargain prices. "Everywhere the old order was crumbling," wrote George N. Kates, an American living in Beijing, "its once fine possessions no longer usable by many now lacking even the necessities of life."[4] Mary Benton took advantage of the situation so well that she was later able to open an Asian arts shop on New York's Madison Avenue displaying "dazzling rolls of silks, priest robes, and wall hangings from the Imperial Palace," whose designs were licensed for use by companies producing fabrics for the home.[5] She lent her antiques for fundraising events for China relief in the 1930s, and they provided her and Pauline entrée to the society of such prewar expatriate Chinese celebrities as Mme Wellington Koo and writer Lin Yutang.[6]

The spoils of another vanishing Asian world intrigued Helen too. She became interested in Japanese costume and history through an exhibit of Buddhist priests' robes at the Metropolitan Museum of Art in New York City. Asking questions of the curator, she was astonished to learn that there was no information she could study in English. From Manila, Helen went to Japan to acquire such a robe for herself, as well as to find a ceremonial kimono. There she met the Japanese textile expert Shojiro Nomura at his richly stocked studio, where she at once won his respect with her tasteful selection from his kimono collection. Helen began her studies with him, and soon realized that with his fluency in English and her passion for sharing his vast knowledge of Japanese costume, they could rectify the lack of information that had so dismayed her in New York City. They ultimately collaborated on and published a book, *Japanese Costume and the Makers of Its Elegant Tradition* (Charles E. Tuttle 1963), which brought this history, little known outside Japan, to the wider world for the first time.[7]

A pre-existing interest in fabrics or garments, together with the orientalism prevailing in 1920s America, with its acceptance of collector expertise in Asian art and craft as fashionable for middle-class American women, may have rendered both Mary and Helen Benton susceptible in Manila. But next to her mother and sister, Pauline is a mystery – a circumstance (and ultimately a role) that she promoted for the rest of her life. Up to 1922, all that is known of her is that she was born Pauline Corinth Benton on 25 January 1898 in Baldwin City, Kansas, where her father was teaching at Baker University. One of the few surviving childhood images of her shows her as a twelve- year-old bystander in 1910 Italy, captured by a roving photographer.[8] Standing in hat, coat, and gloves, she gazes admiringly as President Theodore Roosevelt strides purposefully out of the entrance of a Venetian hotel. A bystander she would remain for the first two decades of her life, overshadowed as much by her surroundings as by her renowned father. While Dr Benton worked with the YMCA in France and Germany, she lived with her mother and sister in New York in an apartment on Riverside Drive, not far from Grant's Tomb and the sliding gray breadth of the Hudson River, and only a few blocks from the campus of Columbia University. From the cradle and almost to the grave, Pauline lived on or near the grounds of several major universities.

A childhood spent rubbing elbows with students from all points of the compass was a privilege not accorded most girls her age, but they were one of Pauline's few connections with the world that lay outside the campus gates. This seems to have inspired her to wonder what the wider world had to offer her. Perhaps this explains the polite detachment that seems to infuse a photograph taken shortly after Pauline's

Pauline as a girl on holiday in Venice, seen here with President Theodore Roosevelt in 1910

arrival in Manila.[9] She wears an embroidered Filipino dress, its *terno*, or butterfly sleeves, jutting sharply up at either side of her slender neck. She looks into the camera with a gaze that seems both charmed and bewildered by the novelty of the experience. It is as if she is not yet sure that this is the channel she is most comfortable with. This Pauline appears to have been content to look on as her mother and sister pursued their enthusiasms, waiting patiently, yet puzzled. While approved women's interests such as printmaking, pottery throwing, or collecting Asian fabrics or antiques fulfilled her mother and sister – both of whom were more conventional than she – convention was never to be a characteristic of Pauline's style or life. And the answer to her question, the need to discover a part of the world not yet staked out by anyone else, would come soon.

Although Manila was on Asia's outermost Pacific frontier, it was a place redolent with the "Orient," the closest many tourists ever came to that fabled locale. The core of Manila's Asianness was in its Chinatown, Binondo, which contained the "most truly oriental bit of Manila streets," some of which were so narrow "that two persons abreast can touch elbows with the walls on each side." This closeness and darkness was considered sinister, as were the people who lived and worked there. Foreigners who did venture into it were urged to take advantage of "being able to get out into the fresh air within thirty seconds, if need be." Considered an outpost of the East, Manila was Western enough to permit a Chinatown to flourish, albeit within the restricted area common to most ghettos of marginalized populations. It is easy to comprehend the concept of Chinatowns in foreign cities, those places where, in John Tchen's potent words, "cultural geographies [mapped] districts of light and shadow."[10] That such geographies could also be mapped over a city long seen as a meeting place of Asia and the West shows how deeply rooted was the question of whether the Chinese or their culture belonged anywhere but safely back in China.[11]

It was in the shops of Binondo that most tourists bought their souvenirs of the Orient, whether new or, as was often the case, old remnants of a world that was disappearing. Frequently such shops were the last resting place of the figures used in shadow theatre, a form of

Pauline wearing traditional Philippine gown in Manila, c. 1922

which, patterned after Asian-influenced European shadow theatre, had been in the region since the late nineteenth century.[12] When Li Tuochen, the shadow master with whom Pauline would study in the mid-1920s and 1930s, shared with an American writer in Beijing his fear that his shadows would end up "scattered in curio shops and picture stalls, sold for a few coppers as toys for children, or to foreigners who do not know Kuan Yin from the Dragon Princess," he was speaking as one who had seen other masters' treasured figures come to that ignoble end. According to Genevieve Wimsatt, with whom Li shared his fears, figures ended up as decorations on lampshades, "a static role," she notes, "but one not altogether inconsistent with their former state."[13] Is this how Pauline first glimpsed these figures, sold or abandoned by troupes no longer able to perform with them? Did the Chinese shadow theatre, which she first saw performed in Beijing two years later and which was to become her life's work, meet her more than halfway in the dark shops of Manila's Binondo?[14]

Compared with Pauline's early years, the short life story of American puppet master Paul McPharlin, a colleague from whom she would come to learn a great deal, is rich with information about what formed and nurtured his interests. A near contemporary of Pauline's, McPharlin was born in Grosse Point, Michigan, in 1903 and had what can be called the classic upbringing of many who later transmute childhood obsessions and instabilities into a career in the performing arts. "The field of puppetry is a haven for eccentrics and misfits," says Stephen Kaplin, co-artistic director of Chinese Theatre Works in New York City. "[They] may possess extraordinary talents, but are also saddled by all sorts of social peculiarities and emotional oddnesses." Socially peculiar and emotionally odd certainly describes both McPharlin and Pauline. McPharlin had a close relationship with an artistic, ambitious mother and a distant, fractious relationship with an often absent father. He manifested an early attraction to theatre as actor, director, and playwright, specifically in the creation of miniature stages and towns and, of course, marionettes. Pauline, too, had an artistic and ambitious mother, and a father who seemed to belong to the world rather than to her. Like McPharlin's family, Pauline's moved often, which perhaps for both children made the passive world of puppets – a world they could marshal and control at will – not only familiar but consoling. Both Paul and Pauline grew up being attracted to anything that was "other," having school friends who were foreign-born or outside the ordinary run of American kids, with whom they could feel a sense of belonging that was paradoxically set apart from the mainstream.[15]

But where McPharlin had little in common with his father, Pauline seems to have shared a particularly vivid interest that had been her father's since he was young – his love of spectacle, which played out on every college campus of which he was executive. For Pauline, this love took the form of a deep fascination with the dance of history and art, the sacred and the profane, and how much the one tells about the other. She also inherited her father's love of theatre. As a student at Ohio Wesleyan University, the young Guy Benton had been willing to risk censure by breaking a college rule forbidding student attendance at theatre performances in order to take in a production of *Richard III* starring Frederick Barkham Warde. Benton and fifty-nine other students were expelled for flocking to see Warde perform at the Delaware City Opera House in October 1885.[16]

Where education was concerned, both Paul and Pauline benefited from fortuitous guidance. Paul's path is clearly traced through a series of mentors in high school and university, while Pauline was fortunate in the fact that Miami University had one of the earliest theatre programs in the United States. Founded in 1905, at the start of Dr Benton's watch as president, the theatre department was headed by Professor Loren Gates, who for his first production staged a performance of *A Midsummer Night's Dream*, most unusually in the open air along the banks of the Talawanda River. It is quite likely that Dr Benton attended this performance. Is it too much to presume that seven-year-old Pauline accompanied him? With its fantasy setting, shifting identities, and its gems of truth buried in comedy, the play would have touched on the same territory as puppet theatre. *A Midsummer Night's Dream* is also one of the plays in which Shakespeare refers to puppets directly. After

Opposite top: Pauline (second from left) with friends at Miami University in Oxford, Ohio

Opposite bottom: Her face turned toward the camera, Pauline laughs with fellow graduates at Miami University

Puck has sprinkled his love potion and Demetrius falls for Helena, the spurned Hermia bitterly upbraids her friend, who calls Hermia "you counterfeit, you puppet." Hermia's life has suddenly careened out of her control, making her truly a puppet of circumstances, a situation with which Pauline, who followed others until she took control of puppets herself, may well have found much that was familiar.[17]

The conundrum with regard to Pauline Benton is that so little is known of her life that it is tempting to assume she came upon shadow theatre as she describes – as an epiphany, a sudden realization – just as it is tempting to overlay any number of theories about what drew her to the art form in the first place. But if we accept her explanation, given in an article written two decades after her year and a half in the Philippines, the story becomes even stranger because, according to Pauline, Chinese shadow theatre first reached out and grabbed her in, of all places, Chicago, and through another foreigner whose heart belonged to China, Dr Berthold Laufer.

"As a child, Berthold Laufer was much interested in dramatics, especially in marionettes," wrote Kenneth Scott Latourette, the China historian. Born in Cologne in 1874 to a well-to-do German Jewish family, Laufer and his siblings had been indulged in their childhood theatricals, many of which featured Laufer's original scripts. His dream was to become a professional playwright, but family pressures turned him toward more academic pursuits.[18]

The theatre's loss was ethnology's gain, because it was in this realm that Laufer found his most brilliant expression, one that was not without an element of the stage he had to abandon. Laufer had the gift – possibly through his sensitivity to the uses of the stage – of taking what to Westerners seemed most arcane in Asian culture and in effect allowing the bright light of his searching intelligence to penetrate and project its substance to a wider world. He was certainly the most qualified Western anthropologist to explain Asian theatre, especially shadow theatre, to foreign audiences. While Laufer was working for the American Museum of Natural History in New York, he travelled to China for the first time, with the Jacob Schiff expedition in 1902, and while he was in Beijing he decided to explore its shadow theatre scene. This was, like so much of the city, still in chaos following the Boxer Uprising – the anti-foreign riots that had exploded into a fifty-five day siege of the diplomatic quarter two years earlier. Six years later, Laufer was in Chicago, serving as curator of anthropology at the Field Museum of Natural History, a post he held until his death in 1934. As head of the department, he would have found that his interests and the department's administration contended for his time, yet he managed to turn out monographs at an astonishing rate on a wide range of topics: the history of jade, for example, or the study intriguingly titled *Insect-Musicians and Cricket Champions of China* (the arthropods, not the sport). And while the Anthropology Department's scope was as broad as Laufer's interests, his "chief interest, of course," wrote Latourette, "was in the Chinese exhibits." And most especially in the shadow figures he had collected in Sichuan Province.[19]

In 1923 the Field Museum had on exhibit what was perhaps Laufer's most comprehensive collection, the puppets and shadow figures he had gathered from all over Asia. Nearly thirty exhibition cases were filled not just with figures but with other tools of the puppet and shadow trade, displayed in order of geography – ironically, from west to east, the direction shadow theatre would travel later in the century, when the figures Pauline had commissioned in 1930s Beijing returned to perform there in 2004.

Cases 1 to 4 contained displays of Chinese religious drama, showing the ten purgatories; case 5 explained the lion dance; cases 6 and 7 displayed Chinese masks from an imperial play, illustrating gods and heroes of the Daoist religion; cases 8 and 9 were devoted to Chinese shadow-play figures; masks and masked figures of Tibetan mystery plays were shown in cases 10 to 17; Javanese puppets and orchestra accompanying performances in cases 18 to 21, and masks, actors' headdresses, and costumes in cases 22 to 24; and cases 25 to 28 were given over to masks from Sri Lanka. These were, Laufer insisted, united by a common theme. "It must not be supposed," he points out for his American reader, "that the Chinese have ever in reality practiced the tortures demonstrated in the ten courts of Purgatory." A Chinese, like the average Midwesterner, was skeptical and rationalistic, he explained. "On the stage, moreover, for which these models are designed, everything is mitigated and permeated by a willful, grotesque humor which makes it difficult for the spectator to take these punishments too seriously." Like vaudeville melodrama, shadow and puppet plays were meant to bring about a heightened state of suspense, but unlike the Western variety they offered lessons that tended to stick: Even amid slapstick, there was always the possibility of grace. "The keynote of this drama," wrote Laufer, speaking to the religious theatre behind all the displayed masks, figures, and puppets, "is not misery and despair, but hope and the possibility of self-perfection."[20]

In the summer of 1922, Pauline sailed back to the United States to attend Helen's marriage in Minneapolis to Dr Dwight Minnich, son of the dean of Miami University. Helen had returned to America with a substantial collection of Japanese costumes and would soon return to Japan for more study with Shojiro Nomura and more collecting. Many of these robes, obis, and accoutrements may have been on display in the Minnich home. Was Helen already talking about writing a book with Nomura, of making Japanese costume her life's work? Did Pauline already have shadow theatre in mind as a focus of her own study, to devote herself to as Helen gave herself to her subject of interest? According to Pauline's account, it was artist friends working for *Women's Wear Daily* in New York who, inspired by the Laufer collection to make "the figures the basis for a fashion collection," persuaded her to go and see the exhibition. If she went only out of curiosity about how something like "puppets" could influence the season's fashions, the results were significant enough to alter much more than her wardrobe.[21]

Chapter 2

SHADOW PEOPLE

It is possible Pauline actually met Berthold Laufer at the Field Museum in 1922; he was in Chicago, and his willingness to give enthusiastic tours of the collections is well known. From everything we know about him, Laufer would have been glad to devote his time and expertise to someone as intrigued by shadow theatre as Pauline was. He had carefully recorded on film and on wax phonograph cylinders as many of the shadow performances as he was able to arrange in Beijing. On such authority he alone could have informed her that these facsimiles, like his displayed figures, were to live performances what descriptions of concerts are to live music. Pauline discovered on this visit that if she wanted to see a live shadow play, the best place to go was "the Broadway of the Chinese stage," Beijing – which only Laufer could have told her. What makes the Laufer collection even more important to Pauline's story, and underscores its influence on her, is that while her main interest would revolve around the contents of cases 8 and 9, containing a variety of Chinese shadow figures from different parts of China, the figures and puppets displayed alongside them, and Laufer's colourful explanations set forth in a special guide book, *Oriental Theatricals,* would seem to prefigure her lifelong study of *all* Asian shadow and puppet theatre. When she came to write the program notes for an exhibit of her Chinese, Indian, and Indonesian shadow figures at the Minneapolis Museum of Art in 1970, the depth of her knowledge of all forms of shadow theatre proved to be as wide-ranging and exceptional as Laufer's own.[1]

When the energetic young Berthold Laufer had arrived in Beijing in 1902, he was looking for someone – anyone – who could make him a set of shadow figures to take back to the American Museum of Natural History in New York City. Like any ethnologist, Laufer would have been as interested in seeing whether these figures were still being created – in a city that had endured such upheaval – as in finding older figures that could be bought for a few coins in the streets and shops. Finally locating an elderly artisan, Laufer asked the man if he would carve a set for him and was promptly turned down. "[T]he workman counted that it would take him at least a year and a half to accomplish the whole set," Laufer wrote, and would come in at a cost of over a thousand dollars. Given the man's age and that he had only one good eye, Laufer did not believe he could achieve such a feat.[2]

Undaunted, Laufer eventually found a shadow troupe that must have been on its last legs, for its performers readily sold him everything they had – over five hundred shadow figures, along with their stage, instruments for the orchestra, and scripts – for $600. According to Laufer, haggling started at $1,000; he countered with an insulting $250, and both parties settled for something in between, a pittance for figures representing untold hours of labour and artistry. The creation of not just the figures but the stage props appropriate to them – the furniture, utensils, weapons, palaces and temples, mountain and water landscapes – was a painstaking process that began in a blood-stained abattoir and ended on an artist's paint-stained table. A master carver started with the stretching of carefully scraped donkey skin – that from the belly region being regarded as most desirable – which, once dried, was flattened and smoothed to a silky translucence and then cut into the required shapes. Up to eleven separate pieces for a human figure were painted according to the colours and designs necessary. They were then knotted together with silk thread, allowing just enough play at the joints to give the figure (from eight inches to as high as twenty-four inches tall) a lifelike flexibility – a kind of art in motion that presaged mid-twentieth-century art media in the West.[3] "In creating these small actors for the screen," wrote Genevieve Wimsatt, "the Chinese artist has expended skill, sympathy, humor and affection, achieving small masterpieces of line that would do credit to an Aubrey Beardsley or a William Blake."[4] Once created, and if well cared for, a shadow figure or set piece could last a century or more. Pauline owned several that dated at least to the late 1700s, while Wimsatt claimed to own figures even older.[5]

Six hundred dollars was a lot of money in the early 1900s, especially to anyone in Beijing in the lean years after the Boxer Uprising. For these performers and artisans to have let their theatre collection go so easily seemed to indicate to Laufer that all was not well in the health of the art form. Indeed, he felt that it was on its way out. "So the [pi]ying-hsi will soon be a matter of the past in Northern China," he wrote home, "and I saved them in the last hour," a pronouncement that came to be taken as fact far too credulously.[6] But long before Laufer's visit, trouble had been brewing for the parchment gods and princesses of shadow theatre. As early as the thirteenth century, a Buddhist movement called the White Lotus sect rose among the poor and disenfranchised Han population of China, which was to have a dire effect on shadow theatre. This reaction against the Mongol Yuan dynasty was later reawakened in the late eighteenth century and into the early nineteenth under the equally foreign Manchu Qing. One of the more widespread legends attached to the White Lotus sect was that its adepts could bring to life paper cutouts of whole armies of soldiers and horses to aid in battling the Qing military, a claim that was co-opted by those who took part in the supernaturally-influenced Boxer Uprising in 1900. Thus suspicion attached to shadow theatre, perhaps due to the tradition that figures be left headless after performances lest the bodies come to life and wreak havoc, and likely by the belief among country people that the figures possessed supernatural powers. "[Shadow theatre's] inception," affirmed Laufer, "is purely religious and traceable to spiritistic séances," an activity that appeared especially subversive to the Qing. "To the Chinese, the shadow is particularly meaningful," wrote Dr Brunhild Körner. "To them the shadow is a true image of the person and is considered one of its souls ... Accordingly, when a magician conjured up the ancestors, he called for their shadow souls." Feared for this magic, shadow players were seized and jailed; many escaped and went underground.[7]

Yet under the Manchus, China found itself controlled by emperors who enjoyed shadow theatre as much as the Han Chinese did, if not more so. Under Manchu rule, Chinese society was shaped by the military culture imposed by the banner system, in which soldiers apportioned among companies bearing eight different flags were garrisoned in Beijing, where they lived off stipends from the state. By the end of the nineteenth century, this system, like most bannermen, was past its prime and the stipends long past due. As their glorious past moved farther away from their precarious present, Manchus began to settle into a lifestyle focused on the amusements and hobbies for which they had always been known. They took "a continued pleasure in the folk arts of the Northeast," writes Pamela Kyle Crossley, "an emotional attachment to the orally transmitted history of the clans and the emperors, a fascination with the aesthetics of Chinese culture, and the taste for trivia that can best be fostered by those who neither reap nor sow, and have few cares beyond the acceptance of permanent communal indebtedness."[8] They pursued with equal passion the flying of kites or the keeping of caged songbirds or pet crickets. The more literary Manchus spent their time at calligraphy, landscape painting, and the composition of poetry. Some still had gourmand appetites that had outlived their ability to pay for them. And many became devotees and even performers of shadow theatre. As Li Tuochen told Genevieve Wimsatt, "The Manchus have always loved the stage, the puppets and shadows." He said that in fact most of the troupes in Hebei, Beijing's province, were Manchu.[9]

Because the Qing government restricted theatres to certain neighbourhoods and districts, and regulated who attended performances as a way of controlling crowds, many people circumvented this by inviting theatre companies to their homes. This practice obtained for shadow theatre also.[10] Even for chronically indigent Manchus, shadow theatre was relatively inexpensive, a kind of portable opera, and for all its affordability it was rich in entertainment, ranging from comedy to tragedy, sacred to profane, sometimes all in the same lengthy play. There were fierce battle dramas between warrior princesses and invading armies; the comic adventures of the Chinese monk Xuanzang as he crossed into India in search of Buddhist scriptures, accompanied by Monkey, Pigsy, the Sand-Ogre, and the son of the Dragon King transformed into a white horse; tragic romances like that of the White Snake, an immortal demon who makes the classic error of falling in love with a mortal man.

The majority of these plays were identical to those performed in Beijing Opera; but unlike Beijing Opera, with its bare thrust stage, shadow theatre had the added attraction of colourful sets, replete with houses and furnished interiors, landscapes with lakes, forests, and mountains. Shadow theatre offered a range of special effects that would not be realized until the advent of motion pictures: forests or temples going up in smoke, magical transformations from human to animal and back again, gorily realistic executions, gods and goddesses who floated eerily on clouds, startling explosions of fire, and boats gliding over waves from which fish leapt and played. "Here exciting clashes actually take place," Pauline wrote, "warriors are dismounted, heads slashed in two and even severed from the body. If the battle becomes too heated and too many characters thus dismembered, another shadow warrior will start to clean house by swishing all the headless bodies and bodiless heads off stage with the tip of his spear." This may sound bloody amusement for a peaceful people such as the Chinese, she pointed out, but that was not what excited most aficionados of shadow theatre. It was "the art of manipulation of the figures," she explained, "and perfect coordination between the action and the music."[11]

All these effects were made the more eye-catching by the animators' ability to change the size and even colour of their figures – and therefore transform their characters with only a slight movement – by adjusting proximity to the light source. Pauline once saw a performance in which she watched "a whole endless procession of foxes running across the screen. Doubting that the players actually owned so many foxes," she wrote, "I guessed there were probably about a half dozen which were being reentered on the screen after they had made their exits on the opposite side. A peep backstage, however, revealed only two which were being zigzagged back and forth in front of a candle a few feet away from the screen."[12] Little wonder, with this entertainment arsenal at their disposal, that shadow masters were seen as intercessors between the worlds of the living and the dead, mortals and gods.

Although shadow theatre was performed over wide areas of China, in Beijing it had a unique flavour. As Pauline described in "China's Colored Shadow Plays,"

The Luanchow School is not the only school of shadow players left in China. The division is made right in Peking, where those players operating in the East-city are known as the "East-city" or Luanchow type and those in the West-city as the "West-city" or Chueh Chow type. The East-city type covers all the Luanchow territory, or the northeast corner of Hopei Province I have just been describing, Jehol, and Manchuria ... The "West-city" type embraces several small villages including Chueh Chow, southwest from Peking toward Paoting, and the provinces of Honan, Shensi, Shansi, Kiangsu, and Szechuan. [13]

The eastern portion of the city had always been the most desirable, favoured by its proximity to the Imperial College and two major temple fairs, at which more conservative and thus more literary shadow theatre would be offered by east side troupes. The western portion of Beijing was considered more remote and far more deeply suffused with the culture and colour of bannermen and their families. Thus, the east was known for its performance from elegantly styled scripts composed by scholars, as well as its highly coloured donkey-skin figures, while the west, with its taller figures, rich with filigree but more muted of colour, was full of broad impromptu humour and earthy references. Pauline took elements from both "schools" in crafting her own version of shadow theatre for America.[14]

※

Books and articles have been written over the past century attempting to trace shadow theatre to some logical source in recorded history, but there is no one conclusive answer concerning when it began or how (and it should be pointed out that there is very little logic in the development of any performance art). The oldest recorded mention of shadow theatre is said to have described how when a favourite concubine of the Emperor Wu of Han (141–87 BCE) died, the emperor's mourning was so intense that a magician was brought to court to alleviate his suffering. According to a translation by Alvin P. Cohen, the magician Shao-weng, "by means of his methods (or formulas) [and techniques], presumably at night caused the images (*mao*) of the concubine as well as the Ghost of the Hearth to arrive (appear) ... The Son of Heaven, from inside his hanging curtain (*wei*), gazing at a distance (*wang*), saw it."[15]

This account appears to describe silhouettes moving behind a curtain, not shadow figures, but it became fixed in the literary and popular firmament as the art form's birth. Only during the Song dynasty

(960–1279 CE) was shadow theatre actually mentioned by name and in recognizable detail, with figures made of painted leather. Whether these were the jointed figures of the shadow theatre of the Qing is unclear – images from the period seem to show animators holding rigid figures by a single stick.[16] As Pauline noted, historians described these figures as being "cut from paper ... and unjointed," merely moved around inside a lighted paper box while storytellers "droned and sang." Another theory, which Pauline espoused late in life, is that rather than developing from one source, shadow theatre sprang up independently in various locales, perhaps enhanced by borrowings that came through travel and trade.[17] Though the old masters claimed that the shadow theatres of Indonesia, India, and Turkey are all descended from a Chinese source – what one scholar terms "cultural nationalism,"[18] appropriation of a foreign invention as Chinese – it is not likely they were correct. India has the strongest claim to being shadow theatre's birthplace. It was from India that Buddhism was brought to China, and as some of the earliest confirmed shadow shows were connected to lectures in Buddhist temples – with figures used as a demonstration tool – and retained a sacred context well into the age of secular shadow plays, this may well be how the art form arrived in the Middle Kingdom. It may also explain how the religious-themed shadow theatre that Buddhist Mongols enjoyed from an early date was secularized under their imperial successors, the Manchus. Certainly, the shadow theatre style that Pauline knew was an innovation of no earlier date than the reign of the Qianlong emperor (r. 1735–96) and thus contemporary with Beijing Opera.

In the late Song dynasty, shadow theatre distinguished itself in a way that it never did under the Qing: there were female shadow masters, one account describing a company that was entirely female. Significantly, this was in Hangzhou, the setting for that most feminine of shadow theatre romances and Pauline's favourite play, *The White Snake*. Only when Pauline came along hundreds of years later did a woman join the "under-the-lamp" gentlemen once again.[19]

Pauline fully understood shadow theatre's original religious affiliation. As she wrote years later, shadow theatre "soon became identified with religious rites in recalling the souls of the Dead, an important function in a land imbued with Ancestor Worship."[20] Yet she was among those who, in the West, helped perpetuate its mythic Han dynasty

origin – the romance of a lost love, Western style. Perhaps shadow players' marginal role in society also intrigued Pauline. Emperor Wu's story
could have been elaborated by shadow masters as a badge of defence
dignified with antiquity (however illusory), for like all performers in
old China, actors were cheered on the stage and scorned on the street.
Pauline's sympathies and biases are well stated in the preface to her
program on shadow theatre, published in Beijing in 1940: "We ... are
descended from a long and honorable line of ancestors. It was during
the reign of that noble Han dynasty monarch Wu-ti, in the year 121
B.C., *they say*, that our span of life began" (Italics added).[21] The inter-
jection "they say" seems to concede that whatever the facts of how
shadow theatre began in China, whether as a borrowing from India
or Indonesia (both of which had early documented forms of shadow
theatre), a combination of some indigenous Chinese shadow theatre
with that of these cultures via the trade routes, or an original invention that arose later but was assigned an earlier and more glamorous
genesis, the magic and attraction of shadow theatre ultimately lay in
what "they" said it was all about – "they" being the audience, those
co-conspirators in the fable that is the power behind all theatre. This
meant, in twentieth-century terms, that for all its connections to
Manchu nobility and the imperial court, shadow theatre was an art
form of, by, and for the people. It was a definition that would resonate
distinctly in 1930s America.

For Pauline, "the magic is not that of memories, but of make-
believe."[22] Yet in her opinion, shadow theatre was a visual record of
past events, so that their acquaintance with the repertoire would give
most spectators at least a passing idea of Chinese history. Unfortunately, as the twentieth century shook off its nineteenth-century trappings, the Chinese public was losing interest in both. When Pauline
arrived in Beijing two decades into the century that promised to change
the face of the globe with its flashy new inventions and social theories,
she found that shadow theatre had become a memory of itself and
almost irretrievably make-believe. Shadow theatre was a folk art, noted
Wimsatt, that like snow in sunshine was "dissolving before my eyes."[23]

Chapter 3

WILLOW-PATTERNED CATHAY

Beijing in the 1920s "was still unique among the great cities of the world in its reluctance to break with the past," wrote Englishman John Blofeld. It seemed a place that would never change. Yet even then, insisted the Oxford graduate turned Buddhist monk, in this capital of decaying palaces and temples, and its "lanes where the soft felt shoes of the Pekingese fell noiselessly upon layers of yellow dust or heavy drifts of crisp snow," there was evidence that "this ancient way of life was doomed." Warlords from within and invaders from without were weakening an already compromised body politic.[1]

For Blofeld, Beijing's effect "was first to evoke and then forever obliterate the charming willow-patterned Cathay of [his] childhood imaginings, for even the prettiest willow-pattern scene could not do it justice."[2] Yet in the decade since the Qing dynasty's fall, both porcelain illusion and daily reality were shattered by the chaos spreading from the north. This began almost immediately after the death in 1913 of one of the last representatives of the old regime, Grand Empress Dowager Longyu, niece of Empress Dowager Cixi and consort of Cixi's nephew, the Guangxu emperor. Even then, after Longyu joined Cixi and Guangxu in the Qing mausolea, the drugging incense of the throne hung in the troubled air of Republican Beijing. In 1914, Puyi, Guangxu's briefly regnant child successor, claimed to remember that "there was a feeling that this was to be the year of [imperial] restoration." But it was more a Restoration comedy, a burlesque of the lost refinement the royalists were seeking to return to, as Yuan Shikai, former viceroy of Zhili, prime minister and second provisional president (after Dr Sun Yatsen) under the Republican government, made his own bid for the throne in 1915. Yuan, who had exploited the weaknesses of the Manchu throne throughout his career, should have known the dangers of the imperial seat he so longed to occupy. After he died in disgrace, the republic picked its way across the surface of increasingly fraught Chinese politics, so soon to fracture into Nationalist and Communist fragments.[3]

At least throughout the first three decades of the twentieth century, walled Beijing was, as David Strand points out, one of the few Chinese cities that "looked so traditional and Chinese and at the same time harbored the essentials of modern and Western urban life."[4] It was a city at once a precise tool of *feng shui* design, meant to align the unseen energies of the earth to benefit the emperor and his subjects, and a place of disruption, fear, political and military jockeying for power, assassination, and greed. The ambiguities of a city with a foot in the past and another in the future, dimly envisioned as it was, "provide a metaphor for the uneven and incomplete social transformations of the Republican period," writes Strand.[5] American Grace Thompson Seton was a visitor in the mid-1920s, and in that period when past and present coexisted, she contrasted Beijing's two distinct personalities. "Bitter poverty cheek by jowl with glittering magnificence," Seton observed, "endless contortions of Rites and Usages strung on a character fundamentally simple," for nowhere in China were the Chinese so practical, even hard-headed, and yet so given to the intricacies of etiquette and rank as in Beijing. But it was also a friendly place, especially for foreign visitors, even when, as many Beijingers discovered, to offer too much to foreigners was to give up much that was never returned. As Seton found (and as Pauline would experience herself), "Peking hospitality is famous."[6] Along with welcoming people, the energy of the place was unlike that of any other major city. "The streets are marvelous," stated Ellen LaMotte, another American admirer. "Those in the Legation Quarter are well paved, European, and stupid; but those in the Chinese and Tartar cities are full of excitement. A few are wide, but the majority are narrow, winding alleys, and all alike are packed and crowded with people and animals and vehicles of all kinds. Walking is a matter of shoving oneself through the throng, dodging under camels' noses, avoiding wheelbarrows [used for human, animal and produce transport], bumping against donkeys, standing aside to let officials' carriages go by."[7]

The Tartar Gate in Beijing. Camels carrying coal from the north were still a daily sight in the 1930s.

This was the Beijing that greeted Pauline in 1923, its chaos and colour as "interesting to hear as well as to see," she wrote, "for its music is a strange, rhythmic intermingling of sounds."[8] It confused her at first. Although Pauline had had Chinese friends since childhood and studied Chinese culture, she felt "wholly inadequate to cope with Peking," she wrote; "the destiny that pervaded its walls and palaces, the temples, courtyards and gardens, the curio shops and markets, the theatres, all bespoke a history and philosophy that could not be penetrated by cursory observations or desultory reading."[9] One had to plunge into Beijing and truly live in its everyday as well as imperial atmosphere to truly get a grip on not just its meaning but on how people lived. Into one of her most popular shadow plays (adapted from Li Tuochen), which years later she performed at the White House, Pauline packed as many of her street experiences as a shadow stage could hold. "Across the screen in turn come the figures you would see and hear on the old Peking street," she wrote when describing it in a 1944 article:

> The flower vendor calling "Mei hua'rh, lai, mei hua'rh!" (Buy flowers, come, buy flowers!); the candy seller with his shop on his back; the scissors grinder who toots his slender horn, and the shop-keeper with his short-handled broom sweeping the street in front of his door. You see the barber, too, his equipment swinging from the ends of a long shoulder pole. He twangs a large iron, two-pronged instrument by means of an iron stick to call his customers. You hear, then see, the two men carrying goods, who trot along to their tuneful "Hi! Hi!" And perhaps there will come one of those decorative two-wheeled carts pulled by a Mongolian pony and still used by some farmers; or a vendor selling pork dumplings or other hot foods from his wheelbarrow equipped with a little stove; or a lady in a rickshaw.[10]

The sometimes comic altercations between rickshaws and pedestrians, camels and automobiles, the jugglers and fire eaters and other entertainers to be found on street corners, the salesmen of everything from candies to immortality elixirs, toys to *dim sum*, and the vast human drama occurring in the streets and alleys by day and by night impressed Pauline deeply. Compared to the chaos of the warlords and, later, the madness of the civil war that ravaged the entire fabric of China, this moving circus of "old Peking" was something to celebrate and remember. Through shadow theatre, this China was for Pauline "a beauty and romance of promise, courage, amazing achievement." It was to be shared with the world, even if shadow theatre was not the real China that surged through the capital's dusty streets; but musings about it, conjured in a quiet walled garden, gave rise to the displays that were later offered to American society folk on New York City's Park Avenue. Yet if these elements were as yet only pieced together from exotic recollections of a distant world fast fading from the screen of the modern era, after 1932 they would become potent symbols of a China that must not be lost, though it might have been and almost was.[11]

For Pauline's Aunt Emma Konantz, "old Peking" had been home since 1919, the year of the student demonstration known as the May Fourth Movement, which brought modern China to birth. It was a long way from Ohio Wesleyan University, Emma's alma mater, where she had taught since graduation, but was even farther from her rural Midwest beginnings. If the vast western states at the other end of the Santa Fe Trail were the ultimate in manifest destiny for easterners wanting or needing to leave the familiar behind, eastern Kansas in the nineteenth century served as another kind of frontier for European immigrants. It was there, in small towns drifting like skiffs on a prairie sea, that Pauline's mother and her sister Emma were brought up, daughters of Germans who had found that there were few obstacles to self-improvement in democratic post–Civil War America if you worked hard enough. John and Rosa Konantz had brought little from Baden-Württemberg except their work ethic, which served them better than wealth on the Kansas plains. They made sure their children were educated – and more, that they aspired to achieving something bigger in life than their parents had known.[12]

Physically, Emma was very unlike her niece, taller and with hazel eyes that were as searching and direct as Pauline's blue gaze was placid and trusting. She was the sort of spinster who could be expected to describe her hair as she did in her passport application, with a touch of middle-aged vanity: "brown – a trifle gray."[13] Like Pauline, Emma never married, and like her niece she filled her life with the same great love: Chinese people, Chinese art, Chinese history. Not long after Emma arrived in Beijing to take up a temporary teaching position in Yenching University's mathematics department, she began collecting Chinese art and artifacts. She also collected theories on Chinese history, culture and science. Like the Cambridge don Joseph Needham more than two decades later, she developed a fascination for Chinese mathematics and science, believing that many firsts claimed by the West should more properly be credited to the Chinese. For Emma, China and math came together in the Chinese system of algebra, first described by Zhu Shijie in his 1303 treatise, *Siyuan yujian* (Jade Mirror of the Four Unknowns). In higher mathematics, Emma saw a language that transcended languages and the source material behind all that was beautiful and harmonious, and not only in China. "Mathematics and art were her life and long-loved specialities," one of her Chinese friends pointed out; "very seldom one possesses the combination of the two."[14] When Pauline visited her in Beijing, Emma was assisting her Yenching colleague, mathematician Dr Chen Caixin, in the translation of *Siyuan yujian*.[15]

While Pauline's interests would range in almost diametrically opposite territory, Emma's passion for understanding the Chinese people through their culture was to be echoed in Pauline's study of shadow theatre and her efforts to trace its ancestry, just as Emma sought to prove the lineage of Western higher mathematics in the *Jade Mirror*. Most of all, they shared the same compassion for the Chinese and concern for what appeared to be their fast-disappearing culture. This compassion was part of what made Emma such a successful teacher; the other part was the sincere humility with which she approached Chinese language and history as she tried to learn all she could of both. "To be able to understand is my sole aim," she told a student friend. To take care of her friends was another. Emma once literally gave the coat off her back to a young Chinese student accompanying her on an outing, catching cold in the process. These things were remembered by those she helped. "Nothing was special in what she said," remembered the girl to whom Emma had given her coat, "but it was full of latent light and strength."[16]

Emma lived in a suburb of Beijing, probably situated not far from the campus of Yenching University, which then was in the process of being transferred from the city to the eighteenth-century country estate of Heshen, a notorious favourite of the Qianlong emperor. Emma's was a courtyard house (*siheyuan*), in which courts with pavilions of one or more rooms on each of the four sides interlocked with others to form a rambling but geometrically balanced compound. The pavilions that edged the courtyards often had porches in front so that one could move from one room to another without getting wet in the rain. Gardens were cultivated within the courtyards, where birds hung in bamboo cages and goldfish darted in cool dark pools. The wealthier the family, the more numerous the courtyards of their compound, which was itself surrounded by high walls to protect the privacy of the family, the virtue of its women, and the family's money and valuables. These walls in turn formed the sides of the many *hutong* that snaked through Beijing, some wide enough for two rickshaws or an automobile, some allowing just space for one person to walk with ease. Such was the pri-

Moon gate in a courtyard
house in Beijing that was
once the home of General
Wu Peifu – typical of the
house in which Pauline's
Aunt Emma lived until
her death in 1936

vacy obtained in this manner that in the middle of one of the most
populous cities on earth, one could sit in a courtyard of an evening
after supper and listen to the crickets or birds, sip tea or wine beneath
the full moon, and never know that a noisy world lived just the other
side of the garden wall.

As Pauline later described it, Emma's house was all this and more,
"a shrine of beauty for all lovers of Chinese art [and] a haven for students in need of counsel and sympathy." One of these students, Pauline
Ch'en (who had not only adopted Pauline's name but her aunt as well)
remembered the garden's beauty. Unlike most who owned such fine
gardens, Emma tended hers herself, wrote Miss Ch'en. Beneath a row
of east windows, she had planted a stand of bamboo which Miss Ch'en
loved to watch shifting in the moonlight; a persimmon tree stood nearby
loaded with rich fruit that drew exclamations from passers-by. Sitting
with Emma in the garden of an evening over tea, Miss Ch'en remembered how "a row of camels [passed] through the pine grove outside

her garden," almost as if she had dreamed it. It was in this magical garden that the course of Pauline's life would change.[17]

"I had gone to Peking with the deep desire to see a Chinese shadow play," Pauline wrote.[18] How long she looked for one and by what methods she does not say, but Aunt Emma seems to have leaned on her connections at Yenching for help (possibly Professor Y.P. Ma and Chancellor Dr Wu Leichuan, who were cited by Wimsatt as shadow theatre aficionados).[19] When even these connoisseurs were not able to bring forth a shadow company immediately, Pauline began to think that the art form must indeed be dying out, if not already dead – a diagnosis she could certainly have heard from Berthold Laufer in Chicago. If there was no theatre and no company of performers, Laufer must have been right when he wrote that he had "saved" shadow figures in "their last hour." Pauline later pointed out that "the few companies left in the city were those that had been employed by the wealthy families under the monarchy and, with their support taken from them, had fallen on hard times." She was told by some of the Americans who had been brought up in China that they had not even known that shadow figures were for performance purposes. They had been given them to play with by their Chinese nannies, who bought them in the markets for a few coppers. It was not the most promising news to hear.[20]

But what Pauline was looking for – a dedicated theatre like that for an opera or dramatic company – had never existed, even at the height of shadow theatre's popularity. As Pauline learned, this absence "did not mean that this ancient drama, beloved for two thousand [sic] years by emperors, fragile court ladies, and weary laborers had become a lost art."[21] It was still very much alive. She was simply not looking in the right places, and a fixed place of performance was rare. Pauline soon discovered that shadow theatre was something that had to be collected and assembled, brought to one's own home, "like the shop-keepers who come ... to spread rare silks, jades, and porcelains at your feet." Meanwhile, Emma continued her inquiries; she was not one to give up, no matter how much trouble or time a search cost her. "She would hunt a whole day in the city," related Miss Ch'en, "for the right ornament for a certain corner."[22]

In the end, Aunt Emma did round up a company, which was "engaged to come to our home," Pauline recounted, "to give an evening's entertainment."[23] Just like a merchant of jades and porcelains, the shadow master would have asked Aunt Emma her preference of his goods, showing her a list of plays from which to choose. Genevieve Wimsatt wrote of placing such an order with the troupe that performed in her garden for foreign guests in 1933. One of the big hits "was a work depicting in terms of stark realism the variety of punishments meted out in the courts of Yen Wang, King of Hell," showing that, like Broadway melodrama, shadow theatre had its seasonal fads. Knowing her audience's stomach, or lack thereof, "I marked off two dealing exclusively with the affairs of this not-too-bad mundane world," Wimsatt explained. Aunt Emma seems to have used the same criterion for Pauline's first shadow play experience; the tame but entertaining plays and scenes she selected were not so different from those performed for other foreigners in Beijing.[24]

What was Pauline expecting as she waited in her aunt's courtyard? What we do know, from her description, is that she was not impressed when the shadow company arrived that summer evening, "a procession of eight or ten blue-clad men, some walking beside rickshas heaped with blue cotton bundles and others carrying oddly shaped paraphernalia on long poles slung over their shoulders." Pauline admitted her dismay that these could have been the appurtenances of any kind of theatre. "Neither did the men look like actors," she noted doubtfully, "nor did their baggage appear to be one bit shadowy."[25]

Aunt Emma's servant offered the men tea and something to eat. Then, with Pauline watching, the players began to assemble their stage. They used "bamboo poles tied together, a paper screen, a lamp hung carelessly behind it, and sagging pink and red cotton draperies," all of which they set up in the middle of the courtyard. Inside what seemed a kind of tent, with a large lighted paper window in front that measured some three feet high and five across, the men then removed their painted parchment "actors" from a trunk – "warriors, emperors, court ladies, dragons, servants, comedians" – and draped the headless bodies over wires strung at right angles to the back of the window.[26]

The evening's program set the standard for what Pauline would later offer to her American audiences: one or more episodes involving "exciting battles in which the victor was aided by breathtaking acrobatic and juggling feats, the mischievous pranks of the Monkey-god and the burning of a bamboo forest." These were followed by lyrical excerpts from romances and *tours de force* of technique and special effects. The most recognizable of the scenes she mentions watching that evening in Emma's garden came from *The Burning of the Bamboo Grove*, a famous play celebrating a female warrior. In program notes published years later, Pauline described the plot with gusto:

> This is a typical military play in which the forces of the Northern Sungs are represented by a lady warrior and those of the Southern T'angs by a magician priest. The two battle first with spears. When the lady proves to be the more skilful, the priest tries to frighten her by changing into a demon. She fights the demon until she succeeds in splitting him in two with her spear. Finally, admitting his defeat, the priest hides in the shelter of the bamboo grove. She calls on the fire gods to her aid, each appearing on a cloud and carrying appropriate fire symbols, such as fire birds, gourds and fire wheels. They surround and destroy both the grove and the defeated priest with their flames, thus leaving the lady warrior and her forces victorious.[27]

If she had in fact seen shadow figures displayed for sale in Manila's Binondo, Pauline would have known them only as dark and lifeless silhouettes. In Chicago, she encountered Laufer's more artfully displayed figures, replete with detailed context, but in just as static a setting. But here they were dancing, fighting, and praying in scenes that filled the white screen with flashing colour and the air with music. She was overcome by their beauty, but above all by the artistry with which they were manipulated.[28]

She marvelled at how deftly the man in charge of stage property selected the correct heads, with an admirable "knack of getting each character ready for his or her entrance at just the moment he received his cue from the manipulator." As anyone who has stood backstage during a theatrical performance knows, the precision of what happens in the wings is what allows for the free play of creativity of the actors in front of the footlights. Yet unlike the backstage engineers of human theatre, these shadow masters had to be both directors and actors, prop men and musicians. Pauline discovered this at a second performance, again arranged by her aunt, which was organized entirely for the purpose of viewing the action from behind the screen.

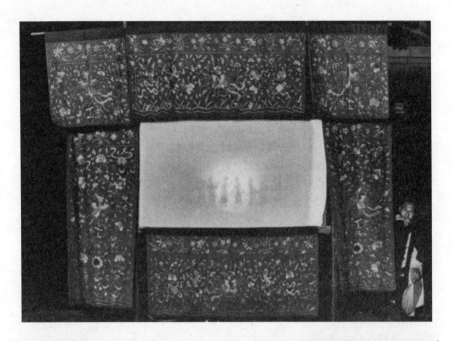

Top: The embroidered silk stage of Beijing shadow master Li Tuochen

Bottom: Li Tuochen in performance.

"I watched the performance by teetering back and forth between the front and back sides of the stage," Pauline recalled, "in an effort to see the 'cause' and the 'effect' all at the same time."[29] This meant breaking a time-honoured rule. While it was permitted for devoted fans of shadow theatre to go backstage after a performance to meet the animators and see the figures, during a performance no one but the players was ever allowed behind the stage screen. For a woman to penetrate to this secret space was especially unusual, because women were not allowed to join men in performance. Li Tuochen claimed this was because only the educated could perform shadow theatre (meaning the literary Eastside variety), and as few women were afforded the education available to men, they never had a chance to try their hand at the art. Perhaps the real reason was China's infamous misogyny: women who mixed in male affairs were thought to bring bad luck. On this occasion, it is likely that the performers were openly indulging a foreigner's curiosity, perhaps even spurred to greater feats of technique to impress her.[30]

Pauline was never one to ignore the manners or mores of old China – in fact, she became very knowledgeable about them and cautioned those she trained to be mindful of them. But only by observing the action from such close quarters could Pauline understand just how the animators held and manipulated their figures, using a stick affixed to the body to control each figure, a stick for each arm, connected at the hands, and sometimes threads that operated blinking eyes or opening and closing mouths. She also took careful note of how special effects were created. To suggest the burning of the bamboo grove, they lit a pile of coarse paper, blowing smoke and using the brief flames to light up the parchment canes from behind. (With American ingenuity but little thought for his pulmonary health, Pauline's collaborator Lee Ruttle was to accomplish this scene with half a dozen cigarettes in his mouth.) Then the forest was gradually pulled away and down from the screen, as if collapsing in a smoldering heap.

Pauline watched figures sweep across the sky as gods flying in on clouds to help the warrior heroine in the fierce battles that filled the screen with action and colour, and delighted in the knowledge that what was happening behind the screen was just as exciting as what was seen in front of it. "It was difficult to tell," remembered Pauline, "whether the players or the audience were enjoying the performance more."

When she came to write her book about shadow theatre, she pointed out that "even the more serious plays [have] their comic relief … When a silly old shadow king flirts with his favourite shadow concubine, every move is supported by a back-stage cackle which heightens the realism and indicates that the 'Under-the-Lamp' men are enjoying the fun fully as much as the audience."[31] When this second play was done, the troupe's lead performer peeked out from around the screen, then smiled at Pauline and charmingly said, "Finish."[32]

On these evenings in Aunt Emma's courtyard, Pauline experienced something far more significant than the tourist's entertainment she later claimed it was. Part of it, of course, was the sheer thrill of seeing her first shadow show. As Jo Humphrey, the shadow theatre expert who inherited Pauline's collection half a century later, points out, "Way back when, before film and television were so readily available, to see colored figures moving on a screen was very mysterious. Many of the most popular shadow plays were about actual historic characters who had through this means come mysteriously to life. Shadow masters knew this and kept everything very secret, never allowing anyone backstage except those who were actually working." Pauline had been permitted that glimpse behind the wizard's curtain; yet unlike Dorothy in the Emerald City, she found not ordinary men engaged in smoke-and-mirrors prestidigitation but artists engaged in the animation of the sacred. "She picked up on that mystique," says Humphrey.[33] As Pauline expressed it, "I cannot imagine any explorer having more thrilling adventures than I experienced on my journey of discovery into China's rich and glamorous past through the medium of the shadow play." It was at this time that Pauline claimed she was "seized with the desire to give a shadow play myself." And as she had been inspired by the Laufer figures in Chicago to see a performance in Beijing, she was now moved by the performance in Beijing to learn how to become a performer herself, though again very far from the ancient capital of China – in fact, in the heart of New York City.[34]

Chapter 4

THE RED GATE SHADOW PLAYERS

One day in 1909 Manhattan, a whippet of a man named Harry Edmonds was hurrying up the steps of the granite-domed Low Library at Columbia University. A deeply conscientious employee of the YMCA, for which he headed the organization's Student Christian Movement, Edmonds noticed a young Chinese descending the steps and called out a cheerful greeting. That might have been the end of it – a moment's how-do-you-do – but the young man stopped and hurried back up the steps.[1]

As Edmonds described it later, the student thanked him for saying hello – the first time, he said, that anyone in New York had accorded him a courtesy in all the weeks he had been in the city. Edmonds was shocked and troubled. After all, America was supposed to be the friendliest place on earth, where all were welcome and hospitality was legendary.[2] But Edmonds was not taking into account a whole segment of American history, with its exclusionary policies and state-sanctioned racism toward the Chinese (not to mention the low status of Chinese in New York City), which likely had a part to play in this student's treatment. Since Chinese had first begun settling in the lower boroughs of Manhattan in the 1850s, they had been associated with stereotypes – opium addiction, a strange, disgusting diet, and "heathen" practices – even as they were meshed into the stereotypes overlaid on other residents of these districts: African Americans and Irish, working-class women and men who were seen as frequenting pubs more often than churches and feeding carnal appetites at whim. "New York elites judged entering Chinese by this moral accounting," writes John Tchen, yet never far from this was the missionary zeal that redemption through adoption of American Christian values was always possible.[3] As American merchants made fortunes off trade with China, including the selling of opium, they "presided over the faith in the U.S. mastery of Chinese material culture, people and civilization," says Tchen. Ownership and display of Chinese porcelains and antiques fostered a "patrician orientalism" that "shifted first to emulation and then again to a sense of civilizational mastery."[4]

These attitudes had driven the Chinese into a ghetto within a ghetto. The irony was that when ensconced in their own "Chinatown," Chinese Americans, whose cultural differences were judged too stark to allow them to become an ingredient in the American melting pot, were just as apt to be targeted by the whites surrounding them as when they had lived among them. If even the sophisticated artist Helen Hyde could write of going to San Francisco's Chinatown to see Chinese in their New Year's finery "like hunting for tropical birds," it is easy to understand how in New York's Chinatown well into the twentieth century, tourists primed by the freak-show legacy of P.T. Barnum could take bus rides through the district to "look" at the residents as if they were exotic animals in a zoo.[5] On at least one occasion, when a fatal shootout occurred between rival gang members, tourists had both the thrill they were seeking and confirmation of the dangers they expected to find in so disreputable a quarter.[6]

Edmonds and his wife decided something had to be done about a situation in which international students – particularly, it would seem, those who belonged to what are now called visible minorities – had no one to share in and encourage their experience of learning about life in a foreign land, let alone to have anyone greet them on the streets of the cosmopolitan capital of the United States of America. So with help from Columbia's dean, the Edmondses invited a dozen foreign students to their home, where they offered tea, sandwiches, and a forum for conversation. On the next occasion, these students brought friends, who brought their friends, and soon the meeting grew so large Columbia's Earl Hall had to be put at the Edmondses' disposal. Impressed by the students he had met through the Edmondses, John D. Rockefeller made a grant of $3,000,000 to build a residence to house eligible undergraduates and the activities that were growing up around the Edmondses' concept. In 1924, International House was erected at 500 Riverside Drive, supporting itself through student fees and grants as well as considerable corporate donations. "In an architectural sense," wrote Oscar Schisgall, "it has been called one of the city's finest examples of 20th-Century planning – simple, functional, yet impressive in its beauty." The building's lower floors offered "all the appurtenances of a modern club," with lounges, gym, a cafeteria and music room, and a handsome auditorium with a good stage, over which floated a bas-relief American eagle. The upper floors housed five hundred men and women. Until the Communist takeover of China in 1949 and the cooling that followed in Sino-American diplomacy, many students came from China to study in the United States, and by the late 1920s there was a significant Chinese presence at International House.[7]

Edmonds' grateful student on the steps of the Low Library thus played another interesting role besides serving as the inspiration for International House; his interaction with Edmonds was a link in the chain of events that led Pauline Benton to a professional career in shadow theatre.[8]

❈

In 1923, Dr Guy Benton fell ill in Minneapolis, where he had retired from his position as head of the University of the Philippines, and Pauline's sojourn in Beijing was cut short so that she and her mother could be with him. A sufferer from "sleeping sickness" contracted in Manila, Benton endured increasing paralysis until his death on 29 June 1927. Pauline not only loved her parents, she admired and respected them. As she wrote to cousins after her mother's death in 1947, her parents' generation was one "of true, stalwart, loyal and loving souls – a heritage that is a great inspiration and strength, one of which we may all be justly proud."[9]

While her mother remained in Minneapolis, Pauline went back to the Riverside Drive apartment later that year, and she then took her first known job – on the activities staff of International House. What drew Pauline to work there is not known, but the proximity of her apartment to the residence hall could have played a part, as did perhaps its YMCA connection through Harry Edmonds. It is just as likely that the multicultural flavour of International House, with its considerable Asian student membership, also had something to do with attracting a young woman so recently charmed by Manila and Beijing. Ultimately, International House would serve as a kind of temporary replacement for the China that Pauline had had to leave so abruptly, just as it would set the stage of her future endeavours.[10]

Pauline later explained that while the shadow plays she had seen in Beijing had given her a "craving" to perform a show herself, she had had to satisfy herself by "purchasing a few figures in a Peking market" to bring back to America with her. Since her return, these figures had lain "in drawers for several years ... until, one day," she wrote, "I was prompted to show them to a Chinese friend, whose first reaction was, 'Let's give a shadow play.'" In fact, Pauline's figures had been taken out of their drawers at least once since her return from Beijing. In 1923, on her return from China, she had produced an exhibit of shadow figures and Chinese antiques in the Oxford, Ohio, home of her sister's father-in-law, the dean of Miami University. Given this enthusiasm for exhibiting the figures she had brought back from Beijing, she probably did not leave them for long in their drawers in New York, and she had obviously had them out on display for her Chinese friends there.[11]

The performing arts were a big part of the scene at International House. Residents were encouraged to involve themselves in all manner of cultural activities, sharing and comparing between cultures. As Oscar Schisgall described, education and entertainment merged in a yearly Festival of the Arts. Applied and performance arts pertinent to the various nations present in the student residents were drawn on for a mass celebration, which culminated in what was called the Night of Nations. Students decorated booths displayed on the lower floors, offering food or visuals according to their national origin. Every half-hour, performances were put on in the auditorium and gymnasium. "One can hear everything from African drums to Oriental flutes," wrote Schisgall, "from American jazz to Tyrolean yodelers. It is a night that *proves* the people of the world can play together in peace – if only the effort is made with intelligence and good will."[12]

Pauline is characteristically discreet in her later accounts of her first foray into shadow theatre performance. It is as if a number of her Chinese friends simply disengaged from the woodwork and came to her aid in mounting a shadow performance. The production appears to have been planned rather than impromptu, and it is most probable that the occasion for which Pauline's friends wanted to use her shadow figures was the Night of Nations. They, however, not Pauline, would have performed with the figures. As a member of staff, she would not have been allowed to perform with the students – it was their show, after all. But in any case, for this improvised North American version of *piyingxi*, Pauline would have learned more from the audience side of the shadow screen than behind it.

She was trying something else new, at least for her; she selected one of her Chinese friends to be narrator for the performance. This was a role typically not seen in authentic shadow theatre, in which each major character announced his or her background and part in the play. Sometimes a star singer would station himself near the side of the stage, where he could be seen and bow to applause; but if a narrator was included, the singer was not visible. The inclusion of a visible, dedicated narrator next to the stage would prove useful to Pauline when she toured the United States with her own company. Her friends, "none of whom had ever handled a shadow figure in China and only one or two of whom had seen a performance, moved the figures in pantomime." Watching from a distance was the best test for Pauline to see just what could be done with the figures she had collected. But it was also important for her to observe (one of the most important parts of a shadow performer's education) as her friends "deft with their fingers … presented a performance which received a hearty response from the audience."[13]

The show had none of the artistry of what Pauline had seen in China, and she did not deceive herself by thinking that shadow theatre was easy to learn. What mattered was that she had begun a journey. In Aunt Emma's garden in 1923, Pauline had been fascinated by an art form that seemed both immeasurably remote yet intriguingly close to her heart, so much so that she believed it was possible to give a shadow play herself one day. And now here she was, sitting in an auditorium beside the Hudson River, with Chinese manipulating shadows that belonged to *her*, moving at *her* direction; and people, *American* people, seemed to like them. Even more than in Beijing several years earlier, the thirty-two-year old Pauline suddenly knew what she had to do. "This [shadow play]," she recalled, "aroused my own interest in setting out for 'more worlds to conquer'" – in short, to become a shadow master herself.[14]

In 1930, Pauline proved she was serious: she had a stage built in New York to go with her figures. Not for her the "sagging red and pink"

The red silk stage built for Pauline in New York City in 1930, now part of the
Chinese Theatre Works' Benton Collection. Behind the "window" at extreme
right is a miniature stage where a Chinese-style rod puppet created by Pauline
was sometimes used as narrator.

curtains and bamboo poles of the stage set up at Aunt Emma's. Her
stage had the façade of a Chinese house, with upturned eaves, all covered in embroidered red silk brocade like that used on Li Tuochen's
stage in Beijing. On either side of the screen were what the Chinese
called "leak windows" – openings in interior walls, through which to
see from one part of a garden to another – which in Pauline's case was
silk cut in the interlocked pattern called "Chinese coin." This pattern
was repeated in gold on the white silk panels that formed the stage
curtain hanging in front of the screen. In keeping with Pauline's need
for a narrator, the "leak window" on the right-hand side concealed a
miniature stage, in which a rod puppet in the form of a Chinese lady
served to explain the action to the audience. (Whether this puppet was
used consistently for this purpose or only when Pauline could not secure
the narration services of a professional actor of recognized name, we

do not know; the rod puppet is never mentioned in any reviews of Pauline's performances.) Below the superstructure of the stage, which sat on a large platform, hung more red silk and a panel of silk embroidered with flowers. The dominance of red would determine the name of the shadow theatre company that Pauline founded a few years later.[15]

Pauline kept Aunt Emma busy during this time. While the stage was being constructed, she sent to China for more shadow figures, which Emma was able to procure for her, along with scripts for plays, which Emma had translated. Emma also effected the most important relationship Pauline was to have in her study of shadow theatre. "With my faithful Aunt in Peking acting as interpreter," Pauline remembered, "I carried on a lively correspondence with Mr. Lee T'uo-chen, Peking's popular shadow player, who had performed in the Forbidden City under the late monarchical regime."[16]

Born in the last two decades of the nineteenth century, Li, a slender, bright-eyed man with a shaved head, was himself the son of a shadow master, a practitioner of the Luanzhou (Eastside) Shadows who had turned to shadow theatre as an underemployed scholar. Li was thus brought up in the trade. As a boy, he had joined his father to perform for the imperial court of the late nineteenth and early twentieth centuries, and as a man he brought his company, Qing Min Sheng (Illustrious People's Welfare), to Tianjin in the 1920s for the entertainment of the deposed last Qing emperor, Puyi (reign name Xuantong).[17] Puyi had been fond of puppet plays in the Forbidden City. In the microcosm of that unreal world, peopled with aging concubines and cringing eunuchs, the young emperor had an especial passion for a play in which a father murdered both his child and his wife and was executed. Puyi took this play so seriously that he was mortified to find that the puppets were not real. Like a puppet in the same crazy play, Puyi tried unsuccessfully to poison the puppet master in retribution.[18]

Li told Pauline that he had known "all the players who performed in the palace, from Kuang-hsu's time to the fall of the dynasty." Li also remembered being called to perform as often as ten times in a month for some of the Empress Dowager Cixi's relatives. Occasionally the dowager, who was close to her younger brother, Duke Guixiang, was present for these performances. This tenuous connection to the infamous Empress Dowager's court was to give Lee Ruttle, Pauline's PR man, a chance to claim that Pauline had studied shadow theatre with

Top: Li Tuochen and his father (on left), c. 1936; both had performed for members of the imperial family.

Bottom: Li Tuochen and his father in performance with a third troupe member. Photos by Pauline Benton

none other than the Empress Dowager's own shadow masters, a cachet
that worked wonders in gullible 1930s America.[19] Yet it was a distinct
compliment to be asked to perform for these aristocratic Manchus,
who were true aficionados of the art form. Like his father, Li specialized in the difficult female roles, which required more than ordinary
skill in falsetto vocalization as well as manipulation of figures. They
had to be not just good but excellent to win over this audience.[20]

Li took his craft very seriously. He claimed to Pauline that his father
was "the founder of the modern school of Shadow acting" and was
part of the Luanzhou Shadows tradition. According to Li, this tradition emerged in the reign of the Ming emperor, Wanli (1573–1620).
The founder of this school, which came to be so popular in Beijing,
was said to be Huang Suzhi of Luan county, some hundred miles east
of Beijing. Huang had failed the examinations (like Li's father) and
had left home, travelling north to Manchuria, where he taught school
in the countryside. Huang first used paper and then donkey parchment to create shadow figures as tools in his teaching. This story would
have been passed on to Pauline, and as the daughter and niece of teachers, she probably wanted to believe it, even as she also readily accepted
the story of Emperor Wu and his shadow concubine. Whatever its verac-
ity regarding more remote times, the story does pinpoint an important
documented detail in the Luanzhou tradition: that the Eastside Shadows originally came from north of Beijing, an area that was traditionally
Manchu.[21]

Like Berthold Laufer, Li Tuochen was a keen observer of the health
of shadow theatre in the capital region, constantly taking its pulse like
a doctor that of a sickly patient. He explained that in all of Hebei county
there were less than a dozen Westside performers, and only half that
number in Beijing itself. This is why Pauline saw an Eastside-style performance first, and why this style, with its scripts and more refined
carving and colouring of figures, became her inspiration – though she
was to blend both Eastside and Westside, with its slightly larger characters, in her North American performances. Ironically, the Westside
Shadows probably had a longer history than the Eastside, whose scripts
date back no earlier than the reign of the Daoguang emperor (r. 1820–
50) and did not reach their full sophistication until the late nineteenth
and early twentieth centuries. They had their golden age right at the time
when China was being ruled by the theatre-loving Empress Dowager

Cixi and Manchu high society was making shadow theatre an integral part of its entertainment world. Pauline readily accepted this context. "The Chinese classical stage of living actors is our model," she wrote in program notes of 1940; and in her unpublished manuscript, "China's Colored Shadow Plays," she made an even bolder claim: "The secrets of Chinese costumes, arts, architecture, religion, history and mythology were all held in the quiet forms of the shadow figures."[22] As she explained, "When the now silent courtyards of the Forbidden City were crowded with officials and persons of rank, resplendent in their yellow, red, orange, and purple silks, with their own shadows as the only contrast to the brilliance of it all, eyes bedazzled by the spectacle could well believe they were seeing *colored* shadows."[23]

This echoes another of Li Tuochen's comments: "Those who love the Shadows, it seems, love also the glorious past, and the Shadows make that past glow again" – the past of emperors and court officials and the gods and goddesses of legend, a past colliding with the present like motorcars and rickshaws in Beijing's lanes.[24]

Shadow theatre by correspondence would have been easy in one respect. Li Tuochen, who had been educated at a Methodist mission and was a Christian convert, spoke and wrote English. He could communicate with foreigners and often produced plays that used not classical shadow characters but figures mirroring the modern world of cars, trains, and airplanes (he even created a shadow play version of the Nativity story for Christmas). But how Pauline was able to learn the more subtle shadow theatre techniques via letters is another of her life's mysteries. We have none of the correspondence to allow us to judge how this was done. Of course, demonstration in person was only part of what made one a shadow master. As Li pointed out, speaking of himself and his brother, "Our training was long and arduous; but after a year of steady practice I could make the Shadows move to my father's satisfaction." In training to be a manipulator, Li explained, one "first had to learn to watch, not your own fingers clutching the reeds, not even the figures themselves, but only their shadows on the screen." When she wanted to watch real masters at work, to whom did Pauline turn? How did she learn to hold the reeds and develop the smooth technique that all shadow performers strove to achieve? Pauline did not study in person with Li Tuochen until 1936. Of direct hands-on training of the sort all shadow performers obtained, Pauline had none before she began to perform in public in 1933.[25]

Given that she had seen only a few performances of authentic shadow theatre in Beijing in 1923 and had picked up some tips on technique via letters, what gave Pauline the impetus, not to mention the courage, to form her own company on a professional footing in 1932? She is mum on the subject in "China's Colored Shadow Plays," aside from discussing technical details that confronted her one after the other, which arose from the imposition of her Western ideas rather than absorption of Chinese ones. For example, the fragile paper screen had to be replaced by a more durable cloth one; "the lighting, one of the more primitive aspects of the Chinese performances, called for improvement." Pauline knew that she had to retain "the authenticity and charm of the original plays" but also had to be careful to make them "enjoyable and understandable to an audience unfamiliar with the culture they represented." For all she knew, her audiences might have a superior knowledge of China, or they might know next to nothing, but to take a pedantic approach to the plays, she wrote, "would be to have defeated our purpose," which was the popularization of a Chinese performance art reconstituted for foreign audiences. She hoped through these means to "arouse a curiosity for further and deeper excursions through the labyrinth of China's ancient arts." But she doesn't tell us how she learned to grasp this ancient art.[26]

As noted in chapter 1, Pauline had made contact with puppeteer Paul McPharlin, who was perhaps the one performer whose drive and scholarship hers most resembled in this period. In early 1932, Pauline's associate Lee Ruttle had written to McPharlin seeking his endorsement for a "Cooperative Children's Recreation Center." McPharlin's response was encouraging, but he noted that Meyer Levin, founder of the Marionette Studio Theatre in Chicago, had set up a festival at the New School for Social Research, in which programs specifically targeted at adults were offered. Did this help change the course of an early plan of Pauline's to offer Chinese shadow theatre performances solely for children? It was also at this time that McPharlin's Chinese shadow romance, *The Vixen's Spell* (translated by Dr Yamei Kin), using hundreds of figures and sets collected by Benjamin March in Beijing, was produced in Detroit – probably the first time Chinese shadow theatre, or an approximation of it, was performed by a non-Chinese in America. Like Pauline, McPharlin did not hesitate to make use of distinctly Western technology to "improve" a traditional Chinese art form. To provide arias for his production, he played recordings of Mei Lanfang singing selections from Beijing Opera, a sample of the mixed media in which he specialized.[27]

It may also be that with Mei Lanfang and Beijing Opera in mind, Pauline had had an even earlier inspiration, in the winter of 1930, when that supremely Chinese artist had offered Americans performances of an art form that outside China was rarely understood by foreigners, achieving one of the greatest of unlikely successes on Broadway.

Mei was born in 1894 into a family of Beijing Opera performers and had debuted on stage at the age of ten. Like his grandfather Mei Qiao-ling, Mei specialized in female roles, which until well into the twentieth century were taken solely by men. He eventually played a wide range, from *hua dan* (romantic young ladies) to roles demonstrating brilliant acrobatics and martial arts, and was soon touted as China's greatest actor. As soprano Maria Callas did for long-forgotten masterworks of the Western operatic repertoire, Mei, with the help of scholar Qi Rushan, dusted off antique Chinese stageworks and made them shine again through a combination of extraordinary discipline and brilliant innovation. Like Callas, he brought revitalized productions before a public that knew nothing of them, to great success. A fan of silent screen comedian Charlie Chaplin, Mei was up-to-date with the latest entertainment trends sweeping America, via Hollywood and the stage, and was a sophisticated cross-pollinator of Asian and Western styles. Assembling a number of scenes from his greatest plays, ranging from the lyrical and poetic to the acrobatic and athletic, Mei and his company travelled to New York City, where on 17 February 1930 he took the stage of the Forty-Ninth Street Theatre.[28]

His excellent planning aside, Mei's timing was terrible. Four months earlier, the New York Stock Exchange had melted like the ice sculptures that once adorned rich men's tables. And the history of Chinese opera in New York City was not a happy one. In 1852 the Cantonese theatre troupe Tong Hook Tong had arrived in New York on promises

made by shifty promoters who disappeared when the troupe's performances were poorly received by press and public. Cheated out of
their gorgeous costumes and stage equipment, and without money to
return to China, the troupe ended up in a workhouse. One of them tried
to kill himself, while the others wandered the streets selling whatever
they had and begging for handouts.[29] As John Tchen points out, if
"authentic Chinese culture was too strange for New Yorkers' tastes,"
any effort at trying to effect cross-cultural exchange was pointless. Enter
the "simulated Chinese," trailing his baggage of stereotyped mannerisms, his vulgarized Irish wife and half-caste children, his cigars for
sale and opium pipe and Manchu queue. Once the simulation took
hold, there was no room on the stage for the real thing, not to mention
a public appetite for it.[30]

Not much had changed, and into this unpromising atmosphere Mei
brought his art to share with those shell-shocked New Yorkers still able
to buy a theatre ticket and summon an interest in something Chinese
that was not a chow mein restaurant or a sideshow freak display. And
as snowflakes fell past the lighted marquee like the plum blossom whose
name he shared, a sort of miracle occurred: Mei's program took off.
People kept coming back, and critics kept raving, to the point where
many lost all grasp of the facts. Though Beijing Opera was "born" only
in 1790 when the Four Great Anhui troupes performed in Beijing for
the Qianlong emperor's birthday, people chose to see in Mei's sinuous
dances and swordplay a performance art dating back several thousand years, to "dance of the Chou dynasty of 400 B.C." As one scholar
of the period has noted, the world of Asia seemed one in which there
was no change, "a world of timeless, atemporal customs and rituals,
untouched by the historical processes that were 'afflicting' or 'improv-
ing' but, at any rate, drastically altering Western societies at the time."[31]
Having watched its most trusted systems fail in 1929, by 1930 America was ripe for the perceived timelessness and classic forms of Asia.
This was part of the magic of Mei's art at this stage of his career – it
paid no attention to the exigencies of the clock and calendar. The fantasy of imagined ancient art forms transferred intact to the lights of
Broadway fed the public's hunger for the exotic and exciting, the bizarre
and *outré*. Confidence men, imposters cashing in on the vanished
thrones of Europe, and Chicago gangsters defending kingdoms of crime
with bullets and bathtub gin defined the 1930s as much as sparkling

Hollywood musicals celebrating beautiful people free of the cares that beset those who bought tickets to watch them. Mei's appearance at this place and time "could not have come at a more psychologically apt moment," wrote A.C. Scott. "The public mood was prepared to be receptive to a dramatic art which ignored realism and whose calm values were those of a civilization with time behind it."[32]

Other than a copy of the souvenir program distributed for Mei's Broadway debut, there is no direct evidence in Pauline's papers that she was in the audience for a Mei performance. But in her future programs she often included a quotation that she attributed to Mei Lanfang: "To know their theatre is to know, in no small degree, the Chinese people." This line actually derives from the preface to George Kin Leung's book *Mei Lan-Fang*, published in Shanghai in 1929. The book was undoubtedly available in New York for Mei's 1930 debut (the author owns a copy autographed by Mei during his New York run, suggesting it was sold during the performance period). The quote, however, is not Mei's but Leung's. Pauline had a copy of the book, from which she pulled this quotation for use in one of her own programs and in haste (or deliberately) misattributed it. Where Mei and shadow theatre are concerned, it is also interesting to note an account of a conversation with Mei that Genevieve Wimsatt recorded in 1932. During their interview, Mei told Wimsatt that he had not only loved shadow theatre performances but had set up his own little stage at home as a child, manipulating the characters in plays of his own devising. Pauline may well have heard of this from Li Tuochen or even from the Chinese actress Soo Yong, who during Mei's Broadway run served as mistress of ceremonies for his performances, explaining plots for audience members as she later did for Pauline. This, too, suggests that Pauline could have seen Mei perform in New York that winter of 1930, as she ventured carefully into her own unknown theatrical territory.[33]

There is still another factor. Shadow theatre is filled with warrior maidens, heroic goddesses, women of power and cunning, like the martial maiden Mulan. Many of the Beijing Opera scenes that Mei Lanfang offered in New York featured these same Chinese women, and through his research into American entertainment he must have known that strong women were a stock-in-trade of the Broadway stage. When fabled Broadway producer Charles Frohman told one of his star actresses of the 1900s that Americans love to see a woman triumph over men, he was referring to a formula that not only Mei and Pauline would have understood by 1930 but that their audiences would have expected to see. If that female dynamism was not a sure sell in the age of the New Woman, what was?[34]

※

At least Mei's performances involved a flesh-and-blood figure, dancing, leaping and singing. Eastside shadow theatre used by Pauline had boasted a screen no more than four feet long by three feet tall, and figures a mere fourteen inches, which even to people sitting close to the screen looked like delicate images emerging from a mist. Expecting people to sit still for this was like asking busy commuters to stop for a poetry reading. Americans also had no frame of reference for what they were seeing. They were familiar with puppet shows, which were commonly seen as entertainment belonging in carnivals or held on street corners and definitely the province of children, not adults. That shadow figures are not puppets, and the great shadow romances and tragedies not the stuff of children's entertainment, is a difference that is difficult even today for many non-Chinese spectators to grasp. As Stephen Kaplin points out, the 1930s was "a Golden Age of American puppet theatre," adding, "The art of puppetry had broken through artistically and had also achieved an unprecedented popular acclaim (thanks to folks like Tony Sarg, Sue Hastings, Remo Bufanno, and the Yale Puppeteers on the east coast, and Blanding Sloane and Ralph Cheese in the west, among many others)." For some, puppet shows as art were not hard to grasp, but what Pauline was offering added something more – something attractively mysterious but also strangely opaque, rich with symbols that might confuse rather than explain, and mannered in a way that would challenge the sensibilities of those who took their cultural familiarity cue from New York's Chinatown. So the learning curve would have been a steep one.[35]

On top of this, Pauline was a complete unknown. Ticket buyers would have to be both curious and credulous to put down money for a performance art which they had never seen and might not understand. She could hope to be taken seriously only by offering sophisticated programs carried out with disciplined professionalism. This is where she needed help, because she had no theatrical background, one of the basic prerequisites for anyone contemplating a life in the theatre. Anyone who had taken the stage professionally would see that, as with Beijing Opera, there were many similarities between shadow plays and live theatre. Superlative pacing, timing, and technique all needed to be part of any live performance worth putting before the public. In the case of staging, blocking the scenes and arranging the sets could make or break a performance. And music was another problem. In Beijing, Pauline had watched shadow figures being manipulated to vocal and instrumental accompaniment. She believed herself capable of manipulating her figures, though only when she returned to China to study under a shadow master did she realize how little she really knew. But who would provide the soundscape so necessary to shadow theatre? "The personnel of a fully equipped Shadow company includes an orchestra of from three to five musicians," noted Genevieve Wimsatt, "who, collectively, are masters of some twelve or fourteen distinct instruments." Some companies with enough talent and manpower could offer accompaniment in most of these instruments, but the typical shadow theatre ensemble was no more complex than a trio or quartet which often included strings, such as the *erhu* (two-stringed fiddle) and the *xianzi* (three-stringed guitar), as well as drums, cymbals, and flute. Pauline did not collect these instruments until 1936, on her last trip to China. Even if she could have somehow rounded up a musician or two capable of accompanying a performance, she needed someone to help her stage and manipulate her figures, block out scenes, work the kinks out of scripts, and smooth stiff translations into fluid dialogue, as well as helping her deliver the lines in a convincing and entertaining fashion.[36]

All told, Pauline's situation looked no better than the Dow Jones averages in late October 1929. But even with the odds against her, she was to find just the right people to assist her in bringing the shadow theatre of imperial China to life among the skyscrapers of art deco New York City.

Ethnomusicologist, composer, and jazz specialist William Russell (real last name Wagner) was born in Canton, Missouri, in 1905. By age ten he had taken to the violin the way he would one day take to the rhythms of Jelly Roll Morton. He graduated from the conservatory in Quincy, Illinois, and went on to study at Columbia University, where in the ruins of Depression-era New York he found a silver lining: rare jazz recordings by Ma Rainey, Morton, and others available for pennies, which formed the foundations of his magnificent and enormous collection of jazz recordings.[37]

How Russell learned to play Chinese instruments is not known, but he became not only proficient in the techniques of the *yang qin* (dulcimer), *yue qin* ("moon guitar"), and the *erhu* but was eventually able to play another dozen Chinese instruments – wind, string, and percussion – and to compose music for them in what seemed to American listeners an authentic sound and style. As well as mastering the instruments, he was able to use most of them during a given performance. Years later, even Lou Harrison would need two assistant musicians when he helped Pauline perform *The White Snake*. As his notes for *The White Snake* show, Russell also manged to create music for Chinese instruments that somehow sounded Chinese while avoiding the "cacophony" believed by most foreigners to constitute "real" Chinese music. Examining his meticulous scores, it is easy to see how the sinuous and ruminative melodies he composed could have lent an atmosphere of otherworldliness to the romance of the White Snake and her mortal lover.[38]

Although Russell is not as well known as his compositions' quality and influence warrant (his works for percussion ensemble were to inspire better-known composers such as John Cage, Henry Cowell, and Harrison), he is nonetheless recognized as the "first composer in the western tradition to integrate African, Caribbean, and Asian instruments with western instruments and found objects." Perhaps the claim to fame that he himself would most readily have acknowledged was as pre-eminent expert in New Orleans jazz. It was a visit to New Orleans with Pauline's company in 1937 that brought him back yearly to listen to and record all the local jazz artists he could find; he gathered one of the largest collections of jazz music and memorabilia in the country. In 1958, not surprisingly, he became curator of the jazz archive at Tulane University.[39]

Unlike the formally trained Russell, Lee Ruttle was one of nature's artists, who seems to have entered the world with the fully formed gift of drama. He was born Leo Francis Ruttle in Rhode Island in 1909, and a disrupted childhood perhaps accounted for his flight into the fantasy world of the stage.[40] Ruttle was very much of his time, in that he came before the public when the most extravagant claims in press

Left to right: Pauline Benton, William Russell, and Lee Ruttle

releases were taken at face value. Aging stage beauties claimed in advertisements that Lux Soap kept them looking younger than their age, which was itself a fiction; vaguely European entities fetched up along Park Avenue claiming lost coronets and the attention of a title-hungry republic. In almost every piece of promotional material released by Pauline's shadow troupe, most of which were written by Ruttle, he claimed to have been a member of the original Provincetown Players. This group of experimental actors and playwrights was founded in 1915 as a reaction against the florid and foreign-authored melodramas reigning over Broadway in the years after the First World War. Writers such as Eugene O'Neill, John Reed, and Edna St. Vincent Millay took part, as did a number of painters, producers, and revolutionaries – artistic and political. From this emerged the so-called Little Theatre movement to bring more intimacy and human scale to theatre productions, which included puppet theatre – perhaps a source for Ruttle's interest in shadow plays.

The trouble with Ruttle's story is that there is little proof of a theatrical career at all, let alone as a member of the *avant-garde* Provincetown Players. Before appearing in walk-on parts in a single, albeit important, Provincetown Players production – e.e. cummings's *HIM*, in New York in 1927 – Ruttle seems to have performed in no other production with any company.[41] In fact, after performing in *HIM*, from 1928 to 1929, he served in the Marine Corps, stationed in various bases from South Carolina to Guam and Guantanamo Bay, Cuba, where the only drama he encountered was when he was convicted in two summary courts martial. Clearly, the structured environment of the military was not for him, at least in peacetime.[42] Yet by the end of his career with Pauline, he could congratulate himself on having made a place for himself in American theatre history, as both performer and as promoter.[43]

Pauline could have met Russell through contacts at Columbia University – he was the sort of person whose itinerant lifestyle kept turning him back to college campuses throughout his career. How Pauline met Ruttle is unknown, yet he was as important to her as Russell, if not more so. It was Ruttle's innate theatrical know-how, combined with his quick ability to learn shadow theatre techniques, that would hold her company together. Ruttle offered something that Pauline lacked – the swagger of a showman, a sideshow barker's vim and vigour, and a shameless talent for promotion and prestidigitation, without which theatre, especially the touring variety, cannot exist. Ruttle churned out press releases and programs making extraordinary claims for Pauline as for himself, catching the wave of American fantasy like an eager surfer. He was as comfortable approaching Hollywood as he was the White House or the Metropolitan Museum of Art, with a nothing-ventured, nothing-gained chutzpah, which in the end helped thrust Pauline's company into the limelight. In contrast to shadow theatre's audience demographic in China, Ruttle aspired to performances that would impress spectators of wealth, power, and prestige. Whereas shadow theatre had become the cheap entertainment of farmers and rickshawmen and curious tourists in the embattled China of the 1930s, Ruttle helped Pauline ensure that in America it played only to audiences of the elite. This factor would prove of great assistance to Chinese relief efforts in the 1930s and 1940s, as well as to wider acceptance of the art form in North America's halls of higher learning.

Pauline had already experimented at International House by adding a narrator to her shadow performances. For her professional engagements she evidently felt she needed a Chinese emcee who could effect a bridge between the unfamiliarity of the art form and the meaning in

Pauline (left) and Chinese American actress Soo Yong, a cast member in Metro-Goldwyn-Mayer's 1937 film version of Pearl Buck's novel *The Good Earth* and narrator for Red Gate's New York performances

it she sought to convey through the common medium of the English language. She required not just any narrator but a professional actor, able to speak in clear English so that no spectator would be in any doubt about what was going on or be alienated by the Chinese "optics" of the performance. The answer was found in Soo Yong, the Chinese actress who had made her public debut in the winter of 1930 as Mei Lanfang's mistress of ceremonies at the Forty-Ninth Street Theatre. Born in Maui in 1903, and a graduate of the University of Hawaii and Columbia University, Soo reached Hollywood in 1934. From then on, the educated and graceful Soo played mostly stereotyped servant or bitch character roles (the latter, ironically, thanks to her perfect diction) which the movie industry felt were proper for a native Asian actor. Soo's roles in *The Good Earth*, the 1937 film based on Pearl S. Buck's successful novel of rural China in turmoil, are a case in point: she was

Pauline in front of her shadow stage

given the roles of a serving maid and of a cantankerous elderly woman who bristled with racialized Chinese mannerisms. Not a single major role went to an Asian actor; Soo and the others played second fiddle to white actors in "yellow face" and were confined to bit parts and comic cameos that were more a part of the scenery than integral to the drama.

It is worth noting that Soo was not the only Asian actor from *The Good Earth* to be drawn into Pauline's orbit. Later in the 1930s, Oakland-born dancer Caroline Chew, who went by her Chinese name of King Lan Chew, played a role in shadow theatre not unlike Soo's – providing the glamour of authenticity to performances in which none of the participants behind the screen were the slightest bit Chinese, though when she was offstage she was able to talk reassuringly and behave the same way as her occidental audience. Something about what Pauline offered obviously felt more comfortable to these assimilated Chinese artists than anything the Hollywood of the 1930s had to offer. (Chew also came to play a romantic part in the life of Lee Ruttle: she became his wife.)

With the troupe complete, it now needed a name. It had to be one that would align with the public's fantasy of Chinese imagery and symbolism, inviting its occidental senses through a magic doorway into the Orient; it had to be catchy and colourful, yet breathe the very incense-shrouded mystique of a temple, thus a sort of sacred experience as well. There may have been deliberations between Pauline, Russell, and Ruttle, or with Pauline's Chinese friends or her aunt; or perhaps Pauline simply looked at her red silk stage and had a eureka moment. As it turned out, the name she chose and incorporated in 1932 attracted all the interest she had hoped for, and then some: *The Red Gate Shadow Players*.[44]

Chapter 5

ORIENTAL CURIOSITIES

China had fascinated Americans from the days when George and Martha Washington collected blue and white dinnerware from Guangzhou, when the serenely self-contained Flowery Kingdom was seen as a nation whose idealized civilization and philosophy were aspired to by the fledgling republic.

As Britain and the United States both sought markets in China and finally pried the door open with opium, the gradual disintegration of the world they knew from willow-pattern plates changed from admiration to scorn, even as fortunes were being built in London and New York on the sale of the drug that was helping create the conditions inspiring this disgust. Missionaries arrived to save souls from Buddhism and bodies from opium, while foreign nations moved in to carve out huge tracts of the Chinese coastline for the betterment of their commercial interests. Pressures built from within both society at large and the increasingly conservative microcosm of the imperial court. Exacerbated by drought and famine at the end of the nineteenth century, northern China exploded in the mayhem of the popular uprising named for one of the many groups involved in it, the kung-fu practitioners and street magicians known as Boxers. Diplomats and Chinese Christians were besieged by Boxer and government forces from June to August 1900. The breaking of the siege by allied forces devastated imperial China and made Beijing one vast fire sale of purloined *objets d'art*. If foreign purchasers could not afford a bit of loot alleged to have been removed from the Empress Dowager Cixi's abandoned Forbidden City bedchamber, there were plenty of other items available to acquire and show one's post-conquest refinement and cultural superiority.

The Chinese who came to North America in the late nineteenth and early twentieth centuries suffered there much of what their brethren back home endured under foreign occupation in the coastal concessions; they were abused as cheap labour and scorned as opium addicts, as bearers of disease, and for their "un-Christian" religious practices; laws were passed to exclude and control them, relegating them to less than second-class status (for example, Chinese Americans were not permitted to vote until 1943). Yet Chinese culture, as strained through art and artifice, lived in a parallel universe. If male America passed laws limiting the civil liberties of Chinese Americans and the immigration of Chinese, female America allowed their cultural contributions to live freely under the guise of fashion, art, decor, and manners. From being the main consumers of Asian-themed culture a decade earlier, by the first decade after 1900 American women were becoming active participants in the spectacle of Asianness. Owning a fan, umbrella, *obi* – or, even better, a house utilizing elements of Japanese design and detail – became a sort of emblem of civilization for white American women of the middle class. They could be certain that their *japonisme*-inflected silverware or grass-papered dining-room walls would impress their female friends with their status as "sophisticated, refined women." But by 1930, Japan was viewed as not so much a western ally as a predator, both to the West and to China. Because of Japan's attacks on the latter, the West was viewing China with more sympathy, while the opening of its treasure houses since 1900 had revealed to the world the refinements of Chinese culture, samples of which it was fashionable to display in one's home in Peoria or Pasadena, marking one, much as the Japanese fad did, as a member of a civilized elite.[1]

In 1914 one of New York's richest socialites, Alvina Belmont, put on an elaborate show at Marble House, her Newport mansion, to celebrate the building of a Chinese teahouse in her garden. A Chinese ball followed, with guests invited to come dressed as Chinese worthies; so fearful was Mrs Belmont that some might show up in evening gowns and dinner jackets that she ordered an army's worth of "Mandarin jackets, or coats, or camisoles, or whatever it is they call them" to clothe those who arrived without proper "Oriental" attire. The craze spread from high society to that intermediate world inhabited by female stars of the Broadway stage and aristocrats by marriage or alleged descent.

Woolworth millionaire Barbara Hutton became a devoted Orientalist, writing Chinese-themed poems that were set to music by Elsa Maxwell and collecting Chinese art picked out for her by author Princess Der Ling, the part-American Manchu noblewoman who had served at the court of the Empress Dowager Cixi.[2] For another woman, Pearl S. Buck, China became a kind of performative masquerade. Through her hit novel *The Good Earth*, China – with Buck as a kind of Chinese woman wearing a Western mask – became a symbol of the injustices perpetrated against the weak, the defenceless, the "other," which would come to embrace the injustices suffered by women and African Americans. "It was not incidental," writes Mari Yoshihara, "that the Orientalist performances by white women took place at the same time that many white woman were becoming New Women of the twentieth century, who challenged Victorian gender norms and the ideology of the separate sphere of art."[3]

Thus, the sphere of performance and influence available to a woman such as Pauline was still circumscribed, because so much of what she had to offer had perforce to be staged in the realm of high society, where "Asia" meant incense and luxury, impenetrable rituals, and untold sensuality, and nothing was to be taken seriously. The only influence that most women, rich or middle class, could claim was that of exercising their taste and judgment as supported by a husband's or a father's purchasing power. While Pauline's fledgling troupe needed the support and connections provided by the people of wealth and position for whom it performed, it needed even more to prove, against other kinds of theatrical performance, that shadow theatre was a viable presence on the American artistic scene. Above all, it needed to make itself accessible to ordinary people, as it was in China. Shadow theatre had to be allowed to grow roots in the public consciousness, so that it could thrive as a transplanted alien.

In January 1932, Pauline announced a public display of her shadow figures (Chinese as well as Turkish [*karagöz*]) at the Benton Oriental Shop, her mother's place of business on Madison Avenue.[4] Mary Benton had worked in Minneapolis as a decorator, where her theme had likely been much the same as in New York City: Asian antiques, with an emphasis on textiles. Displaying her shadow figures and sets became Pauline's theme for the next few years as the "shadow people" went from posing in shop windows or university and museum display cases to being "on display" at a variety of society events in the city. The first of these, a charity ball thrown in the autumn of 1933 by the Seventh Regiment Armory on Park Avenue, served as Red Gate's debut in public, both as a performance and in the pages of the *New York Times*.

Popularly known as the "Silk Stocking Regiment," the Seventh of the National Guard was as much exclusive club as it was regimental barracks, its muster roll studded with names that meant something even after the stock market crash: Livingston, Vanderbilt, Astor, van Rensselaer. The Armory itself owed its splendour to these rich men, who brought in some of the greatest architects and designers – from Louis Comfort Tiffany to Stanford White – to beautify it. And of course, an armory of this kind could only be commanded by a social climber *par excellence*, in the person of Colonel (later Brigadier General) Ralph C. Tobin. Tobin was a confirmed bachelor who had risen above his station as the son of a New York real estate agent. In his late twenties he was working as a file clerk; at the age of fifty-seven he was adopted by the elderly Lina Post Webster, wealthy widow of Hamilton Fish Webster. Though reported at the time as "dimming," Lina was still a light on the high-society circuit, in which Tobin served as "a dashing escort for Newport social functions."[5]

Only Tobin could have had the verve and insouciance to put on a show which, in the darkest days of the Great Depression, was described by the *New York Times* on 5 November 1933 as "A Fascinating Pageant ... Two Thousand Guests Enjoy 'A Siamese Fantasy.'"[6]

As guests filed into the entrance hall, they found "a scene suggestive of a market place in Bangkok." The hall was lined with booths staged by "market-place characters" in what passed for authenticity in 1933 New York: rug merchants, water carriers, vendors of food, jewellery and whatever else appeared appropriate for a Thailand setting, set against the Armory's backdrop of Gilded Age panelled opulence and wall-hung weaponry. In the Drill Hall opposite the entrance, a space that stretched almost from Park Avenue to Lexington, a temple had been erected to contain a statue of the Buddha, towering over the merrymakers below.

Coloured lights played over the temple's "glittering walls," around which had been arranged tropical plants approximating a jungle. Within this – artfully caged or chained – were "an elephant, monkeys and a tiger." As the Buddha gazed on, the guests danced to an orchestra whose players wore "tropical uniform."[7]

Outside the Drill Hall were several rooms abutting the foyer. One of these, the Veterans' Room, had been designed entirely by Tiffany, which was also responsible for the Armory Library adjacent to it – the only two rooms in the world designed by that company. An amalgamation of Moorish, Japanese, and Celtic influences, the Veterans' Room was where Pauline and the Red Gate Shadow Players put on their first public performance. Significantly, the *New York Times* reporter covering the event commented not on any aspect of the performance itself but on the figures, "brilliantly colored and intricately carved," as if they were merely an extension of the room's already eclectic decor. Described in the same breath was an exhibition of "rare Siamese curios" in a room at the other end of the entrance hall. It did not seem to matter that Chinese shadow theatre was presented at a Siamese fantasy ball. Asian was Asian, just as, to many Westerners, all Asian people looked alike. And exoticism was not to be categorized at this level of high society. To do so would be far too like those unsophisticated scholars who made no interesting contribution to Park Avenue dinner parties (unless they were in some way connected to scandal). To most of these people, shadow figures were obviously not the shades of heroes or ancestors but puppets, ornamental and "Oriental" curiosities, unsuitable for children in the way fragile Chinese fans or ivories were meant only for the appreciation of adults, yet stereotypes of the Chinese themselves – childlike, naïve, not part of real life.[8]

This was much the same attitude greeting Red Gate on its next public foray, the Beaux-Arts Ball at the Waldorf-Astoria Hotel. Coming two months after the Armory's Siamese fantasy, the Beaux-Arts Ball was of a different Asian theme. "Magnificent Robes of [the] Period" were worn as New York's elite donned Chinese or Venetian costumes, taking part in a huge pageant with a cast of five hundred depicting Marco Polo's Chinese travels. Dancing followed in the ballroom, everyone wearing medieval Italian headgear or Chinese silk robes and anachronistic Manchu queues.[9]

It is possible that Colonel Tobin of the Seventh Regiment played a part in bringing Red Gate to the ball because it was he who "permitted many of the young men [of the Seventh] to assume various military roles in the pageant," reported the *New York Times*. As with Mrs Belmont's Chinese Tea House celebration of nearly a generation earlier, invitees "made pilgrimages to Chinatown in quest of suitable raiment," implying that the district was worth braving only to co-opt a bit of the residents' traditional garments (seen as costume, not clothing). The ball even boasted a real Chinese princess – or so she called herself – when Princess Der Ling, newly moved to New York with her American husband, took the role of a Mongolian empress wearing raiment given to her by the Empress Dowager Cixi (Der Ling would serve as patron for several of Red Gate's future performances). Make-believe and costume were so much a part of the event that it should be no surprise that Red Gate was given space for its performance in a room next to the ballroom – shadow theatre, after all, had been known to the imperial court, where it had formed a component of celebrations as much as in the homes of the emperor's subjects. But that it was not seen as more than some kind of strange puppet show using figures of more interest than the plays being performed, and that on the whole shadow theatre was seen as something more appropriate for a carnival than a legitimate form of dramatic art, is evident when we discover Red Gate stationed next to another performer dealing equally in "Oriental" mystery, "Myra Kingsley, astrologist."[10]

Shortly after the Beaux-Arts Ball, and in a small newspaper far from New York City, Pauline had what can be called her first real review. On 24 February the *Herald* of Tyrone, Pennsylvania, reported that Red Gate had performed at the Birmingham School. By this time, Ruttle and Pauline had begun to perfect and circulate the press material that later fed their and Red Gate's legend. While the *Herald* reporter repeated the erroneous claim that shadow theatre dated to 121 BC (the discredited Emperor Wu story), he or she made a cogent observation: that Red Gate's offerings should not be confused with the miniature theatre of Tony Sarg, the famous children's puppeteer.[11]

Pauline backstage in performance

Sarg was a master of design; his gift for the piquant reached from marionettes and the first Macy's parade balloons to children's books and interior design. His round-eyed, toylike animals and people showed how closely related his children's art was to advertising principles of the day, where goofy exaggeration was the norm. To compare Pauline Benton and Tony Sarg was like comparing shadow figures and marionettes. Sarg represented the commercial flank of marionette theatre, which performers like Paul McPharlin shied away from and as Pauline was to avoid as well, with some exceptions. As McPharlin's biographer Dr Ryan Howard points out, "Artistic puppeteers rarely took their shows on the road," as Sarg and his students did, making their living at teaching or other work when they were not involved in mounting their productions, which usually took place near where they lived.[12] Pauline would emulate Sarg in taking Red Gate from town to town, like Sarg's popular children's theatre, but aiming instead at adult audiences and on higher artistic ground. She would also copy one of his children's shows, *The Chinese Willow Plate Story*, which she made into a sparkling romance for adult audiences.[13]

The *Herald* writer accurately described Red Gate's offerings not just as figures but as components of a performance, as actors are part of a performed play. Also noted was the fact that the action took place against a translucent screen. Other newspaper accounts had implied the figures were set up in some sort of static display. What the reviewer saw was performance, not puppets, which despite its small scale conveyed a range of drama that human theatre could not, and was by definition not entertainment for children. "The fascinating Red Gate Shadow Puppets with graceful motion, and given voices by their manipulators, dramatize some of the Chinese legends and fables, and also depict a bit of modern life in China," runs the report – evidence that Pauline was already performing with modern as well as historic figures, just as Li Tuochen was doing in Beijing (and as Paul McPharlin did with his shadow show *The Vixen's Spell*). This review is also the first to refer to "special music, arranged to carry out the Chinese atmosphere in terms we can all appreciate," though without mentioning William Russell by name.[14]

This small-town newspaper review was in the vanguard of more prestigious notices that came over the next few years. As Red Gate progressed through the northeastern states and into eastern Canada, more reviews appeared, excerpts of which were included in future Red Gate programs, many of them showing that other observers were increasingly understanding what Pauline was trying to do.

"The figures are so adroitly jointed that their movements are surprisingly agile," wrote the *New York Evening Post*, "capable of a rhythmic flow appropriate to the Oriental dance." "No one could imagine what shadow plays could be like," claimed the *Worcester Telegram*. "The reality was charming ... Voices were piquant and added to the

Oriental atmosphere of the Chinese legends with their imitations of
Peking street cries. The light, the Oriental color, the sprightly dialogue
riveted attention from start to finish." Although the play referred to
was far more Western than Eastern, in plots and in the plastic material from which Pauline had created its figures, the *Ottawa Journal*
was the first to draw a parallel between shadow theatre's resemblance
to animated cartoons and the most famous cartoonist of the day: "No
Walt Disney fan could fail to be intrigued by 'Elephant Gay,' a Chinese fable. His antics, high kicking and the accompanying catchy tune
would inspire that master of caricature ... the sense of artistic composition was cleverly maintained, and the music so delicately blended
with the action that one lost all sense of the Chinese theatrical con-
ventions and sat enthralled by the unfolding of an exquisite story."[15]

After a performance in Cleveland, the voice of a respected art historian was added to the impressions shared by journalists. Thomas
Munro, education curator at the Cleveland Museum of Art, spoke to
Red Gate's effort as conservator of an ancient tradition, protector of
a valuable piece of Chinese culture. "The glimpse which the Red Gate
Shadow Players have given us," wrote Munro, "of the shadow plays
of ancient China is enough to indicate that a folk art of great value
and immediate popular appeal is within our reach." Munro touched
on an element of Red Gate that was to serve it well in the next few
years – that the company was not just a performing troupe offering
pure entertainment but a kind of ethnological Ark, gathering and pre-
serving the art form from the Japanese deluge inundating China with
each passing day.

But even with this recognition came the realization that Red Gate's
history over its first three years was still very much that of a company
which needed to find its *raison d'être* – namely, to avoid being classed
as some kind of display of Chinese curiosities and to be properly
embraced as vital performance art. The company performed in several
eastern states, none farther west than Ohio. Some of their venues were
fashionable (Miss Porter's School in Farmington, Connecticut); some
were venerable (the Chicago Art Institute, Columbia University, Bryn
Mawr); at least one, a performance for Sir Bede and Lady Clifford at
white-columned Government House in the Bahamas, was a brush with
the colonial British upper classes. But most performances took place
at schools or colleges; none in theatres.[16]

A passport photo of Pauline
Benton, c. 1936

In many cases, the impressions recorded of Red Gate's offerings
smacked of those earned by Mei Lanfang during his tour across America a few years earlier. Like many who flocked to museums or galleries
for shows of some new artist's latest abstract painting or sculpture, or
to the concert hall to hear a piece of new music incorporating bull horns
and oil drums, some of the euphoric response to Mei's oeuvre was due
less to an educated appreciation than to the time-honoured act of going
bananas over some new cultural phenomenon, which critics rave about
unquestioningly, its sheer oddness being inescapably compelling. That
this was happening during the darkest period of the Great Depression
says much about what the public had an appetite for – dazzling musicals from Hollywood, Mei Lanfang from China, and shadow theatre by
way of Riverside Drive, entertainment that had found its time and place.

Pauline and Lee Ruttle must have considered many questions in
establishing Red Gate's "brand." Was the company seen as a touring
exhibit of shadow figures, and how could they correct the impression?
What sort of audience and what sort of performances were needed if
shadow theatre was not to be taken as sideshow entertainment? Was
it of the same nature as Afong Moy – "first Chinese woman in America," displayed in a diorama in 1830s New York, "trapped in the American taste for cunning visual display"[17] – or as eye-candy at society
balls, or as an activity for private-school children? Or could it be presented as the heir to a dramatic tradition a thousand years old? As one

observer noted caustically, "This show, during the years of the Depression, did quite well, with the sort of people who read the wrong books and liked the bad poets. They went for this kind of thing."[18] Was Red Gate to be "that kind of thing," or was it to be taken seriously? And how was that to be achieved?

Chapter 6

SHADOWS PASS

While fantasies of a timeless, ever-mysterious China were helping Americans cope with the Great Depression, a harsher reality was settling over the Beijing of 1935–36. Almost ten years earlier Pauline's aunt, Dr Emma Konantz, had been listed with other Americans in China living in the "danger zone" of northern China.[1] To the south, in Shanghai and Nanjing, to which the Chinese capital was transferred in 1927, Americans were reported as endangered or killed in "anti-foreign riots," in reality nothing more than had always occurred in China on the eve of great upheaval. And for the next decade the fractious coalition between Nationalists and Communists unravelled. Warlord infighting became a part of life. By 1932, the ex-emperor, Puyi, now in Manchuria, accepted the "throne" of the Japanese-backed Manchukuo, a kingdom which even the sympathetic regarded as mere sham. China was being prepared for slaughter, not just by the Japanese from without but by Chinese gangsters and unscrupulous politicians from within. The economic ruin was so thorough that even government officials and professors at Beijing's institutions of higher learning were often not paid for months. "Many intellectuals in Beijing began to move southward," writes Sasha Su-Ling Welland.[2] Financial support from the warlords became spotty and then non-existent as battle lines were drawn, erased, and redrawn.

Still, Emma did not leave. Indeed, she may well have been in agreement with English expatriate John Blofeld, who wrote of Beijing (renamed Peiping or "Northern Peace" after the transfer of the capital to Nanjing) that had war not broken out he "might have followed the example of many other Westerners in making Peking my permanent mistress, aspiring to devote the rest of my life to enjoyment of her subtly stimulating embrace." As Blofeld points out, the foreigners who did stay in Beijing after the power centre shifted to Nanjing were of a far subtler, more refined cast, including "painters, sculptors, more writers or would-be writers than I could count, and even some serious scholars."[3] These were people like English aesthete Harold Acton, who was to record his experiences in Beijing's foreign community in a satiric novel, *Ponies and Peonies*. There was the American linguist George N. Kates, who wrote of his years living as one with the scholars and rickshawmen of the city. There was the eccentric tragedy that was Sir Edmund Backhouse, whose brilliance as translator and scholar was smudged by what he assumed would be a lucrative career as a forger. And there were cross-cultural personalities like the part-American Mme Dan Paochao, younger sister of Princess Der Ling, who unlike her sister had opted for life in the East rather than West, and was admired as a participant in the last years of the Empress Dowager Cixi's court, as well as for bringing Western dance and culture to Beijing. After Puyi was ejected from the Forbidden City, Madame Dan had rescued homeless imperial eunuchs, providing housing in her palace while recruiting them to produce fine embroidery and musical performances for A-list Thomas Cook tourists, who paid to tour the premises.[4] Madame Dan was to remain in Beijing long after it was safe for one of her class to be there, but she was not alone. These were the kind of people Emma Konantz could relate to. Like her, they loved Beijing, even in its death throes, far too much to leave it.

In this city of dusty *hutong*, crumbling temples, peeling palaces, and the bittersweet air of a culture on the brink of change, shadow theatre, like devoted Beijingers, was still holding on, if just by its fingernails. Visiting Beijing in the late 1920s, the American artist Bertha Lum was struck by the powerful survival instinct of so fragile an art form. "It is strange," she wrote, "that with all the changing dynasties, never-ending wars and political strife, one thing which has remained practically unchanged in China is the theatre." Yet she found just one shadow troupe still performing in Beijing, consisting of an elderly shadow master who, blind, was assisted by his two sons and a grandson. Neither he nor his troupe would have existed at all without the support of the Chinese American woman doctor, Yamei Kin.[5] Adopted as a toddler by American missionaries, Dr Kin had studied medicine in New York, Philadelphia, and Washington, DC, and then brought her expertise and the strange spectacle of being a female doctor back to China, where she took on traditional Chinese misogyny and traditional Chinese medicine, succeeding in spite of the disapproval of traditionalists. Yet like Mme Dan, also educated in the West, she revered the China of the past. "China cannot turn her back on her centuries of history and tradition, even if she would," wrote Dr Kin. "We must consider what she is and follow a constructive policy. We must not destroy to build anew."[6]

Even as court eunuchs would have expired in the streets of Beijing without Mme Dan's help, Bertha Lum believed shadow theatre would have entirely died out but for Dr Kin. "During the summer," she reported, "she often asks as many as can be seated in her small courtyard to see several dramas presented." Lum attended one performance where she was astonished by the male manipulators' ability not just to impersonate female characters but to "imitate the voices of birds and animals, streets cries and all the variations of each." As an artist, she was also impressed by the "peculiar, jointed rhythm" of the figures, "suggestive of the modern art created today."[7] (Like other foreigners unable to resist, Lum purchased several shadow figures during her time in Beijing; the collection is still in the possession of her descendants.)[8]

Washington, DC, native Genevieve Wimsatt took a dimmer view of shadow theatre's future. She believed – like Berthold Laufer – that she was witnessing its final days and made herself responsible for capturing it in print and photograph, even as Laufer had captured shadow figures for the glass cases of the Field Museum. Though they "still caper for the native who smiles in faint derision, as for the foreigner who marvels," Wimsatt wrote in the preface to her 1936 book *Chinese Shadow Shows*, "too soon the Shadows' function as entertainer, instructor, critic and moralist will have yielded to more ample mediums ... to the auditorium and the silver screen, to the stage and the radio."[9] Though Wimsatt searched diligently for functional shadow troupes in Shanghai, Hangzhou, and Suzhou, she found little evidence to contradict her woeful first impression:

In the shops and fairs of Peiping [Beijing] there were signs of the deepening dusk. On Lantern Street, outside the Ch'ien Mên, shadow figures, demounted – that is to say, detached from their reed-and-wire controls – were being sold as lamp-shade decorations ... At the Lung Ssu [Longfu si] Fair only one old dealer still displayed the little entertainers, these mostly of the cheap paper variety designed as children's toys. Outside the Hata Mên, in the scroll shop tucked away in a corner of an abandoned temple, retired behind a thousand-year-old egg factory, book upon blue cloth book of Shadows lay piled on the shelves, mouldy, stuck together with age and disuse. The proprietor had bought the lot from the heirs of an old showman lately summoned to join his honorable ancestors. They were not selling well. Here were entire casts for a hundred plays, stage settings and accessories, properties without end, from lotus pools to teapots. Few of these were less than fifty years old, the shopkeeper assured me, and some were much more venerable.[10]

Wimsatt purchased "entire casts and settings," into which she rubbed "the best cold cream" (in lieu of tung oil, a drying oil derived from tung tree seeds that was used to coat shadow figures and set pieces) and planned to write a book that would record "all that diligence, curiosity and sympathy could gather of the story of the shadow show."[11] She also hired the best shadow master in Beijing, Li Tuochen, apparently not just to give performances at her suburban courtyard house – photographs of which she included in her book – but also to be interviewed about the secrets of the art form. The Li whom Wimsatt depicts in the pages of her book is a poignant but gallant figure, rather like one of his shadow actors, pressing courageously into the darkness of an unknown future.

Part of the tragedy, Wimsatt records, was that Li had no sons. "I know of no company where there is a qualified showman ready to carry on," Li told her, "when the present proprietor is summoned to join his honorable ancestors." But he also mourned the modern distractions that were depriving shadow theatre of the audiences it depended on for survival. "The shadow show is a family entertainment," Li explained, "a courtyard spectacle, and who now stays at home in the courtyard? Young people, children, even women are now going out to theatres and motion pictures; they are no longer inviting the Shadows into their halls and courts to celebrate a grandmother's birthday, a betrothal, or the naming of a son." It did not seem to matter, he noted, that "many Western innovations and importations have found their way to the screen – bicycles, carriages, automobiles, steam

A shadow theatre performance in northern China, photographed by
Pauline Benton in 1936

cars, and even airplanes." These were, in the end, "no more than
extraneous novelties, introduced to amuse the spectators. We produce
no plays in terms of present day life." Perhaps worse than having no
son, Li told Wimsatt, was that he had "no pupils to continue the old
traditions, to make my shadows dance when I am gone. I do not know
who will love my little players and cherish them when I am gone ...
Shadows pass, T'ai T'ai [Madame]." Little could Li know that, in
another few years, just the sort of student he had dreamed of would be
knocking at his door.[12]

On 3 January 1936, Emma Konantz died of complications following
a cancer operation at Peiping Union Medical College Hospital in Beijing.[13] Though her health had been deteriorating at a rapid rate, Emma
had taught her classes up to a month before she died and then was
forced out of the classroom when student protests over China's relin-
quishment of the north to the Japanese closed down the university.

Having come to China nearly twenty years earlier, Emma apparently had never intended to leave – her passport, re-issued in 1927, was found at her death to have expired.[14] Her student Pauline Ch'en wrote of receiving letters from her shortly before her death, "written with indignation, sorrow and dejection. To encounter such a sympathetic person among foreigners," Miss Ch'en noted, "one who follows closely the current of events, is rare," and she lamented that this foreign woman, who had so passionately loved China, had joined with it in tasting "to the last drop the bitter cup of destruction."[15]

Emma's remains were stored in the morgue of PUMC Hospital until March, when Pauline and Mary arrived in the city. They arranged for burial and then began the daunting task of sorting and selling Emma's art- and book-filled home. Judging from objects later exhibited by Pauline at the Minnesota Museum of Art (and in her own home and that of her mother), the house was crammed with antiques and artifacts, some of which can still be seen in photographs of Pauline's Carmel, California, cottage interiors from the 1960s.

While her mother dealt with the house and its contents, Pauline made contact with Li Tuochen, who agreed to give her lessons in the manipulation of shadow figures. This time, the lessons would be not through letters but in person. Yet that did not make things easier for either teacher or student. That these lessons were such a success is a tribute again to Pauline's genius for observation. Although a Christian, Li had been brought up in an atmosphere suffused with Confucian rules, one of which forbade male to female contact unless the woman was the man's wife or his very young daughter. With a male pupil, Li would have held his students' hands and arms to demonstrate various subtle manipulations. Since Pauline was female, he had to sit at a decorous distance. Thus studying with Li in Beijing was not that different from doing so via letter in New York – both at arms' length.[16]

For the most critical techniques there was no substitute for the live demonstrations Li gave. And he was extremely generous with his lifetime's worth of experience and knowledge. Pauline later noted that when she asked him about *The White Snake*, which was to become her signature shadow play in the United States, he would talk about it for nearly an hour. Pauline truly felt that she was now striking to the core of what made shadow theatre so exciting. "The secrets of Chinese costumes, arts, architecture, religion, history and mythology were all held in the quiet forms of the shadow figures," she wrote. "One thing led to another; there was no end of it all." She saw that however much she felt she was learning in Beijing, her studies with Li were merely the tip of an enormous iceberg. As she commented later, "Mr. Lee T'uo Chen ... told me: 'I have been doing this for more than 40 years and am still a student.'"[17]

Li also introduced Pauline to his father, then nearly ninety. Retired from manipulating figures and singing, Li Senior still kept a hand in the business by performing in the orchestra. While capturing a performance, Pauline photographed the old shadow master with his son behind the screen of Li's theatre, the father grave and noble, the son laughing, a difference not just between their ages but between their eras. Not that the elder Mr Li was devoid of a sense of humour. When he was eighty, Pauline recalled, Li Senior "caught the modern spirit [of political lampoon] when, impressed by some long drawn-out newspaper interviews, he wrote a play entitled, 'A Newspaper Man's Interview with a Field Mouse,' a subject vibrant with satirical possibilities!"[18]

Li Tuochen was obviously seen as a respected master by Yenching University, because he often gave demonstrations of shadow theatre there. Pauline began attending these classes shortly after arriving in Beijing, and she took notes on a half dozen of Li's performances and lectures. Not only did she record his technique in close detail, she took down scene-by-scene summaries of the plays themselves. She also noted the meanings and symbols of the various facial expressions and gestures made by each character and the music to be used for certain scenes, many of which were the same as those in Beijing Opera.[19]

For faces, she learned that scholars' visages were open (and even better with a beard, the mark of sagacity and mature years in old China), while faces in black and white signified a character "straight forward and stupid," red a loyal character, and characters with shaggy eyebrows "most wicked." In walking, a scholar always "bent slightly forward, slow walk, slow swinging arms," while a rich man "stands very straight, stomach out, more rapid swing of arms, but very dignified." A lady of refinement never dangled her arms but held them in front of her body, "slightly swaying," while a maid servant or peasant woman robustly did the opposite; warriors swung their arms most decisively of all.[20]

Her notes are often so detailed as to permit the reader to "watch" a performance. Here are her impressions of Li Tuochen's *Street Scenes*, which became one of Red Gate's most enduring and popular offerings:

Plays demonstrated by Li

Street Scene

Four spectators enter. The "ring leader" is a figure like "Father's Servant." There is another with the foreign looking head, etc. They discuss the street entertainments which are to take place and then line up on the side, fighting for front place. They make fun of the one with the Western clothes.

1st ENTERTAINER: a Juggler. Has a large red contraption 2 or 3 times his own height 2 or 3 umbrella effects at top. Juggler is figure we used for drum dancer. First, he puts his foot under [the contraption] and then kicks it up on to his head. Does all sorts of juggling tricks, transferring to his nose, elbow, etc ... twirls himself around etc.

2nd ENTERTAINER: 4 Drummers. They play perfectly synchronized with the real drums. They beat sometimes on the center of the drum and sometimes on the edge. I wonder if we have two or four drummers among those that were sent for musicians.

3rd ENTERTAINER: Two sporting lions. Did not think that they were so much in comparison with our elephant and tiger.

4th ENTERTAINER: Stilt walkers. They had three or four that did very cute stunts. They had to bring in the full number (10) eventually, but the last ones did not do much. Music was hard drum and a special kind of gong the stilt walkers, which are common street entertainers, use.

5th ENTERTAINER: Sword juggler. Don't know whether we could do it or not on account of having to keep sticks and hands concealed. They did it most cleverly. Twirled it around at lightening speed, threw it into the air, twirling all the time.

6th ENTERTAINER: A "Cart full of ladies" (singers)

7th ENTERTAINER: A cart full of actors. They have heated argument with the spectators. Driver of the cart has moveable lower jaw and large hand, to make his arguing all the more effective. While they are arguing, automobile comes and pushes the cart off the stage.

All through the act, especially between the numbers, the spectators discuss the entertainers.[21]

Her notes for Li's demonstration of three scenes from *The Burning of the Bamboo Grove* are just as colourful and instructive, noting where his interpretation resembles that used by Red Gate:

Plays demonstrated by Li

1st SCENE: Yu Hung sits in front of tent and reviews his troops (4 soldiers).

2nd SCENE: Liu Chun Ting sits in her palace and reviews her troops. A reporter comes and announces that Yu Hung is awaiting battle.

3rd SCENE: No scenery. Battle between the two on horseback. Battle very much like ours. When actually crossing spears, horses remain quite stationary. Very effective the way they started pointing spears menacingly at one another. At different times they change places and turn around, fighting from opposite sides. When he is defeated and driven off the stage, she rides her horse back and forth several times. I suppose this is the equivalent of the stage trick of walking around the stage showing that they are walking a distance. Then she exits. Yu Hung comes back with the demon, evidently giving him his instructions and leaves. Demon dances for awhile and then ax floats around and finally splits him in 2. Then there is the contest with the brick. Then the bamboo grove is set up in the middle of the stage. Liu Chun Ting calls on God of Fire who appears on a cloud, takes his order from her and leaves. The four cloud spirits group themselves around the grove. Yu Hung comes and hides in it (she is off stage). Fire is made as Tante [Aunt Emma] has described many times. Light is flashed off at same time. Finally when fire is over, bamboo grove is pulled down while light is out. Yu Hung is left in his scorched form. Runs around frantically – off stage and entering again from the other side with sparks flying from him.

Finally water is set up for about half of the stage – a bridge
effect at open end connecting with the floor line. He jumps into
the water. Puffs of smoke come from him as he swims across.
Then Liu Chun Ting comes and watches him from the bridge
and recites the final lines of the play.
MUSIC: Gong and drum through the play except hu chin for
demon.[22]

As Pauline studied with Li, she continued to collect shadow figures
and stage props. She also commissioned a complete set of figures, made
to her specifications, from the Lu family of shadow masters. This was
a clan for whom artistic survival had been a generational challenge for
over a century and would continue to be in the next. In the early nineteenth century, the founder of the line, Lu Guangcai, had joined a
shadow troupe in northern China that performed in Luanzhou style.
The afterglow of the long and glorious reign of the Qianlong emperor
still masked much of the disintegration of China's autonomy, as upris-
ings within and foreign onslaught from outside its borders increased.
The dynasty was no longer at its zenith, but the shadow theatre it supported enjoyed a golden age of popularity, in public squares and temple
fairs as in private palaces. But shadow theatre's traditional connection
to spirits and magic moved the government to suspect its modern influence on the secret societies that arose throughout the century to bedevil
both Chinese and foreigners. Guangcai escaped arrest, but many troupes
were harassed and disbanded.

The Lu family only regrouped when Guangcai's son Dercheng started
his own company, which was inherited and carried on by Lu Fuyuen,
Dercheng's son. Their troupe prospered, but the challenges to its existence continued. Film, called "electric shadows" in Chinese, was one
of the first threats to shadow theatre; and as Li Tuochen explained to
Genevieve Wimsatt, the breakdown of the family unit and the desertion
of courtyards for movie houses and the boulevards relegated shadow
theatre to audiences of children and the elderly. If the latter was a fast
disappearing quantity, the children usually grew up to avoid shadow
theatre altogether as more and more distractions presented themselves.
Troupes like that of the Lu family persevered by updating their figures
and performances, using electric light to cast more vivid shadows,
adding contemporary props such as automobiles, rickshaws, recog-

nizably foreign characters, and more obvious comedy. After the fall of
China to the Communists, when Chinese culture was more suspect than
welcome, Pauline tried this same technique, but without the Lu family's success; ironically, Americans were more fascinated with authentic Chinese shadow theatre than an updated simulacrum.[23]

It is unlikely that any of the few shadow troupes left in Beijing were
being actively sought to create figures other than for their own use; thus
it was probably regarded as both a windfall and a challenge when
Pauline ordered from Lu Jingda a full set of them – at fifteen to eighteen
inches in height, they were taller than the typical Luanzhou figures, and
costlier to create. It is also highly unlikely that any of the extant shadow
carvers in Beijing were being given such a unique challenge as the one
Pauline posed to the Lu family: on top of the traditional cast of characters, she requested figures based on stories from the Old Testament
(Noah's Ark) and the New (the Nativity). Others appear to show that
Pauline gave the Lu carvers pictures from Western fairy tales illustrated
by Arthur Rackham and Kate Greenaway. None of her extant reviews
mentions performances using these Western-inspired shadows, but the
figures show enough evidence of wear to indicate that they were used
by her, perhaps for performances in private homes or schools, or by
Polly McGuire, the puppeteer friend to whom Pauline gave these figures in later years.[24] A complete set normally took a year to create.
Pauline must have made it worth the Lu family's while to rush the order,
because by the time she left for home in July, four months later, she
took with her hundreds of figures, sets, and furnishings, as well as a full
set of instruments.[25]

Since 1930, China had been a battlefield for the Chinese themselves –
civil war between warlords, for and against Chiang Kai-shek's Nationalists, and Communists against both. Distracted by its own problems,
China could do little when the Japanese grabbed Manchuria and then,
in 1933, the Great Wall region, using the territory as their own "wall"
to buffer Manchukuo and the north while they figured out how to
capture Nanjing. China was pushed by Japan to sign an agreement in
1935 forbidding the Kuomintang from any activities in Hebei province,
which surrounds Beijing, basically handing northern China over to

Japan. By 1936, northern China was not a safe place for native inhab-
itants, let alone foreign visitors. But it was there that Pauline knew she
would find the most authentic performers and figure makers: "When
I heard that Mr. Chang Yen, recognized as the 'best shadow player in
North China,' was playing a limited engagement about two hundred
miles north and east of Peking, I lost no time in boarding a train to
take advantage of the opportunity, which has been enjoyed by very
few American travelers." Some might have seen Pauline's trip into the
depths of northern China as an idiotic risk to take for so flimsy a purpose, but few could deny that it was courageous. And none could say
she was not as professional in her research as she attempted to be in
her performances or that this trip did not help make her truly the professional performer she was recognized as on her return to America.[26]

Pauline was fortunate to have Aunt Emma's Chinese friends planning her journey and accompanying her. The entire trip was organized
by Emma's colleague, Dr Chen Caixin, with whom Emma had worked
on *The Jade Mirror of the Four Unknowns*. A native of Luanzhou, Dr
Chen "not only urged on me," Pauline wrote, "the importance of such
an experience but also made all the arrangements for the trip." Through
Dr Chen and other friends, she was offered the hospitality of his relatives in the north: "True to the Chinese custom of doing everything
possible for a friend's friend, they left no stone unturned to show me
everything related to the shadow plays in their communities." The trip
took Pauline eastward, ending at Luanzhou, the coastal town that
enjoyed a reputation as the pinnacle of shadow theatre sophistication
and performance. There, she noted, shadow theatre was not restricted
to the intelligentsia: "Almost any Luanchow farmer can, when given
a piece of donkey-skin, carve out some kind of shadow figure," and
many spent their winters doing just that. Such was the quality of
Luanzhou figures that they were sold at the Beijing Lantern Festival
and in smaller places too, where Pauline saw them offered for purchase "displayed on a bamboo framework." She knew of one Luanzhou
farmer who walked several miles to a village market just to sell figures
he had made.[27]

The first thing Pauline wanted to do the night she arrived was go
out to a shadow theatre performance in the town. This performance
was a special one, as Chang Yen was the lead performer in it. She had

A shadow performer
hanging up newly oiled
figures to dry in the sun.
Photographed in northern
China in 1936 by Pauline
Benton

been fortunate to obtain tickets, "as his company is booked for weeks
in advance, and always plays to crowded houses, even though their
tickets are sold at top prices." As she recounted, "My hosts were sur-
prised. Since the Japanese occupation it had not been considered safe
to go out at night, due to robbery and general lawlessness." But with
her friends around her for at least a semblance of protection, Pauline
set forth.[28]

A servant had purchased tickets in advance so that Pauline and her
party could enter the theatre without drawing attention. When they
arrived, they found the space completely full, with no place for them
to sit. Then a group occupying one of the boxes gave up their seats,
drawing the attention of the entire crowd. As Pauline blushed, another
group graciously offered refreshing drinks, which were sent to her and

her party by the occupants of the next box, as a form of welcome. Once everyone was settled, a play called *The Empty City* lit up the shadow stage. But this was "suddenly interrupted," Pauline recalled, "by the appearance of a pink slip of paper on which were written some Chinese characters" pressed against the illuminated screen. "A Chinese gentleman in our group laughed and interpreted the words as 'Welcome to the foreign guests.'" Even more embarrassed, and afraid that the delay in the performance would cause trouble for her friends (the Japanese had imposed a strict curfew on the town), Pauline watched as another slip was pressed against the screen: "In courtesy to the foreign guests, there will be a change of program."[29] Obviously, the great Chang Yen, who was standing behind the screen, was as pleased to have Pauline in his audience as she was to watch him perform.

In her unpublished history of shadow theatre, Pauline cited Mr Chang's company as an example of "traditional organization and division of work during a performance":

Mr. Chang stations himself at the extreme right of the stage, where he has a good view of all that is going on on the screen, directs the orchestra, and sings the parts of the bearded male characters. He has become so famous as a theatrical singer that demands for phonographic recordings of his voice have gone far beyond the limits of the area covered by his performances. The two men who manipulate the figures, one on the right side of the stage and the other on the left, are called "Under-the-Lamp-Men," reminding us that the electric light used today is a modern invention ...

A property man stands behind the two "Under-the-Lamp-Men," relieving them of those characters which have finished their acts, and always ready to hand them new characters just at the right time for their entrances. Those characters, which have had appropriate heads and bodies connected before the performance, dangle on a wire stretched back-stage ... The remaining four men seat themselves far out of the way in the rear, hence their title of "Back-stage men." Two of them are the orchestra and the other two singers, who sit quietly until their cues come, when they dash up to the stage in a manner resembling a football rush and begin to sing.[30]

Chang Yen, the famous Luanzhou shadow master, photographed by Pauline Benton in 1936

Below: A shadow theatre demonstration photographed by Pauline in northern China, 1936

She noticed more comic business at performances as well:

> In the country districts, the audiences pay their admission fees
> ranging from a few coppers to sixty or seventy cents, depending
> upon the reputation of the players, or drop their coppers into a
> tin can that is passed around by the collector during the per-
> formance. He is quick to spot any who fail to contribute and stands
> right in front of them, cutting off the view of the stage and jin-
> gling the can noisily under their noses.[31]

Pauline spent several days in the region, travelling to remote areas
just south of the Great Wall and visiting villages where shadow theatre was more sacred ritual than light entertainment. She photographed
rehearsals and performances, and documented such ordinary activities as hanging oiled figures out to dry. She also recorded the use of figures and props rarely seen. It is interesting to see how these village
shadow masters constructed their stages, how they prepared for a performance, and what kinds of play they offered, hints of which can be
seen in the images Pauline was quick to capture. She visited the coal-
mining town of Tangshan, to the west of Luanzhou, which was famous
for its shadow theatre culture. "I found that there were two [shadow
theatres] operating near a modern motion picture theatre!" she wrote.
"Does it sound like a vanishing art?"[32]

And she continued to collect figures and set pieces, which were added
to those completed for her by the Lu family. She was especially fascinated by scene pieces used to establish interior or exterior scenes, which
were as elaborate as the sets of European or American theatre, given
a fairy tale quirkiness through the foreshortened perspective used in
Chinese art. The setting of the scenes had been refined over time, so
that one used merely flowerpots to indicate the formal entrance of a
courtyard house, rockeries, an arching bridge, or a lotus pool for a
garden, "a pair of stone lions for the entrance to a temple or a palace,"
or "a pair of towers and fir trees" for a secluded temple.[33]

Attending a performance in a little country village, Pauline watched
with dismay as the troupe put on a show using poorly made figures,
with no scenery to speak of. Sympathetically, she visited the men af-
terward to ask them why they had no sets. They told her that of course
they had plenty of sets, but that these were not for ordinary use. They

Pauline with her small demonstration stage

had been made by a master and were to be preserved as long as possible. Leading Pauline to a back room, the men "pulled down from a
shelf three large dust-covered boxes filled with the most magnificent
pieces of scenery I had ever seen," she wrote, "such as in retrospect
make you think you have dreamed about them." Seeing a duplicate
piece among these, Pauline ventured to ask if she might purchase it
and earned a shocked stare. "Oh no!" she was told. These were treasures, even if they sat in boxes gathering dust atop a shelf. "I often think
of that bare screen, the dust-covered boxes," she said later, "and wonder – could those have been irreplaceable pieces created by the hand
of a famous or beloved master that the players thus cherished them?"[34]

At some point in 1936, Pauline seems to have also made the more
than eight-hundred-mile journey south to Hangzhou, the old Song capital, where shadow theatre had once flourished; it was also the setting
for the beginning and end of the tragic romance of the White Snake,
known as Baishe (which Pauline spelled Pai Shih in her translation).
Only photographs among her papers tell about what it was she was
looking for there, but they make it easy to guess her itinerary. There
are images of shadow masters she met and of Chinese friends posing

along West Lake. Most prominent are the photographs[35] of pagodas, such as the Thunder Peak tower, under which the White Snake was said to have been imprisoned by the priest Fa Hai for conjuring a flood to engulf the monastery where her husband had taken refuge after discovering her true demon nature. It was in her prison, according to the anonymous *Precious Scroll of Thunder Peak*, that the White Snake practised "the [Buddhist] Way," so that her heart "was at peace." Once satisfied that she had paid for her sins, Fa Hai summoned a "colored cloud" to waft her away to the peaceful realm of the Immortals. Pauline may have been disappointed to find the Thunder Peak pagoda in ruins – it had been struck by lightning in 1924 (though in fact it collapsed because so many of its bricks were being poached), but it was exciting to hear how real the White Snake was to people in the area. They told Pauline that the lightning strike had finally freed the demon, fulfilling the fate decreed for her in fiction.[36]

Back in Beijing, Pauline resumed her studies with Li Tuochen, but they were not to last for long. By mid-July, the situation in northern China had become so threatening that it was no longer safe for the Bentons to remain. On 14 July 1936 they embarked for Japan, landing in Seattle two weeks later.[37]

Chapter 7

WORLD WAR

When Red Gate was invited to perform at the White House of President Franklin Delano Roosevelt in 1936, it was not because the president or his wife had any special sympathy toward the Chinese or their culture. That would come in a year, after the Japanese descended on Beijing and Madame Chiang Kai-shek fled to the United States and won over Eleanor Roosevelt. The invitation came about in part because Eleanor admired and respected the offbeat and the unusual.

Marginalized as a young girl, then enduring years under the thumb of a mother-in-law not unlike the demanding matrons infamous in Chinese fiction and reality, Eleanor developed a depth of empathy combined with a sensitivity to injustice which made her a lifelong defender of the powerless. She coupled this activism with art to bring to the White House performers who had not been featured there before or who were not welcome elsewhere. Black contralto Marian Anderson sang at the executive mansion in 1936, the first black person to do so, and three years earlier, for the Roosevelts' first state dinner, Eleanor had presented the Chickasaw storyteller Princess Te Ata (a friend of Pauline's), later giving her the Lincoln Bedroom to stay the night in.[1] Offering a performance of Chinese shadow theatre at her granddaughter Eleanor's Christmas party in late December 1936 was in line with Mrs Roosevelt's interests and sympathies, and was to have a most beneficial effect on Red Gate's prospects.[2]

Red Gate owed the invitation entirely to Lee Ruttle's chutzpah. In May, while Pauline was still in China, Ruttle wrote to Edith Helm, Eleanor Roosevelt's secretary. "May I call your attention," he typed, "that the Red Gate Ahadow [sic] Players are available for social functions requiring unusual entertainment?" If his typing skills and syntax

were rusty, his list of references was adroitly selected, including, along with Princess Te Ata, whom Mrs Roosevelt considered a friend, Edward Beatty Rowan, formerly an assistant director of the Public Works of Art Project and as of 1936 an official in the Fine Arts Section of Federal Works; Dr Juliana Haskell of Columbia University, a noted translator of Goethe; Arthur W. Hummel, first Chief of the Division of Chinese Literature at the Library of Congress and author of *Eminent Chinese of the Ching Period* (he wrote Berthold Laufer's obituary in *American Anthropologist* in 1936);[3] and Nelson T. Johnson, US ambassador to China. Ruttle enclosed with his letter an announcement on paper embellished with blossoming plum branches that "Miss Pauline Benton is now spending several months in Peiping, China, where she is assembling new plays to be offered on our programs next season." Mrs Helm's response was brief: while "all social functions are over for this season," she noted, she would be glad to place his letter and attachments on file for consideration for the fall.[4]

By the time Ruttle sent his next letter to the White House on 18 September, Pauline had returned from China and a new program had been printed, a copy of which was enclosed. "The Red Gate Shadow Players have revived an ancient art of China, the shadow play," stated the program, citing the Emperor Wu story and pointing out that Red Gate's "shadow actors," intricately carved and coloured, had been brought direct from China. While the medium presented was "inherently Chinese," filled with "the exotic charm of the East," it had been given a "pattern which is fascinating and entertaining to American audiences," young and old. The program included photographs of William Russell, "specialist in comparative musicology," surrounded by the dozen or so Chinese instruments he played, as well as a shot of Pauline and Lee Ruttle seated behind the stage manipulating figures in what appears to have been a scene from *The Legend of the Willow Plate*. Pauline received top billing, in which it was noted that she had returned from a stay in China "where she had studied with the official shadow player of the late Empress Dowager's court" – a slight exaggeration that was

Opposite: Lee Ruttle creating special effects for the conflagration scene in *The Burning of the Bamboo Grove*

to persist and be further embellished over the years. Ruttle's accompanying letter went straight to the point: "We hope that we may have the privilege of playing in the White House this season."

Edith Helm evidently was impressed, for she wrote on the letter, "How would this do for a Xmas week party," suggesting that Anna Roosevelt Boettiger, daughter of President and Mrs Roosevelt and mother of Anna Eleanor Dall (Roosevelt), might reserve a Red Gate performance for the older Anna and her friends, with a party on another day to feature entertainment suitable for the younger children. Anna Roosevelt Boettiger agreed, though she felt that Red Gate needed to keep in mind when choosing plays that her daughter and friends were still all under the age of ten. This was to alter the plans and reduce Red Gate's performance time, but it was a positive first step.[5]

Ruttle was clearly ecstatic to receive an acceptance. He replied the same day with more than the usual typing errors (repaired here): "We shall be very glad to give a performance of Chinese shadow plays at Eleanor Dall's Christmas party, on Tuesday, December twenty second. The program we will present will include: 1. Street Fair (Acrobats, Street Vendors, Jugglers) 2. The Legend of the Willow Plate (A Play in Five Scenes) 3. Elephant Gay." He carefully pointed out that the troupe would need two hours to set up their stage and equipment, and that if the party took place during the day, the room would have to be darkened. Edith Helm did not take long to reply: "I am afraid that three plays would make rather too long a program for the children. Mrs. Roosevelt may have something else for the hour which is to be devoted to the plays in addition to the ones you are so generously offering to give."[6] She set the time for 4:15 PM, and directed Ruttle to discuss arrangements with the White House usher, Raymond Muir, the tall, skinny Bostonian newly risen to that position.[7]

The three plays Ruttle and Pauline had offered were the best in the Red Gate canon, and their program had been well considered. *Street Scenes* was useful for showing off the exciting technical feats and comedic turns that Pauline had learned from Li Tuochen in Beijing. *Willow Plate* offered drama and romance, and *Elephant Gay* (a Chinese version of Kipling's account of how the elephant got its trunk) was a fairy tale most young children would recognize, even in a Chinese setting. So it must have been disappointing when Pauline realized that Red Gate would not have the whole hour to itself, especially when

Left to right: Lee Ruttle, Pauline Benton, and William Russell in costume for Miami performances, c. 1941

they received the official program and found that it was paired with "Miss Wendy Marshall, The Toy Lady" and her singing puppets. But in any case it was an honour and privilege for Red Gate to be invited at all. The White House regularly received over two hundred offers per season, the majority of which had to be turned down; and even Pauline must have seen that the prestige of this performance would offer much in the way of future publicity and increased performance bookings. So they narrowed the program down to *Street Scenes* and *Elephant Gay*, and set forth for the nation's capital in their station wagon crammed with stage, trunk, costumes, and instruments.[8]

The *New York Times* reported on the performances and party the next day, noting that "Anna Eleanor entertained forty guests with a program presented by the Red Gate Shadow Players, and Miss Wendy Marshall." The only apparent rub during an otherwise successful afternoon came courtesy of William Russell, who delayed the performance, as Michael Slatter describes: "At the start of every Red Gate tour, Russell would leave New York with a suitcase full of clothes and at each successive stopover would abandon a part of his wardrobe to make room for more and still more records." Slatter claims that Russell's work with Red Gate was something of a "front" for his collecting. When the troupe began touring the country at large, his opportunities for seeking out and purchasing grew apace, as did the concomitant distractions. "Wherever he went he spent all his spare time looking for jazz records," noted Ross Russell (no relation). "He did go door-to-door, but he was also on the look-out for unsold stocks, sitting in a warehouse somewhere."[9]

Incredible as it sounds, record hunting was what Russell was doing while his Red Gate co-performers were waiting at the White House in their Chinese costumes and with the lamp on, the figures hanging ready, and children giggling in front of the screen as the minutes ticked by.[10] After Russell showed up, flustered after skidding through polished halls, and the performance was given, a displeased Pauline heard that he had discovered Washington's Quality Music Store and had lost all track of time while eagerly searching the shelves. She obviously did not hold his tardiness against him, because Russell continued with the troupe until 1940. (Nor did Mrs Roosevelt have any hard feelings: Russell was given a special White House cigarette case after the performance.)[11]

Regardless of mishaps, this single performance was to pay off for Red Gate over the next several years. The White House was in a real sense the troupe's debut as a mature performance art ensemble. It was never again to be seen as mere decoration or sideshow diversion. Study with Li Tuochen and immersion in the shadow plays of rural northern China had worked a transformation on Pauline that took her and her company far ahead of where they were the year before. Ironically, the golden age of Red Gate and the revival of shadow theatre had begun just as its Chinese birthplace was about to explode.

※

Those who were Pauline's students or colleagues admired her for her skill and her drive, but none seemed to know the Pauline that existed outside her Red Gate persona. She fell in love with shadow theatre, but did she ever fall in love with anybody? Did she ever want marriage, children, a home, like her sister Helen? All we know is that for over ten years Pauline criss-crossed the country with handsome bachelors, chaste as a nun. This gives some of her notes taken during lectures in Beijing a poignant quality. In April 1936 she attended a talk given by a Mrs Wang, who described in great detail, among other Chinese customs, the age-old practices around courtship and marriage. Pauline drank in every smallest nuance of what brought a man and a woman together, through romance and through the realpolitik of

A scene from Red Gate's production of *The White Snake*, in which the White Snake borrows an umbrella from the young scholar Hsü Hsien

arranged marriage. But clearly she was not sighing over something she desired for herself. "If I could only share the joys of men!" says the White Snake Lady in the play of the same name. But as her servant cautions, "I warn you, Mistress, to make a stroke of the pen through the little word 'love.'" For Pauline, all that mattered was that her shadow figures had to fall in love and marry with unerring authenticity, as animated by their unmarried master, who seems not to have loved anything but shadows.[12]

Master puppeteer Alan Cook came to know Pauline after she moved to Los Angeles in the late 1950s. As he recalls, Pauline's social skills were not highly developed, nor was she possessed of the self-preservative cautiousness about dodgy people that most of us obtain once we have entered the wider world. "She was a bit difficult to know," Cook says. "She had a way of holding back, even when it came to individual puppets. It was like she did not trust people who might really care, and yet she seemed to warm up to others who did not have her best interests at heart."[13] All indications are that Pauline thought of her shadow figures with as much seriousness, if not more so, as the living people in her life, writing and speaking of them as if they were miniature living people and animals. Perhaps, given the responsibilities she had undertaken, there was no room left for the appurtenances of so-called normal life. It is said that her New York apartment was so crammed full of shadow theatre apparatus that visitors could scarcely move, as if she were there on the figures' sufferance and not the other way around. The implication is that Pauline was somehow not quite of the adult world, even that of her fellow troupers Ruttle and Russell, who were very much involved with people and events outside their work with Red Gate. Yet that she was a sophisticated performer, as adroit in romance and tragedy as she was clever in comedy, became obvious at this time, and her skill grew with the passing years.

What we can detect through her work after her return from Beijing is a maturing of the person and the artist, as reflected in the critical acclaim Red Gate's performances began to receive. Russell's music – he was continually adding new Chinese instruments to his repertoire and composing new scores – and Ruttle's increasing fluency alongside Pauline were part of this new and improved Red Gate. But clearly something had happened to Pauline in China that deepened and broadened not just her technique but her choice of traditional plays and her development of new ones. Aside from learning from Li Tuochen in person how to depict sword fights and sword dances, fire juggling, and fireworks, Pauline had grown more sophisticated in the lyrical romances of Chinese legends, those slow love stories in which too often mortals and gods mixed to their emotional cost or physical peril. As she wrote, "The keynote to the manipulation of the shadow figures is *rhythm*," and that could be established not only through practised handling of the reeds but also by acquiring the fluency of movement that has to be developed by an actor before she can ever hope to walk on a stage and hold the attention of an audience. Whatever or whoever the real Pauline Benton was, she was most comfortable in subsuming her id, ego, and superego in the dramas of her "little actors"; and as she grew up, so did they. As she wrote in her performance programs in a statement that became Red Gate's motto, "We ask you All to laugh as we laugh, weep as we weep, love as we love, and live with us our simple truths and homilies as we recreate them for you in our Shadow World." Like the legendary Emperor Wu, who had been beguiled into believing that a shadow cast on a curtain was the soul of his deceased concubine, Pauline had a heart as naive as it was romantic. She shared it bravely with a world she knew was rarely kind and might very well have rejected it – so along with her romanticism went no small amount of courage.[14]

Evidence of her growing sophistication is clear in a short film of Pauline in performance, directed in 1947 by the art historian and filmmaker Wan-go Weng. Now in his nineties, Weng was almost a generation younger than Pauline when he filmed her in New York City performing scenes from *The White Snake*. Weng told me he met Pauline through the China Institute in America, the educational institution founded in New York City in 1926 (of which he later became director). A descendant of Weng Tonghe, tutor to the Guangxu emperor, and related by marriage to the family of Puyi, the last emperor, Weng was "borrowed" (adopted) by a childless aunt and uncle at sixteen months of age (though he lived with his biological parents) and was selected to inherit the family estate in Changshu, Jiangsu province, an old courtyard mansion in family hands since the Ming dynasty. With this patrimony also came one of the most fabulous collections of Chinese art, calligraphy, and books ever held in private hands, a collection Weng brought to the United States in 1948.

Weng had wanted to have a career as an engineer. Hu Shih, Chinese ambassador to the United States, was a family friend, who counselled Weng to "keep engineering as your vocation but art as your avocation." The trade-off was too uneven for Weng. After he had begun working in the field, he found the work uncongenial and uncreative, and resigned from his job. Without money or a job in Depression-era New York, he began working as a cartoonist, an occupation that was all work and little pay. As Weng explained to me, it was a camera that opened up a whole new career for him. Chih Meng, director of the China Institute in America, put Weng in touch with the Harmon Foundation, an organization that gave training to filmmakers basically by handing them a camera and letting them choose and shoot their subjects. Through these means, Weng learned how to make films, and his object was to create short subjects with a Chinese theme, beginning with a documentary shot at the Freer Gallery of Art in Washington, DC, titled "Ancient China's Paintings in America." He went on to make educational films about Chinese culture; he also worked as a consultant in Hollywood and later in Washington, DC, making films on American life in Mandarin for dissemination in China. A poet, painter, historian, collector, Weng still considers his films on Chinese history to be his most valuable contribution.[15]

Initially, after meeting Pauline, Weng was interested in her shadow figures only. "I learned she had a number of figures and sets from China," he said. "I found the collection interesting just for the quality of the sets and figures." Then he discovered she was no amateur shadow master: "I wanted to document her performance. I told Pauline that I liked 'The White Snake Lady' best, and she said, 'OK, let's do that.'"[16]

In his youth in China, Weng had seen his share of shadow shows. "Of course, she couldn't compete with them," he said. "But on the other hand, in America she was the only one! I won't even say in America – in the West. No matter whether we're talking of Europe or wherever ... outside China, she was the best. That she was the only woman, and the first shadow master in the West, I can verify as true." The film Weng shot went on to be chosen for screening at the Edinburgh Festival, no small measure of its or Pauline's perceived quality.[17]

What Weng captured on film is a mere few minutes of performance and another few of Pauline behind the red silk stage, manipulating figures and then putting them away (heads still attached) in a silk-bound

Another scene from *The White Snake*, showing the demoness fleeing across the lake from a dragon sent after her by the priest Fa Hai

folder. But what these frames tell of Pauline's technique speaks volumes for how far she had come since Red Gate's first pantomimes at New York society functions. The excerpts shown are the highlights of the White Snake legend, which Pauline described with characteristic sympathy: "The White Snake had passed through many incarnations and was so far advanced toward attaining Perfection that she was said to represent the spiritual side of man's nature ... A beggar found her [in snake form] and took her to the market to sell. A student saw her there, and touched by her tearful, pleading eyes, bought her to set her free. She immediately decided to reward him by becoming his wife, and set forth for Hangchow, where the young man lived."[18]

Pauline's plot closely followed most versions of this story. Transformed into a beautiful woman, the White Snake enchants the young scholar, whose name is Xu Xian (which Pauline spells Hsü Hsien in her translation), and they marry. Later on, however, the White Snake drinks realgar wine, which causes her to resume her true animal form. Xu Xian flees to the Temple of the Golden Mountain, located on an island in the Yangzi River, where he seeks the protection of its abbot, Fa Hai, who promises to make him a monk and keep the demon away. The

White Snake, unable to convince Fa Hai to give up her husband, uses her full arsenal of magic against him – a twist on the typical European fairy tale in which the male hero battles to win the hand of the maiden held captive by a dragon or in a tower. After using her magic sword to battle both the abbot and his guardian, the White Snake orders demons of the wind and water to flood the temple in a huge storm. Fa Hai keeps Xu Xian safe but tells him that his wife is pregnant with a son who will become a scholar famous throughout China. Xu Xian must return to her, and when the child is a month old, says the abbot, he will come to Xu Xian's house to capture the White Snake in his magic alms bowl and bring her to Thunder Peak pagoda on the shore of West Lake. He does so, and the White Snake is imprisoned beneath it. "Years later," Pauline wrote, "her son, having passed the imperial examinations, came to the Pagoda to offer sacrifice to his mother, and the gods allowed a brief reunion between mother and son."[19]

In Wan-go Weng's film, Pauline takes the female voices while her assistant Arvo Wirta – a melodic-voiced young man of Finnish ancestry formerly affiliated with the Neighborhood Playhouse School of the Theatre in New York City – takes the male ones, providing narration and creating simple percussion sound effects. They depict the young husband's flight to the temple for protection; then the White Snake being rowed across to the monastery by her demon maid, Black Snake, to do battle with the temple guardian and to summon the sea demons; and finally the White Snake's vanquishing by the abbot's alms bowl and her son's sacrifice at the pagoda where she is imprisoned.

In order to capture the figures clearly (films of performances at normal speed often fail to show the detail of figures or gestures), Pauline and Wirta were required to manipulate them more slowly and deliberately than would be normal; thus, their technique can be better understood and appreciated. Pauline had learned from Li Tuochen the technique of exploiting the leather figures' flexibility so that the coloured silhouettes appear to actually be alive, with strangely human gestures. It is as if a paper doll should suddenly reach up to adjust his paper collar or smooth her hair. Their movements of heads, arms, hands, and body are fluent, as reactive to other figures on the stage as live actors would be. They seem to have emotions equal to the flesh-and-blood audience watching them. When the White Snake sobs at her

The most moving scene from Red Gate's production of *The White Snake*, in which the demoness's son pays homage to his mother at her pagoda prison

failure to regain her husband from the temple, face in hands in despair, or when she swings her sword at the temple guardian with the dexterity and desperation of a cornered Errol Flynn, or when her son arrives at the pagoda to burn incense to his mother's memory and weep at the altar, we see just what it was that earned Pauline and her troupe the reputation of artists. Despite the set expressions of the figures, somehow Pauline was able to indicate shades of emotion which, coupled with Russell's music, made for a performance that was surprisingly moving.[20]

Wan-go Weng's film helps us imagine in retrospect another of Red Gate's tour-de-force shadow plays, that of *The Cowherd and the Weaving Maid*. Like *The White Snake*, a tragic romance between mortal and immortal, this play, performed in Los Angeles in the spring of 1937, drew raves. *Los Angeles Times* critic Bertrand Roberts went to see it and his review, amounting to five columns, is among the first to provide

Red Gate's performance of *The Cowherd and the Weaving Maid* was
renowned. Here the Queen Mother of Heaven watches as the young lovers
meet on a bridge of magpies. Note the special lighting effect showing the
stars of the Milky Way.

not only detailed descriptions of just what shadow theatre was and
how it functioned, but to state clearly that it was "not to be confused
with puppet shows" – that it was as serious a business as the stage
works of Shakespeare or Ibsen. Pauline described the plot of this play
in a program published in Beijing in 1940:

> The popular belief is that certain stars are maidens who spend
> their time sitting in the sky weaving and spinning. Once a year,
> they were accustomed to make a pilgrimage to the earth to wash
> their silks and bathe in the streams. The Seventh Maiden was
> known to be the most beautiful of them all.
>
> On one of the maiden's earthly visits, a poor cowherd becomes
> enamoured of her beauty, steals her basket, and keeps her on earth
> as his wife. They live happily together until their whereabouts is
> discovered by a heavenly messenger, who leads the disconsolate

young woman back to her heavenly abode. Her husband follows
her, but before he is able to reach her, the Mother of the Western
Heavens, the Guardian of the Maidens, draws a line across the
sky separates the two lovers. This line is the "Silver River," known
in the Western world as the "Milky Way." So great is the maiden's
grief at this separation that the Western Mother's heart softens
and she grants them the privilege of meeting once a year.

Every year, on the Seventh Day of the Seventh Moon, it is said
that all the magpies in the world come together and form a bridge
across the River that the two lovers may meet. Since this is the
beginning of the rainy season in China, the raindrops are said to
be the tears the lovers shed at parting.[21]

Roberts seems to have been allowed backstage during the performance, where he was able to watch Pauline and Ruttle manipulating
and Russell playing his instruments. "Unlike the American theatre,
where you wait to see what is going to happen," he wrote, "the musical cues in the Chinese theatre prepare you for the next action," a factor that was to be noted later on by other critics. According to Roberts,
"The manipulators must be able folk. They must bellow like a warrior, cry like a baby, coo like a love-sick maiden." Their performances
were funny and they were awe-inspiring, but the shadows also touched
the heart, he added. "Your throat catches at remembrance of the daughter's grief and how the mother agreed to let them meet once a year, on
the even of the seventh day of the seventh moon."[22]

Pauline does not seem to have been aware of it, but there is in this
play and especially in her masterpiece, *The White Snake*, the tragi-
comedy of the Italian *commedia dell'arte*, which is strikingly similar
to Chinese theatre, whether shadow or opera. In the theatre of the *commedia*, concealments and transformations akin to those experienced
by the White Snake and the Weaving Maid were the engine driving both
the comedy and the tragedy of the characters' experiences. In the *commedia*, writes Martin Green, "the low forms were accommodated to
high ambitions above all by means of parody, irony, and fragmenta-
tion."[23] Stéphane Lam of Compagnie Asphodèles, which combines
commedia with Beijing Opera, agrees. He remarked to me that "shadow
theatre and commedia both share a sense of complicity and interaction

with the audience. Commedia is not only made of gestures and masks,"
he added, "it is a popular and interactive form of art that questions
social issues."[24] In this sense, shadow theatre, even more than that
enacted by human actors on a stage, was uniquely able to parody both
itself and its spectators. How often did Pauline's audiences laugh at
her "puppets" only to be brought up short by eternal truths not diminished but magnified by the triumphs and tragedies of these fourteen-
inch parchment semaphores?

Pauline Benton knew all about transformations. She had reincar-
nated from university president's spinster daughter, of no particular
identifying characteristics, to purveyor of the mystery and the magic
of an ancient Chinese art form, whose sole exponent in the West she
was. Thus, it is significant that the legend of the White Snake Lady
entered her repertoire after she had been through transformative experiences herself – some of which would come to her as they were
coming to China.

Chapter 8

SURVIVAL

When imperial Japan emerged from feudal somnolence to pattern its emperors after Prussian potentates, it proved itself against that other Prussian standard, military valour, when it fought and beat imperial Russia in 1905. But Japan had bigger plans than putting the Russian emperor in his place: dominance of all of Asia was the driving force. It was thus paramount that Japan control China. Japan had inherited many of its artistic and literary models and culture from the Flowery Kingdom, but this was forgotten, just as in Germany the Nazis ignored how much of their nation's greatness was due to the German Jewish artists and philosophers, architects and politicians, poets and composers they came to denigrate and dispose of.

Japan's efforts to undercut China, sometimes with the help of Chinese, was an undercurrent throughout the late imperial period and into the era of warlords and presidents. The threat of what its next move would be was what had hung over the Beijing of Pauline's 1936 visit like smoke from a rapidly approaching fire. When the invasion came, it arrived in the form of the sort of deliberate diplomatic collisions which the West had used in the nineteenth century to profit from wars with China. On 7 July 1937, a year after Pauline had left China, Japanese soldiers crossed the Marco Polo Bridge outside Beijing on a flimsy ruse. Threats turned to bullets and in a matter of hours, Japanese troops were swarming over the bridge named for China's first cross-cultural ambassador and into the streets of the city.

The Marco Polo Bridge Incident was followed a little over a month later by the Battle of Shanghai, and finally in December by the horrors of the Nanjing Massacre (1937–38). World reaction toward the events

leading up to Nanjing had been tepid at best, especially in the isola-
tionist United States. This infuriated the Chinese in America. "Many
Chinese Americans felt doubly assaulted," writes K. Scott Wong, "abandoned by the international community in the struggle against Japan
and victimized by racial discrimination in America."[1] Several Chinese
American organizations arose to defend and assist their brothers and
sisters across the Pacific, resulting in the founding of the Chinese War
Relief Association. Public demonstrations encouraged solidarity among
Chinese Americans of all backgrounds and political persuasions, but also
and most crucially among ordinary Americans and the Chinese American community. When the atrocities in Nanjing became known, non-
Chinese Americans began to get involved. In 1938, Colonel Theodore
Roosevelt, Jr, organized Rice Bowl parties across the nation to raise
funds for and awareness of the plight of the Chinese. Celebrities such
as Anna May Wong and Princess Der Ling lent their presence and purses
to these and other events. Red Gate, too, responded to the call.

Reporting on New York City's first Rice Bowl party in June, the *New
York Times* noted that "such a crowd as Chinatown probably had never
seen before filled its narrow, winding streets." Some 85,000 people
milled around in thoroughfares that were draped with the flags of the
Chinese Republic and the United States of America; overhead, lanterns
bobbed and papier-mâché dragons lunged and danced in the breeze.
The ticket price included dinner, "such Oriental delectables as bird's
nest soup, fried rice, shrimp foo young, preserved kumquats and jas-
mine tea," which diners enjoyed while being entertained until after midnight by "stage, screen and radio stars – Chinese and American." There
was street dancing accompanied by Chinese bands, and Red Gate,
which performed at the Chinese Center, "renamed for the night 'The
Moon Gate Theatre,'" was singled out as being a sample of "the world's
oldest movies." For the party, 2,500 tickets were sold in advance and
at least 3,500 more were purchased at the gates. At $6 per ticket, the
New York Chinatown Rice Bowl party brought in almost $38,000,
not counting donations and other purchases.[2]

Suddenly the Chinese, who until then had been regarded as feck-
less victims of their own insularity, were transformed into heroes
battling a vicious attacker, the Japanese, who had previously been
regarded as a model of Westernization in Asia. Sister- and brother-
hood between China and America came to be seen as a reality. Given

the "fashion" factor that always accompanies such events, suddenly all things Chinese were acceptable and respectable, whereas all things Japanese were not. This grew to the degree where, after Japan attacked the United States in 1941, innocent Japanese Americans were uprooted from their homes and sent to internment camps, and all good Americans were urged to keep watch for Japanese traitors. Directions for how to tell the difference between a person of Chinese and Japanese ancestry were published in the popular press. According to the 22 December 1941 issue of *Time*, in an article titled "How to Tell Your Friends from the Japs," readers could learn that "Japanese eyes are usually set closer together ... the Chinese expression is likely to be more placid, kindly, open; the Japanese more positive, dogmatic, arrogant ... Japanese are hesitant, nervous in conversation, laugh loudly at the wrong time." In other words, just like a lot of Hollywood stereotypes. There is a striking resemblance between the anti-Semitic screeds being published in Germany, likening Jews to apes, and American ones about the Japanese. They cast shadows across US efforts to help the Chinese, whom Americans once had spoken of in similarly dehumanizing terms.[3]

Even in an era where exaggeration was the norm, Chinese culture as the Chinese knew it was threatened with extinction. Those who flocked to Red Gate's performances would have done so under the impression that shadow theatre was probably already half-dead in the country of its origin. Thus, Red Gate was not just entertainment; it was resurrection, an ancient performance art brought to the safety and security of the American doorstep at a time when American culture would deem itself threatened with extinction by Hitler and Hirohito.

From the summer of 1937 until Japan's attack on Pearl Harbor in December 1941, Red Gate had crossed and recrossed the country, becoming part of the American response to the tragedy consuming China. In an article Pauline wrote for the *Christian Science Monitor* in September 1941, she described what touring the United States with a shadow troupe entailed. "Like our Chinese prototypes," she explained, "we carry stage and actors in cases and bundles to our audiences in schools, colleges, clubs, museums, and homes all over the country. We travel in a station-wagon, which is less picturesque than the ricksha and foot method, but much more practical and comfortable for long trips."[4]

Two images of how tiring yet invigorating these tours could be for all three performers are found in the Benton papers. The first photograph, taken during a stopover in Miami, shows Benton, Ruttle, and Russell beside their automobile shortly after arriving. They stand in their rumpled travelling gear, along with Dorothea Gauss, Red Gate's booking agent, who worked for Pearl S. Buck's East and West Association. Pauline, with her fussy hat, shapeless dress, and swollen ankles, looks far older than her age; Russell looks distracted; Ruttle anxious for a cigarette. Yet in a second photograph, taken once the trio had switched to their Chinese robes, Ruttle and Russell are alert and professional, while Pauline is as radiant as the Florida sunshine pouring down on her. As the Red Gate Players, they were in their element, at one with the embattled Chinese a world away.

Soo Yong, who had been hired for the supporting Chinese cast of *The Good Earth*, left Red Gate before it returned to the East and was replaced by the dancer King Lan Chew. Also known as Caroline Chew, the Berkeley-born performer was a daughter of Ng Poon Chew, the newspaper publisher and author who crusaded for the rights of Chinese Americans. Though Chew favoured the rights of women, his

The performers of Red Gate Shadow Players with Dorothea Gauss, publicist for Pearl S. Buck's East West Association

daughter Caroline had to wait until his death before pursuing a career as dancer, in her thirties, when most dancers had already hit their peak. By 1935, Chew had performed on Broadway and was making her mark as "the only Chinese woman dancer in America" – a claim that echoes Pauline's own of being the only woman shadow master in the world. So Chew was in good company, and she was more than that for Red Gate. Not only did she perform traditional Chinese dances as "entr'-actes" between acts or scenes, but she gave narrations in American English that audiences could relate to. Perhaps to be expected, given that Red Gate's director was the daughter of a famous educator who believed that nets cast widest were apt to capture the most good, the company's purpose became more and more a tool of instruction: not just to delight Americans with shadow plays but to teach them the history behind the plays and the art form.[5]

When Pauline announced her debut "public" performances in New York City in February 1938, Asa Bordages of the *New York World-Telegram* reported that "the 'shadow plays' of ancient China – talking moving pictures, in colors, 2059 years old [sic] – now are being played for the New York public for the first time in history"; public Pauline had made it, by launching this first open performance at the Chow Mein Inn, an eatery at 1761 Broadway. The Chow Mein Inn was a far cry from the Seventh Regiment Armory, but in fact it was not so very different from the tea houses in Beijing, where shadow plays had long been part of the atmosphere. Red Gate's subsequent venues showed that Pauline's notion of public embraced many sectors: the Barbizon Hotel for Women, where males were not permitted above the ground floor, and the Hotel des Artistes, a studio apartment building that had sheltered everyone from Isadora Duncan to Noël Coward, Alexander Woollcott, and Norman Rockwell. Two more engagements took place over the following months, at the Broadway Tabernacle Church in March and in April in the ballroom of the Ambassador Hotel. According to press accounts, proceeds went to the American Bureau for Medical Aid to China – proof that if Pauline's heart was mostly given to shadow theatre, there was ample space in it for the plight of the Chinese people whom she also loved.[6]

In February, the 1939 world's fair opened in San Francisco. The exposition was meant from the start to be a celebration of the Oakland Bay

Bridge, dedicated in 1936, and the Golden Gate, dedicated the following year. But as a "Pageant of the Pacific" it was meant also to be a smorgasbord of culture and commerce of Pacific Rim nations. After numerous sites had been explored and rejected – Golden Gate Park, Lake Merced, China Basin – architects W.P. Day and George W. Kelham decided to focus on Yerba Buena Island, one hundred fifty acres of dirt, stone, and shrubbery supporting the point at which the San Francisco and Oakland spans of the Bay Bridge met. It was their idea to build a new island to its north, on the Yerba Buena Shoals. The future Treasure Island was to have a post-fair role as an airport; but the Japanese attack on Pearl Harbor transformed it into a naval base. Presided over by an eighty-foot goddess, Pacifica, the fair's grounds were enriched and in some cases overwhelmed by temporary but looming art deco architecture, much of it made brilliant with light and colour as well as having buxom female figures on the façades. Exhibitors displayed and concessionaires sold; priceless art works throve beside risqué advertisements for "Sally Rand's Nude Ranch," and the night skies were so full of sparkling jewel lights as to justify the name of the little man-made island.[7]

"When China, impoverished by the war, found it impossible to participate officially in the Exposition," wrote Jack James and Earle Weller, "San Francisco's Chinese went to work and raised over $1,000,000 to create the 12-acre Chinatown which formed one of the brightest spots on [Treasure] Island."[8] This Chinatown was surrounded by a high wall, its sides painted with enticing descriptions of what could be found within: everything from jades, silks, paintings, and curios to "mask-makers, fortune-telling birds, street entertainers, musicians, dancers ..." Above the walls the sightseer glimpsed a pagoda and yellow-tiled roofs with curling eaves and dangling bells, while inside they were presented with a riot of "silken streamers and glowing lanterns against a background of vermilion, tulip yellow and gold," courtesy of San Francisco Chinatown's craftspeople. There was even a pavilion devoted entirely to the Chinese treasures of Princess Der Ling, who had served as consultant on the village's decorations.[9]

Though not listed among the vendors for 1939 or 1940, Red Gate is on record as having been en route to perform at the fair. Driving across the country again in their packed station wagon, the troupe stopped in Reno for a performance. From there, ran a local newspaper

Left to right: Pauline Benton, Lee Ruttle, and Robert Youmans

report, Red Gate was headed for the Golden Gate International
Exposition.[10] While I secured no hard proof that the company was
actually at the fair, Red Gate could have been simply another of the
"exhibits," along with Princess Der Ling's complete throne room and
the mask makers and street entertainers. The latter would, in any case,
have come and gone in the gypsy fashion of all temporary features at
any carnival. Against all the chinoiserie marshalled to give the Chinese
Village a crowded authenticity, even the only woman shadow master
in the Western world would have had to offer something spectacularly
incredible to stand out from the throng. Maybe what Red Gate had to
offer was even a little too authentic for this slice of ersatz China.
Perhaps this is why Pauline took Red Gate's stage on to San Francisco's
Chinatown itself, where the troupe spent that and the next summer
performing.

Chinatown had had a lurid reputation almost from its beginnings in
the 1848 gold rush – as a locus of gambling, gang wars, prostitution
and, of course, opium smoking and dealing. No one seemed to consider that packing thousands of men together in a ghetto (Chinese
women being restricted by immigration policy) would result in the same
sort of testosterone-fuelled frustrations and altercations found in
crowds of males anywhere.

San Francisco's chief of police, Jesse B. Cook, who had known Chinatown since childhood, gave a more nuanced perspective. Like any
other condensed neighbourhood, Chinatown had its "hoodlum element," but not everyone there was an Asian criminal out of the pages
of Sax Rohmer. Cook insisted that the Chinese were not natural gam-
blers. "The old-time Chinese visited gambling houses so much because
there were so few places of entertainment," he wrote. "In the first place,
very few of them were married men. They could not speak English
and, therefore, could not enjoy American dramas, dances or games.
The only things left for them to do were either to visit houses of prostitution, gambling houses, lottery houses or the Chinese Theatre." Cook
believed that Chinatown's men would not have so willingly spent time
in the activities that gave them and Chinatown a lurid reputation had
they been afforded more productive or at least more interesting activities than were shared with the whites who lived around them. Of
course, one obstacle to Cook's belief that assimilation would solve many
of the neighbourhood's problems was that few San Franciscans wanted
the Chinese to take part in their games, attend their dances, or sit in
their theatres. Nor, indeed, after their treatment at the hands of white
politicians and citizens, did many Chinese want to partake of their
neighbours' entertainments or their company.[11]

The venue for Red Gate's performances in summer 1939 was Ross
Alley, the oldest alley in the city and possibly the most notorious in
Chinatown.[12] Before Red Gate arrived, Ross Alley had been the place
to go for brothels and gambling and other forms of what Chief Cook
would regard as the regrettable necessities of a marginalized male pop-
ulace. It is now the address for the Golden Gate Fortune Cookie Factory and is lined with murals of residents engaging in ordinary daily
tasks; in Red Gate's day, it would have been not so much sordid as
down at heel. Which is possibly what made the troupe's offerings that
summer seem even more magical. Old timers who had not seen shadow

theatre since their youth in China, or the young who had only heard about this entertainment, may have stopped in to see what was on offer. Word got around until it reached the offices of the *San Francisco Chronicle* and the ears of Alfred Frankenstein, the paper's art and music critic. Born in Chicago in 1906, Frankenstein had begun as a teacher of music history (he also served as clarinetist with the Chicago Symphony Orchestra) before being named the *Chronicle*'s art and music critic in 1934. An expert in American art, Frankenstein's best-known work was a study of American *trompe l'oeuil* painting, an interest in artistic illusion that may have helped draw him to shadow theatre – optical illusion in motion – in the first place. So Frankenstein had to see what all the fuss was about. He appears to have been more impressed than he expected. "Down in Chinatown – especially, in the little alley off Washington street, between Stockton and Grant, known as Old Chinatown," began his review, "one may witness these days one of the most charming, eloquent, persuasive and novel forms of theatre the world affords."[13]

Frankenstein probably attended more than one of Red Gate's Chinatown performances, because his review mentions nearly all the major plays in the company's repertoire: *The Legend of the Willow Plate, The Cowherd and the Weaving Maid, The Monkey Stealing the Peaches, The White Fox Spirit*. Frankenstein also lists the shorter plays and scenes: *Drum Dance, The Burning of the Bamboo Grove*, and the Kipling-inspired *Elephant Gay*, which had been such a hit at the White House. For a critic so interested in the uses of illusion, Frankenstein was an uncompromising seeker of the basic truths of art and life. In his typical no-nonsense style, he made perhaps the boldest claim ever advanced about shadow theatre, yet one that echoed the art form's reputation in China: not just theatre of entertainment, but theatre of the sacred. "Here, if anywhere," Frankenstein wrote, "is Wagner's synthesis of the arts." Richard Wagner pioneered the concept of *Gesamtkunstwerk*, a performance embracing drama, music, visual elements, even dance, in which all elements of the stage work are interwoven and interrelated, much as they would be in the movies of a later century. He also tuned all his mature works to a pitch of intellectual, emotional, and spiritual rigor that had never been seen or heard before on any stage in Europe, imbuing his operas with a sacred significance. And given Wagner's insistence on controlling every aspect of a production, he could be said to have the signal characteristic of a shadow

master, who controls several figures, sings and gives dialogue, and assists
with scene changes: the ultimate micromanager. (Perhaps it is no surprise that in his childhood, as Wagner describes in his memoirs, *Mein
Leben*, like Berthold Laufer he had been fond of making puppets and
producing outlandishly romantic plays for them to act in.)

For Frankenstein, the figures were "triumphs of design and color,"
the plots of the plays "delightful and forceful," and Russell's music
sophisticated in providing a Chinese "atmosphere" that did not pan-
der to ersatz musical chinoiserie or present so authentic a sound as to
be "deafening and monotonous to the Western ear."[14] Aware that
shadow theatre had been compared to the cartoons of Walt Disney,
Frankenstein dismissed the parallel, declaring that "the shadow theatre has a greater range, purity and sophistication than anything Disney has yet done." This, it should be noted, was two years after *Snow
White and the Seven Dwarfs* made animation history.[15]

Frankenstein's review in that waning year of 1939 was not to be
Pauline's only recognition from an intelligent and sensitive observer.
At a 23 October performance at Mills College in Oakland, a Portland-
born composer named Lou Harrison was sitting in the audience. Handsome but compact, with a solidness that ballooned to Falstaffian
proportions in later years, the twenty-two-year-old Harrison had studied composition with American composer Henry Cowell; later, while
working in the UCLA dance department he also studied with émigré
twelve-tone master Arnold Schoenberg. As unconventional musically
as he was personally and spiritually, Harrison was on his way to creating a genre of percussion music that William Russell, Red Gate's musician, would become known for. Like Russell, he explored found objects
(such as car brake drums) as sources of tone and timpani, as did the
composers whom Harrison championed as a music critic, among them
Charles Ives.[16]

During Harrison's youth in San Francisco, he had experimented with
a wide range of different styles and types of music from a variety of
cultures. The music of Asia, especially that of Indonesia, resonated with
him. Harrison was always fascinated by how instruments were constructed and how their materials affected their sound-producing capacity. So he attended Red Gate's performance at Mills College (where he
was then teaching), as much to study Russell's mastery of Chinese

instruments as for the play itself. And indeed, as Harrison later wrote, through Russell he received an education in another kind of music too. "We got sufficiently acquainted," he recalled, "that he brought stacks of records up to my apartment and sat down very seriously and gave me my first education in jazz, beyond the jazz piano I'd had.'" He came to admire Russell's own works so greatly that in later years he and composer John Cage programmed Russell's percussion ensemble works for public performance.[17]

Yet sound was displaced by sight as the light came on behind the screen of Pauline's red stage. Fascinated by puppetry through his work for the Depression-era Works Progress Administration, where he came to know important puppet masters of the West Coast (he would later leave his substantial collection of Asian and Western puppets to the University of California Santa Cruz),[18] Harrison the dancer and actor found himself overcome as by a magic spell. "On the white screen appeared wondrous figures of the most enchanting beauty and splendid colors. Their movement was as subtle or as robust as that of living actors and the stories were of serene, mystic richness." Watching the "little actors" act out their vast romances against the glittering tonal backdrop of Russell's music, Harrison had as life-altering an experience as Pauline had had in Aunt Emma's Beijing garden sixteen years earlier. "This performance went directly into my heart," he wrote, "and was permanently impressed there."[19] It was an impression that remained strong for the next thirty years and would lead to the little actors' – and Pauline's – rebirth.

Pauline's program of performance, education, and assistance to the Chinese continued to strengthen throughout the war years, and the respect she hoped to achieve for shadow theatre increased as well. In February 1942, the Metropolitan Museum of Art in New York City included Red Gate in a shadow theatre exhibit organized by the museum's curator of Asian art, Alan Priest. Priest was one in whom sensitivity to Asian art, culture, and religion was paired with an incorrigible and sometimes insufferable arrogance that was by no means unusual among highly placed museum curators – "a crusty, malicious character," wrote

James Cahill, "modeled on the then-popular image of the lovable rogue who insults everybody (see 'The Man Who Came to Dinner' etc.), and played the part well."[20]

Priest wrote of the exhibit that it seemed more a species of toy theatre than something more serious. But when the lights were turned down, the music began, and the figures entered the illuminated stage, toy theatre and shadow theatre parted company. At that point, as Priest explained, "instantly the audience is theirs." Priest apologized that the exhibit featured mounted shadow figures, because it was only "in movement [that] they have an especial quality," adding that the "elixir that flows in their veins is the same as that which animates shadows from a log fire or reflections on the underside of boats when the sun shines on lightly moving water." In other words, despite the highly controlled structure behind the white screen, where every move and gesture was planned and rehearsed, shadow theatre had about it the same unpredictable charm as the lights and shadows of nature, further enhancing the magic and myth of the plays the figures appeared in and the dance of reality and fantasy in which shadow theatre specialized.[21]

In the summer of 1943, Pauline took part in a two-day conference at the Institute on Asiatic Affairs in American Education at Harvard University. The education editor of the *Christian Science Monitor*, Millicent Taylor, was present, and among the many experts offering their theories and advice she singled out the address given by Dr Olov R.T. Janse as the theme of the conference. Janse believed that far from being unprovoked, Japanese aggression was partly the result of Westerners' "failure to understand the mind of the Asiatic." For example, Westerners in Asia had not "understood and been generous with the religious feelings of the people" where they had "gone in and sought to introduce a modern economy." Before laying railroad tracks, said Janse, foreign companies in Asia should have allowed the local people to burn incense to their deities of the earth or to ancestors supposed to be buried nearby, to comfort the living and soothe the dead. Foreigners should learn local traditions, he insisted, and seek to accommodate them, instead of dismissing or trampling them – precisely Pauline's tactic in researching shadow theatre in the villages of northern China.[22]

Given that the attendees were not diplomats or politicians but educators, this call for what we would now term a more globalized view may not have achieved much traction. But a retooling of education, addressing the absence of Asia in the American curriculum, was the subject of another speech that day. Dr Howard E. Wilson of Harvard's Graduate School of Education, an expert on Asian and Latin American material in American school texts, noted that "there are two main ways of introducing more about Asia into the schools. One is through special courses and 'units' of work; the other is to inject a great deal of Asiatic comparison and contrast into the prevailing courses in English, in art, in history, so that material on Asia and its peoples is filtered through all the existing studies."[23]

Following Wilson's presentation, Pauline had an opportunity to demonstrate just how Asian art and culture might be made part of the American school curriculum, as a way of teaching American children Chinese history and legend. After performing two shadow plays, she spoke on the art form's pedagogical potential. "Miss Benton, whose theatre is noted for its accuracy in reproducing Chinese shadow plays in the classic tradition, declared that all she has learned about China – and she is considered an authority on Chinese costume and customs – has come through shadow plays," wrote the *Monitor*'s Millicent Taylor, who had championed Red Gate in the past. Taylor added that Pauline had finished her talk by showing sets of shadow figures and even stage sets that had been created by American schoolchildren after seeing Red Gate performances. In 1950, while Red Gate was performing in the New York area, the company was accorded two columns in the *New Yorker*'s "On and Off the Avenue," in which the writer described Pauline as "a skilled artist possessed of a vast knowledge of her métier" whose shadow plays would, in an ideal world, take the place of the "depressingly commonplace" amusement afforded to children by television.

Demonstrating shadow theatre to a rising generation may have given Pauline hope that the art form would have a future beyond her lifetime – would outlive the often shallow menu offered by the television of the day. It may seem counterintuitive of Pauline to have focused to this extent on the role of children in her shadow theatre performances and demonstrations. It was their parents, after all, who spent money on tickets and whose influence might draw more substantial support in the future (nor were performances for children generally reviewed or seen as review-worthy by editors). But then Pauline was not running a nonprofit organization. Red Gate was more like a school, an educational experience, a role not unlike the one she believed it had served in China – a means of celebrating and remembering the glorious past.[24]

In one special case, Pauline's strategy was to pay off, though not until long after her death. When she performed in the late 1940s for a high school in Pittsfield, Massachusetts, the spectators included a young girl who would not only grow up to found a shadow theatre company in New York but would become heir to Pauline's legacy as well as her stage, sets, and figures – indeed, she would spend years restoring those same figures, saving them from disintegration, so that they could continue to perform long past her own lifetime.[25] In focusing on children, Pauline Benton was building more wisely than she knew.

Chapter 9

CULTURAL REVOLUTION

With the atomic obliteration of the citizens of Nagasaki and Hiroshima, the Second World War came to an end for East and for West in September 1945. But the war that had been raging in China between Nationalists under Chiang Kai-shek and Communists under Mao Zedong, temporarily held in abeyance, now resumed with a renewed vengeance.

China lay in ruins after the depredations of the Japanese, and both Chiang and Mao each insisted he had the better plan for rebuilding and reforming the shattered nation. But after numerous losses to the Communists, Chiang began to see the writing on the wall. Having already shipped many of Beijing's imperial treasures to safer havens, he now began to strip the city of some of its greatest artworks, to be crated and sped to Taiwan, where they were joined by the better part of the Chinese gold reserve and, shortly, by Chiang and hordes of refugees in chaotic flight. Down came the blue and white flag of the Kuomintang; up went the red flag with gold stars of Mao's new regime. Between 1912 and 1949, China had lost a decaying monarchy in exchange for a dysfunctional democracy, which in turn had now been displaced by Mao's perfect world of equality for all.[1]

Mao made enemies of those who for a few happy years had been China's friends in the West, when he aided North Korea in its invasion of the south in 1951, precipitating the Korean War and adding China to the blacklist of an increasingly paranoid America. Where China had been a nation of heroes during its fight against the Japanese, it now seemed to Americans a frightening army of robots in blue suits behind impenetrable walls, governed by a man whose aim seemed to be world domination by soulless Communism. China's close relations with Russia, which had just tested its own bomb, gave sleepless nights to Western leaders; a Cold War started a new little ice age that prompted construction of backyard bomb shelters – that quintessential do-it-yourself project of the 1950s throughout America. And when provoking the outside world was not enough, Mao imposed backward backyard projects on his own people. The Great Leap Forward (1958–61), an unrealistic effort to bring China up to the standards of the industrialized West by forcing Chinese to construct their own steel smelters, taking farmers away from their crops, or overplanting crops and forcing inexperienced intellectuals to tend them, led to famine and the death of millions of Chinese.[2]

With American casualties in the Korean War, China's bona fides in America died too (though a strong defence-oriented relationship was to continue with the Taiwanese government). From the heights of respect in the late 1930s, Chinese Americans and Chinese students, academics, scientists, and diplomats were treated in the 1950s and 1960s with the same lockstep suspicion that had turned the United States against Japanese Americans in 1941. These were the Senator Joe McCarthy years, in which Communist witches were thought to convene secret conclaves, casting spells on ordinary suburban Americans and their way of life. The careers and characters of those accused were burned at the stake of superstitions that were as corrosive as those that had lit the fires of Inquisition Europe. Chinatowns across the United States began to be seen as hotbeds of burgeoning Communist activity; telephones were bugged, businesses watched, Chinese Americans with relatives in the People's Republic were questioned. Many Chinese Americans, even those whose parents and grandparents had lived in America, paid its taxes, and since 1943 voted in its elections, lived in fear not so dissimilar from what their cousins in China were enduring under Communist cadres. Each broken shop or house window, ethnic slur scrawled on walls or screamed by white children seemed to indicate to Chinese Americans that the good times were gone; some returned to China, only to find that they had stepped from the frying pan into the fire. This was especially true during the Cultural Revolution.[3]

Technically, the Cultural Revolution lasted from 16 May 1966, when Mao first warned his people that bourgeoisie influence was infiltrating the Communist Party, until the Chairman's declaration of its end in 1969, when even he was dismayed that this effort to retrench his power had caused damage outweighing any possible gain. One of its chief instigators was Mao's wife, Jiang Qing. Always fancying herself an artist – in 1930s Shanghai she had been a second-rate film and stage actress – Jiang Qing appeared on posters showing her declaring that the Chinese were to "let the new socialist performing arts occupy every stage." What this meant was art that had passed the litmus test not just of "Mao thought" but of Madame Mao's agenda; eight model operas were decreed and performed over and over and over again, cheered on by the obedient, the cautious, and the ambitious. Many of these were students whom "Mao thought" had encouraged to criticize their teachers, their parents, and any other authority figure, with methods ranging from public humiliation to torture and murder behind closed doors. Intertwined with this criticism of the traditional arts was the "Destruction of the Four Olds" movement early in the revolution. Though the Four Olds campaign mainly targeted religion, resulting in the destruction of countless temples, mosques, monasteries, and anything related to them, the Olds expanded to include art in any form that had not sprung from the pure cloth of Communism, that is to say, the artistic production of several thousand years of Chinese history. Young people – brainwashed to deny their own history and the value of education, to ignore the traditional bonds of the student-teacher relationship, as well as the even stronger bonds of family, and to scorn as superstitious the reverence of ancestors or of anything except Chairman Mao – attacked, persecuted, tortured, and killed "running dogs" and "revisionists" by the thousand. They eradicated age-old customs, marched intellectuals to labour camps, and left a legacy of damaged and destroyed architecture, antiques, libraries, and whatever else seemed to stand in the way of the free flow of Maoist ideology, with effects still seen today on buildings, in libraries and art collections, and in survivors scarred by the experience.[4]

An example of the senseless violence from this period was the attack on the elderly Mme Dan Paochao, younger sister of Princess Der Ling. Mme Dan had been one of pre-Communist Beijing's premier social figures. A woman who had studied in Paris with Isadora Duncan and brought Western dance to China (for which she is still revered by classical dancers), Mme Dan had served as lady-in-waiting to the Empress Dowager Cixi and then as hostess to several of the Republican presidents of China. In the 1920s and 1930s, she had sought to preserve traditional performance art – dance, music, theatre – at her red-columned palace, offering them to foreign visitors who, as with shadow theatre, seemed more eager to sample Chinese culture than most Chinese themselves. Though she had fled in the Nationalist exodus in 1949, Mme Dan eventually returned to Beijing and published her memoirs of her time at the imperial court during the "Hundred Flowers" period. Though this underscored her feudal origins all too clearly, she managed to live untouched through the turbulent 1950s in her apartment east of the Forbidden City, visiting the British legation for afternoon tea, where she befriended a young Englishwoman, Pattice Hughes, and gave her presents, corresponding with her in excellent English even after Miss Hughes returned to England.[5]

Mme Dan's pleasant old age changed overnight. Sometime in the late 1960s, Red Guards dragged her from her apartment into the street. Though she was a harmless woman in her early nineties, the Red Guards broke her legs – symbolic torture for a woman who had had the gall to bring foreign ballet to China. They then ransacked her apartment, which was filled with scroll paintings by the Empress Dowager and other imperial gifts, as well as foreign books and pictures, destroying everything. "There was little left," says her adopted son, Meng Zhaozhen, "but a few photographs among the ashes."[6] Mme Dan was taken to the hospital by Meng. She died there, and Meng buried her ashes in Beihai Park, former pleasure ground of the Empress Dowager Cixi, whom she had served in her youth (and, incidentally, where the Peking Shadow Theatre was housed in the 1970s).[7]

Although author Han Suyin was assured by young opera singers in early 1970s Beijing that Mme Mao "had saved them from performing as princesses and beautiful ladies," princesses like Mme Dan were actually an exception to the rule among Jiang Qing's many victims. Ordinary artists and artisans were resolutely struck down along with the Four Olds they were believed to promote. Indeed, shadow masters, uniting as they did art and history that were celebratory of the feudal order and the superstitions inherent thereto, were an ideal target.[8]

In 1994, director Zhang Yimou released *To Live* [活着], a film chronicling the life of one family through its fall from affluence in the warlord-riven China of the 1940s to the sweeping changes after 1949. The film chronicles the particularly dire effect of the Cultural Revolution on shadow theatre. In the plot, based on the novel by Yu Hua, a wealthy merchant's son Xu Fugui loses everything to a gambling addiction. Having spent so much time over dice in the tea houses, where shadow plays were performed, Xu often joins the players behind their screen and develops a talent as singer and manipulator. Xu performs shadow plays to support his wife and child, using a trunk of old figures passed on to him by the man to whom he had lost his family's wealth. When the Japanese invade, Xu is conscripted by the Nationalists but takes his trunk along, performing for Chinese troops in the field. This trunk becomes his unlikely salvation when he is captured by the Japanese: he performs for Japanese officers and soldiers, shadow theatre being as popular with the Japanese as Beijing Opera, and when he is captured by the Communists, he performs for them. After 1949 and down to the Cultural Revolution, shadow theatre was not exempt from the Olds that Mao ordered Chinese people to eradicate. Xu becomes a labourer but holds on to his trunk of shadow figures, using them to entertain neighbours during that part of the Great Leap Forward when ordinary Chinese were adjured to fire up smelters in their backyards – an ironic juxtaposition of past culture colliding with what passed for modernity. Only when ordered to do so does he burn his little actors – it was obey or suffer in the new world order. Yet the trunk remains, and it becomes as much a symbol of hope for Xu as his shadow figures had once been. The final scene shows Xu's grandson, very much the China of the future, admiring the fluffy yellow chicks that Xu is allowed to keep, which now live in the empty trunk, symbols like the grandson of the changes to come. It is as if Xu and his family, controlled like puppets by forces beyond their control, may look forward to the day when they may have a say in what dramas they enact on the stage of their lives. Life, says the elderly Xu, with his undying optimism, "will get better and better" – incidentally, a slogan much in circulation in the famine years of 1958–61.[9]

Although it is fiction, Zhang's script does reflect real circumstances, including those that challenged one of the most renowned family shadow troupes in the last decades of the twentieth century. The Lu family of Beijing, whom Pauline hired to carve figures in 1936, is an example not only of what could be endured but of how one could avoid the disaster that fell on many by simply going with the flow.

Throughout the Japanese invasion and into the war period, the Lu family – which included Jingda, the artist who carved Pauline's shadow figures – continued to perform. But when the Japanese invited the Lus to perform in Japan they refused, much as Mei Lanfang did when he grew a moustache to avoid performing his famous female roles for China's Japanese overlords. While Mei was never manhandled into cooperating, and found ways to make a living when he temporarily left the stage, it was a different story for the Lu family troupe. After Japanese agents took two of Jingda's brothers by force, sending them by train to board a ship for Japan, they managed to escape by jumping off their moving car, injuring themselves in the process.[10]

This refusal to obey the Japanese would have stood the Lus in good stead in both the last days of Chiang Kai-shek and under Mao, but life did not get any easier for them. With China now an atheist state, worship of any kind was proscribed, and temples were shut down. Because such shadow performances as there were in 1950s and 1960s Beijing largely took place at temple fairs (as is still true today), the Lus' once certain source of performance income vanished. But the government had other plans to keep shadow masters busy. Though in the mid-1950s Beijing's Foreign Languages Press turned out such books as *Folk Arts of New China*, in which it was alleged that both the Kuomintang and the Japanese had tried to crush such traditional arts as shadow theatre – and even included pictorials showing a White Snake figure made by Lu Jingda and scenes from "feudal" plays – the reality for folk arts performers and creators was not so rosy. Forbidden to perform "feudal" plays of the past, shadow masters were sent into the countryside as bearers of propaganda, shadow-theatre style. The Lus performed plays expounding "Mao thought" in a variety of simple dramas and comedies, among which were lampoons of American President Dwight D. Eisenhower (known as "The Worries of Ike"). "Some of the old style family troupes were given status as big national companies," writes Stephen Kaplin, artistic director of Chinese Theatre Works in New York. These favoured troupes were given "large artistic and administrative staffs, training and support facilities." But while a few classical plays were still permitted to light up shadow stages, by and large the troupes were consigned to political screeds for adult audiences and, for children, the sort of animal fables that Pauline herself would perform in Red Gate's waning years, using garishly coloured plastic figures outlined by brilliant banks of lights.[11]

Lu Yuefang's sons, who took on the family business, did well during this period, even performing at the front during the Korean War (much as the fictional Xu Fugui does for Chinese and Japanese soldiers), staging their plays in the tunnels beneath the demilitarized zone. This won the Lu company more government accolades and support; they became an officially sponsored troupe, with the government paying all their expenses. But this strange new golden age came to a halt with the Cultural Revolution. "The Peking Shadow Stage found themselves in transition," writes Dr Gerd Kaminski. "The Cultural Revolution played hell with them. In 1967, many of their figures, some of which dated back to the Qing dynasty, were taken by fanatical Red Guards, splashed with gasoline, and burned."[12] "The results were disastrous," affirms Kaplin. "Almost all serious intellectual and artistic activity ceased for [the revolution's] 10 year duration. Chinese theatre companies were restricted to presenting eight new plays that had been officially sanctioned by [Jiang Qing]."[13] Persecution reached even these former favourites, so the Lus stopped performing and abandoned their company altogether. The effects of this persecution could be very sad indeed. Han Suyin was with a group of foreign writers who were guided to Tangshan in 1966 by cultural and propaganda officials to visit a "model" brigade of workers labouring to transform wasteland into productive farmland. A banquet ensued, with endless speeches. By midnight Han was one of the few foreigners left, feeling sorry for the shadow performers who were still waiting to demonstrate their "subtle and intricate art." Though Tangshan was famed for its shadow theatre, during the Cultural Revolution it was obviously seen more as a curiosity to flog for visitors, if there was time left at the end of overstuffed programs singing Mao's praises.[14]

Red Gate found itself being reconfigured in America through the pressures of the Pacific War. Robert Youmans, who had taken over from Lee Ruttle in 1939, had joined the armed forces in 1943, as Ruttle himself had done. It was also around this time (1942–43) that William Russell left Red Gate to found the "American Music" jazz record label. He also began to make his name as a composer. "Russell's choice of the percussion ensemble as his genre," states a program note, "assembled in a collage of western and non-western instruments with found objects, qualifies his work as perhaps the first truly avant-garde American music."[15] Arvo Wirta, who would appear with her in Wan-go Weng's 1947 film, became Pauline's new assistant, and it was he who performed with Pauline at one of Red Gate's most prestigious venues in 1943, the Marines Memorial Theatre in San Francisco. By spring 1945, when Red Gate performed at the Royal Ontario Museum in Toronto, the duo of Benton and Wirta was augmented by the addition of William Boyer, but aside from a few other assistants over the years only Wirta continued with Pauline until Red Gate's end; his last known performance with her was in Honolulu in 1954.[16]

Who took over for musician Russell is another of the mysteries about Pauline. Wan-go Weng reports that neither Russell nor any other live musician was present for his shoot of *The White Snake*. Pauline and her assistant seem to have made do providing basic sound effects using chimes, bells, and drum – instruments within their capacity – along with recorded Chinese music. The Russell days of richly authentic accompaniment were past, as was, it appears, Red Gate's attraction for audiences. "The closer Americans got to real Chinese," writes John Tchen about an earlier period of US-Chinese relations, "dispelling their imagined 'Orient,' the more their respect for and emulation of Chinese civilization diminished."[17] It was as if the legendary world of China embodied by shadow theatre was easier for Americans to tolerate during the war years, when supporting the besieged Chinese was allied to American patriotism than it was when faced with the very different landscape of Mao, militant Communism, and above all a China seeking to take its place beside the United States as a world power. And as Stephen Kaplin explains, post-war America tended to be far more fascinated with Japanese than Chinese culture, which has had a difficult time competing with Kabuki theatre and Bunraku puppetry, which he points to as a significant contributor to contemporary American puppet technique, or popular culture as in film, anime and manga comic books.[18]

Alan Cook related to me an anecdote showing that if interest in Chinese culture among many Americans was on the wane in the post-Mao years, Chinese Americans had a different feeling about it. "I did an exhibit of Chinese puppets at the Los Angeles County Fair," remembered Cook, "including shadows once owned by my good friend Frank Paris [the puppeteer famed for creating television marionette Howdy Doody]. In one corner I had a shadow screen where I did improvised shows" – birds that fluttered and scattered as a cat prowled and pounced; a grazing camel; a Pekingese dog crossing a bridge with her puppies. "I was the only non-Chinese person participating in the 'Chinese Living Arts' exhibit in the Arts Building. Before the actual fair opening, we had a preview on Tuesday night for members of the Taiwan Consulate of Los Angeles, a few residents of L.A. Chinatown, and lots of retired American missionaries from Claremont, California ... 'Old China Hands.'" Cook asked audience members who had lived in China if any had ever watched a shadow performance or seen shadow figures. "Some Chinese folks said they now regretted that they had not," Cook recalled. "At the time, the art seemed old-fashioned and they preferred movies. My response: But the shadows *were* the first movies!"

Later on, Cook noticed that children from the San Gabriel Valley Cultural Association, who were performing dragon and lion dances in front of the Arts Building, came to watch his shadow shows, often seeing the same ones several times in succession. Cook asked them if they were not bored by the repetition. "They all shook their heads 'NO,'" he says. "So I said we were going to have them help me perform the shadows." Cook was pleased when, two years later, one of the boys was still at it, "using plastic replica shadow puppets." The boy put on a play he called *The Five Chinese Sisters*, which Cook knew was originally about five identical brothers. "Feminism was making a big political splash in those days," he says, "so I asked if that's why he had sisters in his version. No, it was because he only had a lady puppet – she was used for all the identical sisters." This proved to Cook that if shadow theatre had not interested many older Chinese who had grown up with the advent of motion pictures, it could stick with some of their younger American grandchildren, something Pauline herself had believed was the key to shadow theatre's future. "It was an interesting experiment for me," Cook added, "to transport Chinese culture to Chinese-Americans."[19]

❊

In the late 1950s Pauline crossed the country again, leaving east for west. She lived first for a short period in Hollywood in an apartment not far from the Hollywood Bowl, as Alan Cook remembered it. Just why Pauline decided to depart from there for the sleepy seaside town of Carmel is not known. She knew coastal California well, and San Francisco was clearly a place she enjoyed – it had been especially important to her during her Red Gate years. Perhaps she chose Carmel because it was cheaper than San Francisco yet near enough for day trips. (She was to find the proximity useful when she began giving shadow theatre classes at the Chinese Culture Center there.) It is possible also that she wanted the quiet that Carmel was known for, at least outside the tourist season. Not just the dramatic cliffs and the rhythmic crash of waves, but the layout of the town may have charmed her. Unlike most American towns, Carmel has no proper street addresses, making its residential neighbourhoods not unlike the old *hutong* districts that Pauline and Aunt Emma had known in Beijing. Many of the same rules for finding a house in old Beijing applied to 1960s Carmel: the cottages have names, and one locates them by knowing a cottage's proximity to the other residences as well as to the nearest cross streets.[20]

Pauline first appears in the Carmel records in 1959, though she was mentioned in the 21 July 1958 edition of the *Monterey Peninsula Herald* as having "recently moved to Carmel from New York."[21] She was then living in a house on Olivier Street (now an Indian restaurant), which was also an exhibit space for her: she advertised "An Unusual Showing of Oriental Stone Rubbings" there at the "Red Gate Studio" in late 1959 and in early 1960 – she even had a wooden sign made, shaped like the curling roofline of her shadow stage and painted red, with imperial yellow lettering.[22] It was also at this time that Pauline was listed as working as a clerk at the Carmel Mineral Art Shop. This begs the question of whether she was in financial distress in her last years. Whether she had inherited sufficient money from her father or had saved enough proceeds from Red Gate's cross-country tours to keep herself afloat, or a combination of the two, there is no record, but she does not seem to have lived like a woman in want. Pictures of Pauline in her Carmel cottage show her surrounded by Chinese and Japanese *objets d'art*, furniture, and hangings, inheritances from Aunt Emma, which she surely could have sold had she been hard up. Almost

Pauline Benton in California, c. 1955

Pauline and her pet cat in their cottage in Carmel, California, c. 1960

every artist knows about the dreaded day job, without which bills do not get paid, and Pauline's mysterious employment history may be murky simply because she took temporary jobs over the years that would not have been recorded. And possibly it is no more complicated than that a woman who had kept up a constantly busy life over the course of some twenty-five years needed to keep active even in her retirement (and was perhaps grateful for a little extra income).

Though far from her friends and colleagues in the East, Pauline, with her ginger cat, was by no means leading a solitary life with her. Before leaving New York she had made the acquaintance of a California woman who, though not from the shadow theatre world, was drawn into it by a love and a talent she shared with Pauline – that of storytelling. Pauline McGuire, whom Pauline knew as Polly, was also known among the children of San Francisco as the Story Telling Lady. Polly had worked for the San Francisco Recreation Department since the early 1930s as playground director and the first of its official storytellers. She presided over story hour at recreation centres and playgrounds in the city, where she was dubbed "the gypsy storyteller," not just for her peregrinations but for her costumes. An article in the April 1949 issue of *Recreation* described this habit of "wearing a costume in keeping with the stories she told ... an Indian costume was used for the story of 'Coyote and the Stars'; that of a cow girl for 'The Adventures of Pecos Bill'; a clown suit for 'The Show Must Go On'; and so on."[23]

As the friendship between the women developed, Pauline discovered that Polly shared her love of all things Chinese, including the Chinese American children she told stories to at the Chinese playgrounds. This love included a fascination with Chinese shadow theatre, which Pauline was happy to teach Polly. Soon Pauline began to give Polly figures from her own collection. While many of these were traditional Chinese figures, they also included much more unusual examples – the figures she had commissioned from the Lu family in Beijing using images from European and American fairytale books. In a letter of 28 October 1946, Pauline wrote to Polly: "I sent the set of 'Elephant Gay' right off to you," implying she trusted Polly very much indeed; *Elephant Gay* had been one of Pauline's most popular shadow plays and was one she performed at the White House in 1936.[24]

During her years in New York, Pauline had looked forward to Polly's visits and been disappointed whenever her plans had to change because of health or family issues. But she enjoyed being able to share her ideas with Polly, specifically for a new kind of shadow theatre using the cartoon-like animal characters she had designed and created using plastics. This was a far cry from the works of art carved by the Lu family in Beijing but was in keeping with what Pauline saw as dwindling American interest in the older art form. "I feel there are possibilities of this opening up an entirely new field," she enthused to Polly, little aware that in Mao's China in the next twenty years the old classic shadow figures would be officially supplanted by the sort of childish animal characters she was introducing just after the Second World War.[25] She even had discussions with a toy manufacturer who expressed interest, not ultimately acted upon, in marketing Pauline's modern shadow figures.[26] Polly supported Pauline in all her enthusiasms (including Pauline's diligent work on her book) and was there to share with her the more significant occasion of Wan-go Weng's filming of scenes from *The White Snake*. "They did a beautiful job of the photography," she wrote Polly, "and the colors came out very well, though they did some other things to it that I didn't like at all" (things not elaborated on in the letter).[27]

By the time she moved to Carmel, Pauline had given Polly dozens of her Western-style as well as Chinese shadow figures, and also a small stage with silk curtains, which Polly treasured. (Happily, given how easily collections can be scattered, these figures which had passed out of Pauline's hands found their way back to the Benton Collection when Polly's daughter donated them to Chinese Theatre Works in 2010.) Polly used the figures in her storytelling – she used puppetry of all kinds – but she also became an extremely useful and reliable assistant for Pauline. Polly helped her with the now relatively rare Chinese shadow play performances she was called on to give, which Pauline approached with her typical energy and perfectionism. She assisted Pauline in the repair and conditioning of the figures, in transporting and setting up the stage, in rehearsals, and in operating as chauffeur. She proved to have useful connections, as when she introduced Pauline to her friend Chingwah Lee, a Chinese American actor whose talents had been restricted to a bit part in the film *The Good Earth*. Pauline was fascinated to know what Lee's "appraisal" would be of her shadow performance. She also considered him a wonderful raconteur. "Didn't we have fun at Chingwah's?" she wrote Polly after an especially enjoyable dinner with him.[28]

Since Pauline did not have a car, she came to rely on Polly's generosity to get her between Carmel and San Francisco. One of these trips took Pauline to San Francisco to give a demonstration performance. "The program I am planning to do now will require about two extra pairs of hands to help me back-stage," she wrote Polly in her cursive ballpoint, "and I would love it if you and Mercina could do it." In the letter of 8 May 1969, Pauline lists a half-dozen things Polly needs to remember, and many more that she herself needs to remember, and the pages are crowded with as much thinking aloud as information Polly needs to know. It is like reading the preparation notes of a seasoned professional who after all these years still has the pre-performance jitters and still expects endless rehearsals and total obedience, from herself most of all, until she gets the action right. Oh, and, she adds at the end of the letter, "If you have time to jot down that recipe for your oatmeal cookies, I would appreciate it. I like them better than mine."[29]

Her correspondence shows that Pauline had both an executive strength and an undercurrent of neediness, was a disciplined taskmaster who put in hours of rehearsal, rested like an athlete on the day of her performance, yet was also nervous, obsessive, superstitious. If Pauline Benton was a serious artist, she was also a woman who needed to be loved but knew no way to ask for it except through her "little actors." For people like Polly McGuire, Mercina Karam, and Lou Harrison, and the people who watched Red Gate's performances, there was no resisting that combination.

Chapter 10

SHADOW WOMAN

Besides the odd gig, her day job, and giving shadow theatre workshops in San Francisco at the Chinese Culture Center (two of her students, Andrea Ja and Pamella Ramsing, later started their own shadow theatre company in San Francisco), Pauline kept up her research into shadow theatre by travelling abroad.

In the mid-1960s she went to Germany – for the first time in over half a century – to examine shadow figures and sets in the collections of the Deutsches Ledermuseum in Offenbach, the Stadtmuseum in Munich, and the Berlin Museum für Völkerkunde. It was probably on this trip that she met Dr Brunhild Körner, daughter of the German sinologist Dr Ferdinand Lessing. Dr Körner wrote the forward to a program printed by the Minnesota Arts Center to accompany an exhibit of Pauline's figures in 1970–71. It was an interesting choice, for it demonstrates again the negative assessment of shadow theatre's future by another academic specialist. Sounding very much like Berthold Laufer, Dr Körner lamented that in the China of the day, the art form was disappearing: "As the contents of the historical plays oppose the new ideologies, they are replaced by revolutionary plays. However, should this old and popular art ever completely die, the wonderful shadow figures gathered in this exhibition will remain as a lasting monument."[1]

Pauline's essay in this program shows how different a perspective she took on the topic, refusing to give up hope that the "little actors" had a future, even if it might not be in China. It also shows how far she had come in her understanding of shadow theatre and confirms that her acceptance, and exploitation, of its alleged origin in the reign of the Emperor Wu had possibly always been used as a marketing ploy rather than because of her belief in that origin. This is an interesting insight on Pauline the promoter as well as performer. As she pointed out, "The belief has long been held in the Western world that the shadow plays were indigenous to China ... This belief, however, is now being challenged. There are those who believe they had their roots in India, others that they originated in Indonesia where the art is most widespread today, or that they may have come from somewhere in Central Asia ... While the answer may never be known, speculation is fascinating, for it involves old trade routes by land and sea, the trail of religious beliefs, folk arts, entertainment, customs, and comparative sources of literature."[2]

In other words, shadow plays were as much a mirror of their culture as the plays of Molière, Sheridan, or Strindberg were of their respective places and times, and as such they were no more in danger of disappearing, so long as there were performers and audiences able to bring them to life. In a way, too, Pauline was paying homage to the sacredness of shadow theatre, where the shades of past emperors and heroines of history came back to life on the little screen in order to show their audiences the beauty and the folly of being human. This offered more reason to believe in the art form's durability, for it was tied to rituals that had survived so many vicissitudes as to appear to be as indestructible as the immortals whose romances it enacted.

There would have been nothing more natural for Pauline to do at this point in her life than to sit down and finish her book on shadow theatre. The short pieces Pauline wrote on the topic, appearing in her programs or as articles, are so engaging and rich with details, and the breadth of her knowledge of shadow theatre of India and Indonesia and Asia Minor is so wide that it is no wonder her friends pushed her to write down everything she knew. She actually had begun to put a manuscript together sometime in the 1930s. "China's Colored Shadow Plays," which in its unfinished state comprises 136 pages, along with the entire text of her translation (from a previous German translation) of *The White Snake*, seems to have been an ongoing project right up to the end of her life (though its last date is 1941). In an interview published after her death (in 1976), Pauline described the book as "richly illustrated with color photographs" and as a work that "promises to reward its readers with its unusual firsthand experience in a country newly reopened to North Americans, as well as with its authenticity as a resource and its charm as folklore." Her enthusiasm for the art form she had first seen nearly fifty years earlier had not dimmed, as shown in some of her last writings. "No wonder the people were excited!" she remarked on the advent of shadow theatre. "Here was an animated talking picture unfolding before their eyes, enacting their favorite stories of history and legend. It was similar to the excitement caused by our animated cartoons when they first came into vogue."[3]

The book's table of contents shows how thoroughly she covered her subject: Colored Shadows of the Past; Colored Shadows of the Present; The Figures: Their Costumes and Facial Makeup; Scenery: Effects and Properties; Manipulations and Gestures; Music, Literature of the Shadow Plays; and Shadow Plays Abroad. She included patterns for creating two shadow figures and instructions on how to construct them (out of plastic). She even added a list of the principal Chinese dynasties, the ten emperors of the Qing dynasty, and eight American museums that held shadow figures: the American Museum of Natural History in New York City, the Brooklyn Museum, the Cleveland Museum of Art, the Dudley Peter Allen Memorial Museum in Oberlin, Ohio, the Field Museum of Natural History, the University of Pennsylvania Museum, Princeton University's Gest Oriental Library, and the St Louis Museum of Art.

The one thing "China's Colored Shadow Plays" does not contain is information about Pauline's technique. Her last associate, Mercina Karam, wife of a prominent doctor and mother of two daughters, was a bright, sympathetic, and talented younger woman hungry for just the sort of information Pauline was so qualified to share. She was always asking Pauline her secrets of the trade and, according to friends, was always given the runaround. As Stephen Kaplin notes, "Karam prodded her to publish her writings, based largely on the notes she took in the 30s while studying with Mr. Lee, [but] the manuscript remained unfinished."[4] Pauline had also had at least one contentious wrangle with a publisher, which may have coloured her view of all of them. When Samuel French showed enthusiasm for publishing Pauline's shadow play *The Chess Party* in 1941 – significantly the same year she completed the draft of "China's Colored Shadow Plays" – Pauline was willing at first to complete the agreement. But on examining the contract, she let fly at Frank J. Sheil: "In my letter to Mr. Walsh of May 31st," Pauline wrote, "I stated the conditions under which I would be willing to sell the play. The first of the three stated is the only one you have included in this contract." What Samuel French had left out was acknowledged use of Pauline's writings on the background and technique of shadow theatre, and the fact that she was not asked to sign off permission to use images of shadow figures from her own collection and to make sure they were depicted correctly. Pauline's demands of Samuel French, which regularly dealt with some of the greatest playwrights of the age, seem to have created an impasse that could not be bridged, and the publication offer was dropped.[5]

As any creative person knows, sometimes the longed-for ending of a project, be it a book, painting, or symphony, can feel like the approach of the Grim Reaper, and the artist who cannot wait for a project to end quixotically tries to stave off completion. Pauline had bared so much of her heart through her "little actors" over the course of thirty years of public performance, it is possible that as she shared her knowledge of shadow theatre on the page, she realized she could not divulge everything. She was still the woman who would not tell Mercina Karam which tung oil she applied to her figures or how they had been created, and she was not about to divulge secrets stored in deeper places. And maybe Pauline knew that she still had one more great performance inside her that must come out before she, the magician behind the curtain, could reveal all the secrets of the shadow stage.

※

According to one account, Pauline became reacquainted with Lou Harrison at the American Society for Asian Arts, a summer program in San Francisco. They had not seen each other since October 1939, at Mills College, but Harrison had never forgotten her performance of *The White Snake*, the brilliant figures, or the magic of William Russell's Chinese-inflected music.[6] Pauline's enthusiasm for her work inspired Harrison to ask her if she would be interested in reviving Red Gate, with himself and his collaborators Bill Colvig and Richard Dee, who had formed a Chinese music ensemble, to accompany her in music arranged specially for the revival. She asked him to come see her at her home, and a date was set.

Dee had first met Harrison in his twenties, the same age at which Harrison had encountered Pauline and Red Gate. "He taught me Chi-

nese music," said Dee. Besides Dee, Harrison had taught his own part-
ner, Bill Colvig, to play the *sheng*, a reed instrument long associated
with Chinese folk and opera performances. Between the three men an
ensemble was born, as well as an active partnership in Harrison's creation of puppet theatre. Both Colvig and Dee performed in Harrison's
puppet opera, *Young Caesar*, a parable on romantic and political contact between East and West, as told through the love affair of the young
Julius Caesar and the King of Bythinia. Harrison's fascination with
puppets was nothing new, but it now found its natural Chinese outlet
through Red Gate's "little actors," and when he met with Pauline in
Carmel he evidently turned on the charm, of which he was so capable.
"We took Pauline to lunch," Dee remembers, "and had a lovely time.
Lou talked to her about how he would love to have her come out of
retirement and wondered if she would consider doing so. I don't remember all the details, but he apparently convinced her."[7]

Of Pauline's residence, Dee remembers only a small house filled with
Chinese objects, in the midst of which Pauline, grey haired but bright
faced, was "a charming, very attractive older lady, as sweet as could
be." He was similarly impressed with her associate, Mercina Karam,
who was to take an assertive role in the rehearsals and performances.
A trunk of shadow figures stood in the living room during that first
visit. In an omen of things to come, Pauline had discovered that the
figures had become stuck together, but she was able to show some of
them to the men. Besides the trunk and its figures, which Pauline began
to sort through, she had brought out the translation of *The White Snake*
which Aunt Emma had sent her from Beijing so many years earlier,
and which she had used in Red Gate's heyday. She also seems to have
retrieved some of William Russell's transcriptions of Chinese melodies,
along with his original compositions, for Harrison to use in constructing
his score.

Harrison not only arranged the music but performed it. He was an
expert on the *xiao*, or vertical flute, along with a number of percussion and chime instruments. As Dee said of himself, "I was the pluck
and bow man," but in fact he was also one of the vocal performers,
and indeed his contribution to this portion of the performances was
every bit as significant as Pauline's. Along with several instruments –
the *erhu, sanxian*, woodblock, cymbal – Dee, an experienced actor, performed all the voices except that of the White Snake and Black Snake.

White Snake and Black Snake, figures carved for Pauline in Beijing in 1936 by
the famous Lu family shadow masters, now part of Chinese Theatre Works'
Benton Collection. Photographed by author in 2011

Thanks to a tape made of a rehearsal in Pauline's cottage in 1971, it
is possible to reconstruct through the performance of these men and
of Pauline and Mercina Karam some sense of Red Gate's glory days of
decades earlier.[8]

    Attempting to describe a theatrical performance based entirely on
sound recording is not as difficult as it would be were the performance
one entirely of movement, such as dance. At least we have in this

rehearsal tape the words and music; we know the plot of *The White Snake*, and we have the 1947 film by Wan-go Weng. All the same, one listens as if blindfolded. We cannot know what comic details Pauline added to the Bonze to accord with Dee's characterization of him, so reminiscent of the crafty, creepy Monastatos in Mozart's opera *Die Zauberflöte*; or what graceful, noble details were added for Fa Hai, who Dee modelled on the High Priest in the same opera. What effects of light and shadow did Pauline and Marina produce for Harrison's storm scene which – with its frisson of chimes, like pagoda bells in the wind, and its madly wandering theme on *houguan* (a kind of oboe) – conjures in sound the chaos of the White Snake's flooding of the Temple of the Golden Mountain? What about the duel between the angered demon and the Temple Guardian, with the dragon unleashed by the Abbot Fa Hai? We cannot know. Dee, the only member of the ensemble still living, saw all performances from backstage, his attention diverted by his tasks. What we can hear are the two sides of Pauline as performer. We note her remarkably fluid and effective vocal delivery as the White Snake and as her conniving companion, the Black Snake. We also hear Pauline's careful attention to detail. Though she knew and respected Harrison as a composer and performer, she did not always agree with some of the music he produced for her – her complaint, in one instance, being the heaviness of the wood block underscoring one of the White Snake's pensive scenes. "It's too heavy; she is a *lady*," Pauline protested. She was not satisfied until Harrison, Colvig, and Dee achieved the correct combination of sounds and effects.[9]

Stern on the technicalities, Pauline the actor was silky softness throughout. Vocally her White Snake has the charm and energy of the athletic young heroine she is enacting behind the screen. Throughout the heaviest part of the sword fight, we can hear her marshalling Mercina Karam with the assured authority of an experienced stage director. For a first rehearsal, it is a remarkably taut performance, aided by Harrison, Colvig, and Dee's edgy accompaniment, which offers a cross between traditional shadow theatre music and the atmospheric soundscape of a film score. Some idea of what was going on can be deduced from Pauline's description of the atmospheric deities who crowd the stage during the storm scene. "No account of the scenic effects of the paper screen would be complete without mentioning clouds and cloud spirits," Pauline wrote in "China's Colored Shadow Plays":

Left to right: Richard Dee and Lou Harrison, who performed with Pauline for her final production of *The White Snake* in 1971

Certain cloud spirits who have no occasion to walk the earth as human beings, are carved out of one piece of parchment as stationary, jointless figures, riding on their own individual clouds ... [One] such character is Yu Shih, the Master of Rain. If it is supposed to rain, his figure, clad in yellow armour with a blue hat and standing on a cloud pouring water from a pitcher, is pinned in place on the shadow screen. Likewise, wind is indicated by the God of Wind with his fan and a dragon, a form he sometimes assumes, shooting forth gusts of wind from his mouth. If the storm is accompanied by lightning and thunder, the Mother of Lightning appears, gorgeously arrayed, holding in each hand a mirror from which stream two broad flashes of light; and the

Spirit of Thunder in the form of a bat-winged, eagle-beaked monster surrounded by his drums with which he produces the noise
of thunder.[10]

At seeing and hearing this and the other visual and sound effects,
Karam's toddler daughter, who was present during the entire rehearsal,
can be heard exclaiming in delight.[11] "I remember Pauline as very com-
petent," Dee said, "very clear-headed. I suppose she may have already
been ill, but there were no signs of it. I remember she was very skilful
with her assistant. She seemed fine."[12]

With Harrison's participation lending lustre, the newly revived Red
Gate Shadow Players was invited to perform at the Ojai Music Festival by composer Gerhard Samuel, the festival's artistic director. The
festival had had its beginning in 1947, though it did not have its official launch until two years later. By 1953, Lukas Foss, the German-
born American composer, had made his Ojai conducting debut, as did
Igor Stravinsky in 1955 and Aaron Copland two years later. Samuel,
who had served as music director of the Oakland Symphony, San Francisco Ballet, and Cabrillo Music Festival (co-founded by Lou Harrison
in 1961), was brought in as artistic director in the festival's twenty-
fifth anniversary year. Having worked with Lou Harrison and his Chinese music ensemble, Samuel had heard about Harrison's work with
Pauline and wanted the ensemble to perform during this important
season. "Certainly the Ojai Festivals have been best known for the
music they have brought to the Ojai Valley for the last 25 years,"
reported the *Ojai Valley News* on 23 May, "but in the beginning, drama,
dance and poetry were also integral parts. This is a tradition that has
been revived and expanded for the Silver Anniversary Festival beginning Wednesday, May 26th." Along with Jack Nakano's pantomime
group Les Masques Blancs and Carlos Carvojal's Dance Spectrum, Lou
Harrison, Kenneth Rexroth, and friends performed a concert called
"Sunday Morning of Chinese Verses." And the second night of the festival, Red Gate performed at the Ojai Art Center Theatre. Though there
was rain over the festival weekend, all events were reportedly sold out,
with over four thousand attendees.[13]

Red Gate's next public performances took place in San Francisco,
sponsored by the fledgling Chinese Culture Center, which was housed

at that date in two floors of a downtown hotel. Because of space restrictions there, the CCC arranged for Red Gate to perform at the Fireman's Fund Theatre on two evenings. Critic Alexander Fried of the *San Francisco Examiner* was present for the performance that took place on 5 October, which he deemed "as charming as it was quaint. While experts say 'The White Snake Lady' is full of symbolism," Fried added, with a wink to the gallery, "laymen and children found it an immediately likeable Buddhist fairy tale." Like many a critic before him who focused on the beauty of the figures and sets because of their lack of grounding in the performance aspect of the art form, Fried loved the "puppets": they were "translucent, delicate little figures in lovely colors, seen against outdoor backgrounds." And he enjoyed the music, though rendering his opinion with a dissonant value judgment: Harrison's accompaniment was a "softened, flavorsome version of Chinese theatre scores whose strings, winds and percussion are usually far noisier." It is obvious from Fried's perspective at least that Pauline was upstaged by Richard Dee, "who was both serious and comical in various voices." About the only valuable piece of information Fried shares with his readers in this review is something that tells us about the way Pauline constructed the production. Though the program lists only *The White Snake*, Fried comments on action that included "a tame lion who did somersaults and a stilt dancer who did the split." This sounds so much like Li Tuochen's *Street Scenes* it is likely that for this performance Pauline included a couple of scenes from this most popular show in her repertoire. Was this a gesture to children in the audience, who would be far more interested in the somersaulting lion than the tragic love affair of the White Snake Lady? Perhaps Pauline knew this was one of her last performances with Harrison and his ensemble, and she wanted to show everything she could do, all the tricks Li Tuochen had taught her in the Beijing that was so long ago and far away from 1971 that it might as well have existed on another planet.[14]

However uninterested or dismissive it seems, Fried's review does end on a pleasant note that Pauline may have appreciated. Red Gate had created on the whole, he wrote, "a naïve if bright sense of life." For a shadow master to whom her "little actors" were like living beings and extensions of herself, this was high praise indeed.[15]

Pauline Benton (1898–1974)

Just as the details of Pauline's emotional life are shrouded in the same mystery into which she folded the many secrets of her shadow theatre technique, so are the details of her final illness. A single woman, with no spouse or lover or children, only a few friends, and no diaries to record the truth of her last days, the Pauline who had lived so long with the immortals of shadow theatre proved to be all too mortal.

Diagnosed with a brain tumor, she seems to have believed almost until the end that she could combat her disease. In an obituary written by Lou Harrison, the composer states that in her last two years Pauline was so ill she was unable to perform at all – a double tragedy after the high point of performing with Harrison at a prestigious music festival.

Still, she was "ever hopeful," wrote Harrison, that her condition was treatable and temporary.[16] When reporter Sandy Rookaird interviewed Pauline in March 1973, she found her "a fragile looking woman," but one who "sparkles with enthusiasm when she talks about her beloved shadow figures," insisting that the delicate figures were "really very tough." In the end, they were tougher than their master. Pauline died in Monterey on 22 November 1974, at the age of seventy-six.[17]

She met death as she had lived life and, indeed, as she had performed for audiences across the nation: behind a screen, hidden from view, a continual mystery. In the absence of a will, what happened to her cottage full of Aunt Emma's Chinese antiques is not known. But her collection of shadow figures, scripts, instruments, along with her stage and sets, were all spoken for: she had left them (or, per Lou Harrison, had sold them) to Mercina Karam, the friend who was with her until the end. Harrison, too, was with her, in spirit if not in person, and wrote perceptively of the woman and the performer he had known and worked with. Calling Pauline "one of the most important theatre artists of the century," Harrison affirmed Pauline's careful, authentic approach to shadow theatre and how magnificently her scholarship and perfectionism had paid off. "Everywhere the Red Gate Shadow Players went," wrote Harrison, "were left astonished and moved admirers, who remember the loveliness of what they saw, and also, along with the fascinating music, the expressive beauty of Miss Benton's own voice." Noting with regret that Pauline had not lived to complete her "splendid" manuscript, "China's Colored Shadow Plays," Harrison struck a note of alarm: "The tradition of which she was so ardent and brilliant an expositor is doubtless dead (or at least underground) in Madam Mao's cultural China." But he, like Pauline, still had hope that through the "brilliant" Mercina Karam, "the Red Gate Shadow Players may once more delight living audiences." He had every reason to believe this would be the case. Mercina was still a young woman, and she had the good fortune of beginning a correspondence and friendship with another woman whose life work was shadow theatre, Jo Humphrey.[18]

A daughter of prominent architect Joseph Franz, Jo – a vigorous lady both regal and down-to-earth – was captivated by what she calls the two great loves of her life, China and the theatre. Although twelve-year-old Jo had seen a Red Gate performance staged at her high school in Pittsfield, Massachusetts in the 1940s, it was the figures' colours that she most remembered – she only learned about Pauline's work later, when she was in college, and never saw a Red Gate performance as an adult. She could not have guessed then or earlier that Pauline's legacy would one day become part of her own.[19]

At the time Mercina met Jo, the older woman had had a career as a theatrical director and was now working for the American Museum of Natural History in New York City, where her interest and expertise in shadow figures had literally carved out a job. Having only seen pictures of shadow figures, copies of which she had used to teach a course in Chinese culture, Jo and her daughter were visiting the museum for one of its open house days when she saw a full display of some of the shadow figures Berthold Laufer had brought back from China in 1902. The theme of this particular open house was the preservation and restoration of stored objects. Jo was amazed to discover how ironically appropriate it was for the Laufer figures to be there: they had last been exhibited almost a century earlier, and nothing had been done to preserve them. When the museum found out that Jo knew a great deal more about the figures than they did, she was hired to identify and restore them. The latter proved to be far more difficult, as no one really understood how to care for shadow figures – nor, Jo claims, do most museums care whether they are properly stored or not. "People here [in the US] just don't think much of the shadow or puppet tradition of any kind," she says. "I know of museums of high reputation with wonderful collections of shadow figures, and they're just a pot of glue today, all stuck together. They are simply not considered all that important." For Jo, shadow theatre's preservation was as vital as it had been to Pauline years earlier, and even more so in the aftermath of the Cultural Revolution in China. "We heard horror stories about shadow figures being burned," she recalls, "about shadow masters being punished for having them. Some were hidden under floorboards, in water jugs, anywhere safe, by the bravest of these people."[20]

Shortly after Mercina Karam contacted Jo, she went out to New York to see her and the Laufer figures. "Mercina showed me how the figures I was restoring were animated," remembers Jo, "even though, as she told me, 'These are so small, it's hard to animate them the way we did with [Pauline's] bigger figures.' I knew that although she had learned on small figures, Pauline had developed her own technique using the big ones. Though the size is the same as the Sichuan figures, they were

not constructed in the same way or controlled by the same means. She
had worked on and perfected her own technique for animating her figures; but you know, Mercina asked her many times to explain it all on
tape, and *she would not do it*. Pauline *had* to be mysterious!"[21]

In her last year working for the Museum of Natural History, the
museum received a grant for an exhibit drawn from its collections of
Asian shadow figures and puppets. Jo helped mount the Chinese part
of the exhibit, demonstrating for an increasingly interested crowd how
the figures were animated. After the exhibit ended, Jo and Shirley
Romans, an artist who had worked with her, convened a workshop in
Jo's home; they began giving workshops and performances, and in 1976,
the Year of the Dragon, Jo, Romans, and Evelyn Mei became founding
directors of Yueh Lung Shadow Theatre. The company toured for
twenty-five years, using figures and scenery most of which were created
by Jo and based on Luanzhou figures. In 1993, with the addition of a
research/resource division, the company was renamed the Gold Mountain Institute for Traditional Shadow Theatre. It was just the sort of
organization Pauline would have dreamed of. Herself now ill with cancer, Mercina Karam realized that the safest repository for the Benton
collection was the Gold Mountain Institute. So in the early 1990s, and
not long before her death, Mercina sent the entire collection to Jo. As
her husband Dr John Karam wrote to Jo shortly after Mercina's death,
"She was so happy to be able to discharge the great responsibility left
her by Pauline to find a home for her beloved Shadow Figures."[22]

Before she even looked in Pauline's travel-scarred shadow figure
trunk, Jo was prepared to find the figures just as worn as Laufer's, but
she did not anticipate the degree of neglect they had suffered. "Her
performing figures were in pretty good shape," she remembers, "because she had removed the tung oil and lacquered them – one of the
secrets she wouldn't divulge to Mercina." But it was the other figures,
which Pauline had used for demonstration purposes, several of them
among the oldest in the collection, that caused the greatest concern.
"They had been put in with layers of wax paper, layers of aluminum
foil, and God knows what else. Anything was stuck to everything!"
Clearly, the figures had suffered from vicissitudes in the lives of the
two women in whose care they had been for so many years. The storage method used by shadow masters in China was to keep each figure
between paper sheets in "books" of cloth and cardboard, large albums

like the one Pauline is shown placing figures into in Wan-go Weng's
1947 film. But of course, the best conditioner of all was to use them,
as Jo Humphrey points out: "If they got dirty, [the shadow masters]
cleaned them. This is something few museums understand."[23]

Through Pauline's and then Mercina's illnesses, the figures, stored
in an airless trunk in uncontrolled environments, had deteriorated. In
all her experience with shadow figures, Jo had never been faced with
such a daunting task, which was more of an experiment as she tried
one method and then another to bring the figures back to proper condition. For months that turned into years, Jo patiently pried figures off
wrappings and each other, cleaning them with cotton swabs dipped in
turpentine, and reconditioned those that she was able to save. Though
Pauline had sold or donated many of her figures and set pieces to museums in the 1960s, she had kept back some old and valuable figures. Jo
was able to save the best of these, and her trial-and-error restoration
efforts were a success. "I took a couple of figures to Europe," she recalls.
"We were there to see a famous Chinese shadow troupe and show them
what we were doing. The performers said to me, 'Oh, but these are
brand new!' and I said, 'No, they are not – they were made in 1890!'"
Among the pieces Jo was able to restore was a complete scene of a
concubine's wedding, carved in the nineteenth century, which has been
exhibited everywhere, from Hong Kong to Greece and across the United
States.[24]

On her retirement from the Gold Mountain Institute in 1999, Jo
passed on all the company's materials, including the Pauline Benton
Collection, to Chinese Theatre Works, located in the multicultural
enclave of Jackson Heights, Queens. Founded in 1990 as Chinese Theatre Workshop, the organization was the brainchild of Kuang-Yu Fong,
a Chinese Opera performer who specialized in *hau-san* female singing
and dancing roles. Fong had served as co-artistic director of Gold
Mountain; when Jo retired, the organization was merged into what
became Chinese Theatre Works, of which Fong became executive director. Fong's husband, renowned puppeteer Stephen Kaplin, who serves
as co-artistic director and technical director, captured his excitement
in an essay about the day he received the trunks containing Pauline
Benton's legacy. "Puppetry is a form of bridge building," he wrote, finding inspiration in the sight of the Brooklyn Bridge outside his studio
windows: "At the heart of all [puppetry's] myriad of forms, genres

and subgenres is a play with the distance between the performer and
the performing object. The temporary contraptions we build to span
the gulf between these two distant points we call puppets ... The gulf
between the object and its operator is one span – the gulf between the
object and its image is another. Shadow puppetry bridges both at
once."[25] The nature of bridges, he added, was obvious in the way he
and Pauline's figures "ended up in the same Brooklyn loft, looking out
over upper New York Harbor."[26]

Yet this was not to be the end of the bridges that spanned nineteen-
twenties Beijing and twenty-first-century New York, or the life of a
woman born in 1898 Kansas and those of young shadow masters living and working in Queens, Long Island. In 2004, Kuang-Yu Fong
asked Jo Humphrey to take part in a most unusual shadow play – a
documentary of how the passion that Pauline Benton conceived for
shadow theatre in the Beijing of the last emperor had transmitted itself
to and transformed the lives of two other women, Jo and Kuang-Yu,
in the New York of Mayor Rudy Giuliani. The play would use not
only the White Snake figures Pauline had commissioned in Beijing in
1936 (which she had last performed with in 1971) but also figures that
were created by Chinese Theatre Works from photographs of all three
women. As Kaplin wrote, "A popular Chinese proverb says that wherever there are three women, there will be drama." Far from being quar-
relsome, this group would celebrate the shared passion and shared
concern for the fate of the art form whose disappearance, all three
women agreed, would have robbed world performing arts of a sophisticated form of entertainment and education, and also an ancient craft
that, as Pauline believed, encapsulated all that was best and most brilliant of Chinese culture. Titled *Three Women, Many Plays*, the shadow
show was taken by Fong, Kaplin, and Humphrey to China to the First
International Shadow Show Festival in Tangshan, Hebei Province, the
town where in Mao's China nearly forty years earlier shadow masters
had been treated like quaint performing animals, put on display for
foreigners like pandas at the zoo.[27]

The play ranged over the territory of Pauline's discovery of and career
in shadow theatre, with plastic shadow figures created from photographs of the young Pauline and elderly Aunt Emma, along with figures of Li Tuochen and a street peddler selling old shadow figures – all
against backdrops as varied as old Beijing streets and Times Square. It

Jo Humphrey (left) and Kuang-Yu Fong (right) superimposed on a photograph of Pauline, from the Chinese Shadow Works production of *Three Women, Many Plays* (2004)

also included in its eclectic dramatis personae shadow figures from Indonesia and Turkey, India and Europe, in which the monkey god Hanuman interacts with the White Snake, and *karagöz* figures tussle with *wayang kulit* puppets at a party that ends when all of them remove their heads before dawn to get some sleep. Jo Humphrey and her story of how she came to follow Pauline's path as shadow master intersects with the history of shadow theatre, from its beginnings to its fading years and its near eclipse during the Cultural Revolution, as well as its unlikely resurgence as exemplified by the return of Pauline's figures to perform in the country they had left almost seventy years earlier. *Three*

Women was a parable on the surprising durability of art in its most fragile yet powerful manifestation: the theatre, that clear prism through which are refracted a culture's manifold colours. There could be no better proof that Pauline's "little actors," whose future she had despaired of, had outlived the worst that could be thrown at them by warfare and politics. On the other hand, they were clearly still in danger of succumbing to a far worse threat – indifference.[28]

In *Three Women*, a trio of spectators gathers around an exhibit of Berthold Laufer's shadow figures at the American Museum of Natural History.

"Aren't they just gorgeous?" exclaims a woman. "Imagine all the work that went into making them!"

"But," interjects another onlooker, "how did anyone at a performance appreciate all the exquisite details and colours?"

"*Performance?*" asks another person, stupefied. "People performed with these works of art? Surely nobody does that anymore," he adds, to the sad nods of all present.[29]

Chapter 11

MONKEY KING

When in May 2011 I was taken to see Pauline's shadow theatre collection by Stephen Kaplin, it was in the process of being moved again,
this time to a larger, brighter studio space overlooking a rail yard in
Long Island City. I had already spent the afternoon among the papers,
photos, programs, and paraphernalia of the Red Gate Shadow Players, most of them stored in the apartment of Kaplin and his wife. Across
the Chinese dining table we spread Pauline's collected lifework in paper
form. The archive documents Red Gate performances over a range of
fifty years, from the expensively printed announcements of Columbia
University or the China Institute in America to the mimeographed
leaflets of schools and ladies' clubs in the Midwest and California. The
scores that William Russell composed for Red Gate's performances
are also there, remarkably clean for performance copies. The carefully
notated bars spilled forth plaintive chinoiserie melodies to the mind's
ear against the traffic sounds of twenty-first-century Jackson Heights.
Pauline's scripts, which exist in various versions, were all scrawled with
her annotations, while her source material, including German translations of shadow plays and the occasional appearance of Chinese characters, showed more evidence of the serious, even academic interest,
and above all the enthusiasm she brought to bear on the art form.

Kaplin's own enthusiasm and artistry interposed from time to time.
A showman with an understanding of light and shadow, smacking of
both the scientist and the mystic, Kaplin glowed as he demonstrated
for me how Pauline may have achieved one of her more spectacular
special effects, which was captured in one of the black-and-white photographs in the collection. In the photo, stars shine around the lovers

in *The Cowherd and the Weaving Maid* as they stand together on a bridge of magpies curving against the night sky. Taking up a "light puppet," a small human figure made of mirrored plastic, Kaplin's subtle twists of the form made a little man of pure sunlight – and apparently as alive as either of us – dash and pirouette across the walls and ceiling. "I'm sure that's how they did it," he beamed.

As Kaplin demonstrated, my eye fell on the text of a lecture he had recently delivered at the University of Connecticut. Kaplin had written: "It is quite extraordinary that both sacred and scientific observers (who agree on little else) seem to concur that the physical Universe we all inhabit is a composition of various sub-frequencies and textures of Light … What we perceive is but a faint wisp of [the] original Cosmic brilliance, trickling into the mouth of the dense, material caves where we, Plato's prisoners, are no doubt chained. But even so imprisoned we can perceive out of the images of Light and Shadow thrown onto the walls of caves some glimmer of Reality's primal essence."[1] Here we were, the dancing light man seemed to say, in another cave, painting its walls as we have always done with the drama of the daily and the eternal.

Later on, Kaplin and I drove across town to Chinese Theatre Works' new studio. Its walls white as a shadow stage screen, its high windows facing the bright and lucky south, Chinese Theatre Works' work space is stacked to the rafters with the tools of Kaplin's and Fong's trade: the tinsel and weaponry and satin of Beijing Opera, interspersed with set pieces for puppet theatre of all descriptions and an army of puppets to go with it. Indeed, all seemed frozen in mid-conversation, mortified at our human intrusion into their realm.

From drawers and cardboard folders Kaplin drew forth still-vibrant shadow figures, Pauline's "little actors." With Kaplin's permission and at his direction, I took up the well-worn rods of the White Snake, arguably Red Gate's most famous star. I tried to make her walk and gesture against an expanse of white wall. I did so clumsily and not too forcefully. Given the age of the figure and my total inexperience at handling her, it was more likely I would break her than animate her. Yet the demoness maintained her cool composure. Since being born on a carver's table in pre–Second World War Beijing, capturing audiences across North America and beyond, helping Pauline give her final performance in 1971, and then returning to China in 2004,

White Snake had done it all, and even a rank amateur could do little to dent her dignity.

Kaplin pulled out other drawers, each filled with precisely cata- logued masterworks of shadow theatre craftsmanship, of a delicacy and beauty perhaps lost forever: palaces, pagodas, and gardens, mountains, trees, and streams, set pieces in which a one-dimensional portrait of a god falls away to become the two dimensional "real" thing; another where a rabbit mixes magic medicines in the moon; others in which demons from fearsome Buddhist morality plays about the horrors of hell push carts of blood and urine or wield terrible instruments of torture. And from one box Kaplin pulled the lovely crimson embroideries that once adorned Red Gate's stage. "Look at this panel," he said, "with seven of the Eight Immortals. Only the female immortal, He Xiangu, is missing."

Indeed she was, and I wondered if this was one of those jokes that Chinese artisans loved to play on the observer. When she became an immortal, Miss He disappeared into thin air, not unlike a shadow fig- ure suddenly removed from the screen – or like Pauline, who on being enraptured by shadow theatre became more than a little invisible her- self, at least to her fellow flesh-and-blood human beings.

"Nowadays, this guy is the star of our shows," Kaplin told me. He held against the light of the windows a tiger figure that had been fea- tured in many of Pauline's performances. He is still flame-striped, bril- liant, wide of eyes and toothy of grin. It was easy to see why he was still hard at work, this nearly eighty-year-old beast, in CTW's eclectic shows, where shadow figures mix with hand puppets and the ornate grotesqueries of *wayang kulit* characters. I looked past him to the empty train tracks below the windows and at two alley cats that had been sunning themselves on a concrete pad and were now gazing up at the tiger's gambols, wide-eyed in disbelief. "What is *that*?" they seemed to be asking. Or, as the figures themselves do in Kaplin's 2004 play, "Surely nobody does *that* anymore?"

※

In November 2010 a pair of elderly shadow masters, the husband and wife team Cui Yongping and Wang Shuqin, declared to a *New York Times* reporter in Beijing that they were ready to leave China, taking their shadow figure collection with them. They hoped to start afresh in America, where museums or patrons or both might show more interest in their collection than the Chinese government had done. As Cui told reporter Michael Wines, "You're the first visitors this month." When the Cui Shadow Puppet Museum had opened its doors in 2004, government officials had professed amazement and promised support. But Mr Cui and Ms Wang never heard another word. No support materialized to help them pay for the museum they had carved out of two flats in their south Beijing apartment house that was large enough to house thousands of figures but nowhere near the space they would need for the more than one hundred thousand they had to keep in storage.[2]

Cui and Wang, like their collection, have suffered more than their share of hard knocks. Both were among the best in their fields in China, with Cui writing scripts for and books about shadow theatre.[3] It all ended in 1967. The Cultural Revolution delivered these artists, as it did so many, to menial labour in an industrial hellhole, the Beijing No. 1 Smelting Factory. But if Cui and Wang were afraid, they were not cowards. It took bravery and even foolishness to tempt fate the way they did when they secreted beneath their home, hidden in the foundations, their growing collection of shadow figures. They did not see the figures again until the mid-1970s. With the end of Mao and the beginning of a new China, Cui and Wang were able to resume their former careers in shadow theatre, reviving the famous Beijing Shadow Play Troupe in which they had once been star performers, even touring Europe. They collected more figures, some of them dating back to the late Ming period. They offered their passion and their collection to the nation. But no one in China was listening.

"I opened this museum because I wanted to encourage this art," Cui told reporter Michael Wines. "I wanted it to become popular again." But China had succumbed to the wasting pressures of Western pop culture. This saddened the couple because, in the bigger picture, shadow theatre was not just a Chinese cultural landmark. Turning their backs on China as it had turned its back on their shadow museum, Cui and Wang applied for visas to transport themselves and their collection – and their artistry – to New York City, where their son Jun Cui and daughter-in-law, the former Japanese dancer Mika Saburi, ran a successful restaurant; and to where, ironically, Pauline Benton had believed

The author with Cui Yongping (left) and Wang Shuqin, Forest Hills,
New York, May 2011

she had to bring shadow theatre over eighty years earlier, a cultural
refuge in a new land.[4]

   In May 2011, a few months after they had finally made their way
to the United States and their son's apartment in Forest Hills, New
York, a forty-five-minute subway ride from where the White Snake lay
sleeping in Long Island City, Cui Yongping and Wang Shuqin agreed
to meet with me. In the dim hallways off the elevator on an upper
floor, I saw a stooped male form silhouetted against light from an open
door. Had such a shadow figure appeared on the other side of a screen,
you would have understood instantly that here was a hero who had
suffered more than his share of the world's bitterness. Coming closer,
I recognized Mr Cui. His right arm, nearly paralyzed, hung almost without movement, a stillness sad to see in an artist for whom complete
command of the body was his fortune. I reached out to take his left

hand. "*Nin hao*!" said Cui, with an impish grin. Behind him from the lighted space of the apartment emerged his wife Wang Shuqin, bringing with her a smile that was light itself. "Come in, come in," she urged me, in that sweet Beijing Chinese that catches at the heart of anyone who has ever fallen in love with that city and its people.

Over tea,[5] the life story of these artists came scrolling forth like a painted landscape held delicately across what I knew were the tragedies they had both endured during and after the Cultural Revolution. They had begun their studies as teenagers, in 1961, under Lu Jingda and Lu Jingan, members of the family that had made Pauline's shadow figures nearly three decades earlier. Cui, who is descended from a Manchu family, proved to be the best student, followed only by Wang, who became his wife and co-performer. They later performed with the Beijing Shadow Play Troupe, which the Lu family ran, and it was with that company in 1983 that they went to Europe. Both Cui and Wang were amazed at how seriously Chinese shadow theatre was taken in the various European nations – so at variance with the indifference shown them in China.

At a French shadow theatre museum, Cui was so moved by the care given to shadow figures that he asked the curator if he might be allowed to give a lecture to the museum's visitors. According to Cui, the curator, identified as Jacques Pimpaneau, refused, remarking, "You Chinese don't even have a place to collect [shadow figures]." This was true but it hurt Cui, who decided on his return to Beijing that he would build his own museum for shadow theatre, using the figures he and Wang had made as well as those he had collected by travelling to every corner of China. But the stroke ten years later, which nearly killed him, proved to be just one of many obstacles to realizing this dream. Though he was given up for lost, after emerging from a coma he scribbled a note to his wife: "I cannot go; my shadow figures won't let me go."[6]

Months of rehabilitation followed; the money he and Wang had saved dried up. Yet in 2004, the year Pauline's story and her figures returned to China, Cui and Wang managed to open their private museum of four small rooms far from central Beijing, in Tongzhou District. A treasure in shadow figures and set pieces, antique instruments and scripts, and figure-making equipment was crammed into this space, which was visited more and more often not by Chinese but by foreign tourists. Some Chinese showed what for Cui was the wrong kind of enthusiasm for his collection. He was offered $3 million for the whole museum by a Hong Kong businessman. He turned him down. There was no way they were going to trade their life's work even for the money that could have instantly made their lives easier – that would have been on a par with the destruction of the Cultural Revolution.[7]

Both Cui and Wang spoke to me of their pride in belonging to the Lu tradition, which was worth far more to them than any material fortune. "They were the greatest, the best," Cui told me, adding "Miss Benton, of course, was one of theirs as well," having studied with Li Tuochen, who was also part of the "Lujia." It was a pleasant surprise to hear this, and I asked him to repeat the term "Lujia" – the Lu family. It was as if by some happy circumstance artists could become the children of the mentors who had trained them, and the troupe be their authentic family, and in turn for the parents of future artists to carry on the torch of inherited technique, regardless of such silly immaterialities as the fact that Pauline was born in Kansas and Cui in Beijing. Their shared art made them brother and sister.

Only toward the end of our discussion did the old pain bleed its way through. "Shadow figures were burned – Lu family figures, all of my husband's figures," Wang shuddered. "They were piled up and set on fire. It took them three days to burn to ashes." So there was no better proof, I pointed out, that in bringing shadow figures out of China, Pauline had truly saved them from a worse fate than being stored on a dusty shelf.

Yet being left on a shelf could pose a worse threat, Cui told me. "You do know," he asked, "that the Lu tradition is broken?" For the first time, I saw tears in his eyes. "It was broken in the sixth generation, when the son didn't follow the footsteps of his father and grandfather. So the Lu theatre is done." As he said this, I could not help but think that much the same could be said for the tradition that Cui and Wang had hoped to hand on to the future. Though Cui had trained his son, the latter had soon seen that there was no way to make a solid living by performing shadow theatre, and like his two sisters he had entered other fields. Remarkably, since many Chinese consider it unfilial for their children not to follow the course set by their parents, Cui and Wang concentrated not on their biological children but on finding those other heirs who were able to take on a tradition that was both fragile and weighted with centuries. They had to find a home for their greater legacy, their performance history and the shadow collection that was their life's work, because the place where shadow theatre had begun no longer wanted it.

Echoing Pauline, Cui said, "Shadow theatre is about China – it *is* China. It is our art, our history, our manners and mores." To preserve it, he and his wife had thrown over any of the self-preservative mechanisms common to most retired people, who normally look forward to a quiet and secure place in which to live out their elder years. Instead, like intrepid characters from a shadow adventure, they had leapt on a magic cloud powered by jet engines and landed in a city and country as foreign to these lifelong Beijingers as the strange landscapes of the west were to the Buddhist monk Xuanzang and his travelling menagerie. But they had come not to seek the treasures of the ages but to bestow them.

It was not easy talking about these things, which excited them and, as a fire flashes through flimsy paper, then died down into cold ashes and made them ruminate sadly. One does not want to see Cui's and Wang's artistry die, though art forms and customs and whole languages are dying out every year at almost as great a rate as animal and plant species, and there seems to be little that anyone, even those who live to preserve them, can do about it. Above all, it hurts to see elderly people who have suffered so much take on an additional challenge flung at them not by life but self-chosen, which possibly might prove the final straw. I wanted to urge them to go back to the Hong Kong millionaire, accept his cash, and drop this burden that was becoming too heavy for them or anyone else to carry.

Wang suddenly darted up, flashed me a brilliant smile, and asked me to come with her. I followed her into the small bedroom that had been her and Cui's only private space since leaving Beijing: two narrow beds, some shelves, a table. Figure-carving tools lay neatly stored in a wooden box. I recognized the blazing colours of shadow figures in the paint-stained palette nearby. And spread across one of the beds was a collection of shadow figures, both animal and human characters, from fierce bearded generals to gentle ladies. They lay as if frozen in the middle of some urgent conference about Cui's and Wang's heroic act to save them from oblivion – some puzzled, others brooding, and still others laughing as if none of it mattered anyway. Through the window thrummed traffic noise interspersed with the flutings of pigeons.

"Here," said Wang, "take him!"

She handed me an amber and black striped tiger, one not unlike the version the Lus had made for Pauline a lifetime ago. The New York cloud cover did what it does best and suddenly fell away; sunshine flooded the room, so that the tiger glowed like flame. As I took the rods and made him dance stiffly across the bedspread, onto his back leapt Sun Wukong, the shape-shifting Monkey King. Up and down we went, monkey and tiger, me and Wang, as the tiger tried to buck off that prince of mischief and Monkey held on for all he was worth, my laughter mixing with Wang's. Cui stood behind us, smiling. "Chinese shadow theatre is the art of China," he told me. "But it is also the art of the whole world."

Mr Cui and Ms Wang have attracted the interest of another North American who has been tracing the winding journey of Chinese shadow theatre from remote past to uncertain future. Annie Katsura Rollins is a young actor, dancer, set-and-costume designer, puppet designer, and puppeteer based in Minneapolis, Minnesota. Her mother was the child of a Japanese father and Chinese mother living in Hawaii, for whom assimilation – and the learning of English only – was the norm. When Annie was in high school, she was frustrated by the lack of information about her mother's Asian heritage. At age sixteen, she was allowed to spend a semester in China. It was a trip that (like Pauline's) changed her life and led to her discovery of Chinese shadow theatre. "I love puppets," she writes. "I love theatre. I love China. Put all of those together and you get Chinese shadow puppetry. It's the culmination of my three passions."[8]

In 2008, Rollins spent a summer in China apprenticing to the Hu Xian Shadow Troupe in north central China, learning how to animate and carve figures, and publishing a fascinating blog about every step of the way. Her love for the art form is palpable. "Of all forms of puppetry, I believe [shadow theatre] is the most exciting," Rollins told me.

"The glow of the lamp and the ambiguity of the shadows plays upon a very special and dark corner of our imagination. It digs deeper and stirs harder than any other form. I love its limitlessness and its mystery."[9]

Rollins was awarded a 2011 Fulbright Fellowship to spend a year in China researching shadow theatre. Over the ten months of her project she visited all the provinces that historically had specialized in the art form, working with extant shadow masters and their troupes – a journey not unlike Pauline's almost eighty years earlier. Having read the 2010 *New York Times* interview with Cui and Wang, Rollins wanted to meet them and made arrangements to visit their shadow figure museum in Beijing. The couple greeted her warmly and took her on a tour, but like others before her, she found the museum to be "a small, cramped and chaotic place." Nonetheless, it seemed to celebrate the world of shadow theatre itself: "resourceful, cluttered and passionate." When the couple told her of their plans to move to the United States with their collection and their reasons why, Rollins had mixed feelings: "Part of me is glad to see Chinese shadow puppetry making its way west towards America, but much of me is sad that the Cuis had to look for opportunities away from home." Yet she expressed a hope, which again echoes Pauline from a half century earlier, that Cui's and Wang's leave-taking from their and shadow theatre's native land was "just a new chapter in Chinese shadow puppetry's evolution for survival." The China of today, says Rollins, is focused on the future, "racing there so fast, I think they'll arrive and regret they didn't move forward with more thoughtfulness. Isn't this the case everywhere?" She notes there are many other Chinese folk arts that also are falling by the wayside.[10]

For the rest of the year, Rollins immersed herself in shadow theatre, recording minute descriptions of lessons in manipulation that were given to her, in one example, by the shadow master of the Zhonghua Shadow Company. Most romantically, this company is located behind the artificial hill crowned with the pagoda known as the Tower of Buddha's Fragrance, at the Summer Palace near Beijing. In such settings, and again like Pauline, Rollins found that in the figures themselves were reflected whole eras of Chinese history – design, styles, symbology – relating shadow figures to real Chinese life. The fragile art form's history has been "so long, and troubled, and also celebrated," Rollins told

Annie Katsura Rollins in 2008 during her apprenticeship with Master Wei
of the Hua Xian Shadow Troupe, Shaanxi Province

me. "To think that shadow puppetry has been the receptacle of China's
oral storytelling tradition for about 1500 years is incomprehensible.
The richness overwhelms."[11]

And thus came another discovery that paralleled Pauline's conclu-
sions. In the 1930s, Pauline had seen that most shadow theatre was to
be found in the remote villages of northern China, having been chased
out of the cities by movies and a rapid pace that was breaking up the
old communal courtyard life of extended families. Though Rollins
was only vaguely aware of Pauline's work in shadow theatre and knew
nothing of her research trips to China, she came to the same conclu-
sion, but with a twist – that through China's relentless urbanization,
the rural culture that best fostered shadow theatre is disappearing
because the rural people who enjoyed it are now being transplanted to
urban centres for jobs. Rollins concluded that "the new audience has
moved to the city." To test her theory, she offered shadow theatre performances in miniature in the streets of Beijing, using a small screen
fixed to the back of her bicycle and with the shadow figures depicting

people with ordinary modern conveniences, such as bicycles. To her delight, Rollins found that far from failing to draw spectators, her performances were enjoyed and appreciated. Children, for whom each day brings a new animated computer game or movie cartoon, gathered to learn how to make the figures move across the screen. "The audience is there," Rollins believes, "and hungry for more."[12]

Of course, this hunger can come at a price too high for many would-be shadow artists, performers, or carvers. In China, Rollins saw that wherever shadow theatre is "commoditized," as it is for Xi'an's lively tourist trade, it can secure local and government support. Performers and carving do continue, depending on the circumstances of a particular area. "I was most impressed with the officials in Bazhong, Sichuan province, and Tai'an, Shandong province," says Rollins. "Call it intuition, but I felt that they had more than just a political interest in their performers, met with experts for recommendations on how to improve and how to publicize and much more." But where shadow theatre has not established itself as a money-making activity, the shadows and the masters who keep them moving are increasingly unwilling to devote their lives to what can seem a hobby that is both expensive and singularly isolating. "There are few apprentices for the traditional troupes," explains Rollins, "as most believe that the demand for traditional performance is nearly finished." Many younger people want to get into the carving of figures just for the tourist trade, turning them out not so much to take the stage as to be framed and frozen on a tourist's wall back home. They may sell figures this way, Rollins points out, but they will never be the kind of masters who showed her the tricks of their ancient trade, whose mentorship is needed if a new generation is to take over from them and push shadow theatre a little deeper into the future.[13]

Rollins's lavishly illustrated Fulbright blog, "A Year in Shadows," gives many reasons to believe that shadow theatre may survive. One ray of hope came ironically through a man who may be the last of the Lus. During her journey, Rollins met Lu Hai, a member of the shadow theatre family who carved Pauline's White Snake and other figures in 1936. Though Lu told her that his son (the seventh generation of Lu shadow performers) is "the end of the line," he made this observation without apparent regret, focusing instead on shadow theatre's possibilities for the future. He agreed to teach her, much as Li Tuochen – who also had no heir to whom to pass on his artistry – had taught Pauline. "He's pushing it forward with new stories, new characters and an infusion of animal characters," Rollins wrote, "that he assured me 'make the kids happy.' They must." She had already seen this on the street corners of Beijing, just as Pauline had recognized it in her young audiences.[14]

Rollins had just returned from China when I asked her to share her frank opinion of the present and possible future of Chinese shadow theatre. "When I look at it with my realistic hat on," she said, "I know that traditional shadow puppetry must evolve – just as it's done for 1,500 years – into something we have yet to know." Perhaps this means changes that will make the average traditionalist mourn that the end has come. "I simply remember that shadow puppetry has survived much worse," she explains, "and done so with its characteristic tenacity. I don't know why I should expect that this should be its end. It's not." Like all art forms, she says, shadow theatre is "always on an evolutionary continuum." Rollins hopes that foreign interest in shadow theatre performance – and engagement by scholars and performers like herself – will lead to more enthusiasm for the art form in China. "As much as I want to simply preserve the living art as is," she says, "I know it will never survive that way. Art must reflect the change we make as a people, a society." Rollins plans to continue her work as an educator, researcher, and practitioner of the shadows, "to encourage innovation and foster a new wave of Chinese shadow puppetry."[15]

EPILOGUE

One warm spring evening in Manhattan, as I finished research for this
book, I escaped the noisy mugginess of Lexington Avenue for the cool
calm of the church of St Vincent Ferrer. The building is located across
the street from the Seventh Regiment Armory, the grand setting with
its Tiffany rooms where Pauline and Red Gate made their public debut
in 1933. I looked at the windows and thought of how often Red Gate's
parchment dramatis personae were compared by the American press
to "stained glass in motion." And I wondered whether Pauline, too,
had slipped into this church, built in honour of the peaceful saint of
reconciliation, for some quiet before the riot of the fashionable affair
that February afternoon. Although not conventionally religious, Pauline
was intensely tuned to the art of the sacred. That, after all, is what
shadow theatre is: drama as intermediary between men and gods, much
as these stained-glass saints rainbowed in the early evening sun and
these friars lifting sweet voices to heaven were for those few of us seated
in the gloom of the pews.

As so often, the press opined more wisely than it knew. Shadow figures were, in a sense, China's church window heroes, telling in motion
what these static glass worthies had to impart, frozen in lead mullions.
Churches, like many a shadow show, are lacking the audiences they
once enjoyed and perhaps took for granted. But the sacredness of
shadow theatre – that jewel in the lotus of whatever faith or art moves
the soul, the beauty and message recognized as unique and useful by
all – is still a very real thing. This energy lives not just in the artists
whose arms, hands, fingers, voices and hearts are the power that brings
them to life, but in the figures themselves. Pauline's journey was to the

East, and her companions on the long pilgrimage were her actors – the emperors, clowns, demigods, and warrior maidens – in whose very shapes and movements were to her the proof of what had made China great once, and could make it so again.

Whether shadow theatre will enjoy the renewed life that Pauline Benton predicted was possible for it in the New World remains to be seen. But as long as there are those who reach for the sacred in life, whether on the Beijing street corners where Annie Katsura Rollins drew crowds to a tiny illuminated screen, or Wang Shuqin making the Monkey King dance for the pigeons on a Forest Hills windowsill, the shadows will continue to inspire us all in our individual journeys to the West.

THE WHITE SNAKE

The White Snake was the shadow play nearest to Pauline's heart: material related to it in her collected papers far outweighs that from any of her other productions. It was the one play from which scenes were filmed (by Wan-go Weng in 1947), and it was the last one she performed before her death in 1974.

Pauline did not read Chinese, and her Aunt Emma ("Tante"), who provided many of her early shadow play scripts from Beijing, seems to have relied on Chinese friends to provide English translations. However, Pauline discovered that the shadow play scripts included in Wilhelm Grübe and Emil Krebs's *Chinesische Schattenspiele*, edited by Berthold Laufer and published in 1915 by the Royal Bavarian Academy of Science, so closely resembled the translations Aunt Emma had sent to her that she translated and adapted them for her use in America. Grübe and Krebs's translation in turn is heavily informed by various versions of the story: *The Precious Scroll of Thunder Peak*, Feng Menglong's account in *Stories to Caution the World*, and other sources down to the nineteenth century. The tale is not as ancient as Pauline believed it to be (nor did it derive, as she thought, from ancient India). Dr Wilt Idema, translator of *The Precious Scroll*, makes clear that the story of the White Snake seems to have been first circulated in China no earlier than the sixteenth century. Such additions as the son conceived by Xu Xian and the White Snake came from improvisations incorporated by actors in the eighteenth century as melodramatic crowd pleasers.

Pauline updated her scripts where she deemed it necessary – and as we have seen, did not include arias, with instrumental music provided only as atmosphere or for dramatic emphasis – but did not modernize them, so that as the twentieth century wound on, some of the text reads like the corny lines from film comedies from the 1930s. The script for *The White Snake* is, however, in a class apart. Given a fine simple translation, with any unclear usages explained by Pauline in footnotes, the play offers a plot that has the romance and tragedy of Western opera – the woman not of this world who, like Hans Andersen's Little Mermaid, loves a mortal man and suffers unspeakably to be his wife; the man who, shocked that he has taken into his life a woman not subservient but equipped with magic powers, flees to a monastery to escape her; the White Snake's murderous battle to regain the father of her unborn child, knowing that once the child comes, it is her duty to pay for the sins she has committed against both gods and men by giving him up; and the poignant homage paid by her son to his mother. It is, Pauline points out, a parable on filial devotion. But it is also about something even greater: it is about what we will do for love. The tragedy of the White Snake is that in this immortal's desire to share the pleasures of mortal life, she sees human love as a kind of eternity that even the gods cannot give her, which despite the shortness of all mortal endeavour seems to her a worthwhile exchange. There is something in this that smacks of the risks Pauline took to record and preserve shadow theatre in her time, and those same risks taken by Cui Yongping and Wang Shuqin in our day; and, of course, the passion they all share for this art form suspended between heaven and earth, gods and men.

Pauline included the full script of *The White Snake* at the end of her manuscript "China's Colored Shadow Plays." With the permission of Chinese Theatre Works, who hold the rights to the text, I have the honour to reproduce it here in full. I have retained Pauline's romanization of Chinese characters as well as her footnotes; my own are interspersed where needed and are headed "GHM." I have also remained faithful to Pauline's mixture of American and English spelling, as used in her typescript of the play.

I dedicate *The White Snake* to the memory of my mother. Like Baishi, she was a warrior for love.

Grant Hayter-Menzies

THE WHITE SNAKE

BY PAULINE BENTON

The White Snake is an ancient Chinese legend, derived from an Indian source, which has been dramatized both on the human stage and the shadow screen, where it is a popular favorite. The last scene, especially, is one the audience never tires of seeing because it bespeaks to them a beautiful example of Filial Piety.

According to the legend, the White Snake had lived a virtuous life, devoted to consecration of spirit, for hundreds of years. Her abode was a cave on the side of beautiful O-Mei-Shan, the sacred mountain of Szechuan Province. One day, she wandered outside and fell asleep in the warm sunshine on the side of the mountain, where a beggar seized her and took her to market to sell. A young student saw her there and, feeling sorry for the little white snake with her tearful, pleading eyes, bought her, and set her free.[1] She immediately determined in her own mind to compensate the young man by becoming his wife.

To fulfill her purpose, she set forth on a cloud to visit Hangchow, where the young man lived. On the way, she met a Black Snake,[2] who joined forces with her and accompanied her in the guise of her maidservant. Assuming the form of a beautiful young woman, the White Snake became enamoured with Hsü Hsien, the poor young student, and, through the connivance of the Black Snake, succeeded in inveigling him into marrying her. After they were married, Hsü Hsien opened an apothecary's shop. While he was still ignorant of the fact that he had married a demon, she used her magical powers to bring about an epidemic which caused her husband's business to flourish. To this day, many people in oriental countries believe that pestilence and disease are due to the machinations of the White Snake.

They lived happily together for a year until the Festival of the Fifth Moon, when she drank some wine to which had been added a potion as a protection against demons. This caused her to turn into her natural form of a large white snake, whereupon she raised her head toward her husband and spit forth tongues of flames which frightened him so that he dropped dead. When the White Snake became conscious of what had happened, she changed again into her human form and set out in search of the Herb of Immortality. The gods were very angry with her, but, since she was destined to give birth to a son who would become the head of the literati of that day, they directed her to the God of Long Life who gave her the desired herb.

After she restored her husband's life, he was still so terrified that he fled to the monastery, where the priest Fa Hai, who had power to exorcise demons, would have destroyed her if it had not been for the protecting influence of the God of Literature, desirous of saving the life of her unborn child. This, however, was not until after she had directed such terrible floods against the temple, destroying millions of lives, that the gods sentenced her to everlasting punishment under the Pagoda, called "Lei Feng-t'a,"[3] on the West Lake, to take effect as soon as her son would be one month old. The Priest, therefore, ordered Hsü Hsien to return to her until such time as she would have fulfilled her earthly destiny. When the child was one month old and the guests had arrived to celebrate the occasion, the Holy Man appeared at the door to take her away to captivity. She changed back into the form of a small white snake, while her husband tried to plead for her release. It was too late, however, whereupon he left the child to the care of his sister and entered the monastery to become a monk. Years later, after the child had grown to manhood and passed his examinations, he came to the Pagoda to offer sacrifice to his mother, at which time the gods permitted a brief and touching reunion between them, when she told him the pathetic story of her life.

In 1928, the old Thunder Pagoda was destroyed by lightning. Freed thus by the aid of her own elements, the country people rejoice that at last the White Snake has made complete atonement and been reborn into the Region of the Gods.

In the story, we find the two snakes playing the part of the temptress, a role which seems not to be confined to the Christian religion. As one who has devoted many lives to consecrating her spirit, the White Snake is looked upon as the good woman, believed to symbolize the spiritual side of man's nature. Since the Black Snake is inferior to her in attainment and virtue, she represents the physical side. When the two are shown far apart, the spiritual element is dominant; but when the White Snake comes under the physical influence of the Black Snake, her demonical nature comes to the fore.

The play concerns itself with the earthly sojourn of the White Snake. It is difficult to secure a text of the complete play, since one troupe of shadow players seems to have only one or two episodes in its repertoire. Even on the stage it is difficult to see the entire play given in one evening. Mr. Lee [Tuochen] tells of a Mongolian prince who had had a complete shadow play text, which he lost along with other valuable material during the Boxer Rebellion. The Grübe-Krebs collection includes five episodes of the play, which covers the whole story by indicating in dialogue those scenes which have been omitted. By comparing this with the various texts of single episodes I have been able to collect here and there from the shadow players and Chinese play books, I have found them to be so nearly alike, that I have used the Grübe-Krebs version as the basis for the English translation, making such combinations with the other texts as seemed advisable.

The text, as presented here, is the version we[4] have made for our American production. It has been our purpose, through a simple prose translation, to retain the spirit and form of the original as far as possible. The references to Chinese proverbs and typical Chinese ideas, which enhance the beauty of the story, have too often been omitted from translations of Chinese plays. The one thing we have attempted to eliminate has been repetition of thought which occurs in Chinese plays due to the fact that the idea presented in spoken words is usually repeated in singing. This, of course, would tend to grow monotonous in an English rendering.

The stage directions are not indicated in any Chinese text, since the players are well versed in the action. In most of the shadow play texts, in fact, the lines run along continuously without any indicated as to which characters is speaking. The directions which I have indicated here, wherever they would seem to help in visualizing the drama, are from my own notes taken at the performances.

CHARACTERS IN THE PLAY

HSÜ HSIEN, the young student. He appears in the blue costume, decorated with a youthful floral design, and simple blue hat of the scholar.

PAI SHIH, the White Snake. Her costume is always white, with a "fairy collar" and tight sleeves for her acrobatic and battle scenes. She wears a traveling hat with a small white snake coiled through her hair.

HSIAO CH'ING, the Black Snake. Her costume, in black, is identical with the White Snake's.

FA HAI, Abbot of the Temple. A high-ranking Buddhist priest or abbot wears a straight robe, draped over one shoulder, squared off in a patchwork pattern symbolic of the rags and tatters of Buddha. He wears a paneled crown, each panel of which is decorated (embroidered or painted) with a small image of Buddha. He carries a duster in his hand, taken over from the real stage, that is carried by priests and celestial beings as a symbol for dusting away the sins of the world.

A BONZE, or Buddhist monk. The costume is a long straight robe and black hat. The pock-marked, two-eyed face indicates the comedian type.

WEI T'O, the Defender of the Faith. The image of this god, who is supposed to defend the Temple against demons and evil spirits, is found at the entrance to all Buddhist temples, facing the inner courts. His costume is that of a warrior, and his headdress of a Buddhist warrior.[5]

THE WATER DEMONS, including the Turtle, Frog, Snail, Fish, Crab, and Lobster. The fact that these demons all have human legs indicates that they are copied from the stage actors.

KWEI HSING, the God of Literature. The warrior's costume of the shadow figure differs from the traditional short flowing robe in which he is usually portrayed. He has an ugly green face.

THE SPIRIT CHIEH-TI, the Guardian of the Pagoda. He appears in the costume of a spirit, with shaggy eyebrows, large eyes, and long Taoist hair.

HSÜ MÊNG CHIAO, the son of Hsü Hsien and the White Snake. Having attained the rank of "Chuang-Yuan,"[6] he wears a red cos-

tume, as the "Official of Low Rank," with headdress decorated
with laurel blossoms.

The White Snake

FIRST EPISODE
"The Borrowed Umbrella"
On the shore of the West Lake, Fifth Day of the Fifth Moon

HSÜ HSIEN

(*Enters, walking slowly toward the center of the screen.*) I give no
thought to the spinning wheels of love that weave their threads
about men's hearts. On long summer days, I spend the dreamy hours
in deepest contemplation. I am a poor student who dwells in the
proud freedom of the mountain wilds and studies only such books
as are useful to mankind. My family name is Hsü, my name Hsien.
I am a native of the prefecture of Hangchow. Unfortunately, my worthy parents are dead and I have no brothers. Our household possessions have dwindled away and, although my head is full of the most
beautiful thoughts, I still do not have any employment for them.

It happens that today is the Fifth Day of the Fifth Moon and the
lotus blossoms are just in their prime. What is there to prevent me
from taking my light umbrella that swings around in the breeze like
azure waves, and going out to the West Lake to view the flowers
that I may become intoxicated by their beauty? (*Walks into a pavilion which is placed in front of him.*)

I will tarry for a while here in the Shrine of the Lotus Flowers on
the West Lake. See how the waves ripple, how in boundless dis-
tances blue shadows scurry, how the breezes spin a thousand patterns on the surface of the water, and the sunbeams sparkle like
pearls on the waves. Green waves, blue mountains, and the winding
waters encircle the strange deserted mountain in the distance. Such a
picture as I see there! It would be difficult for even the artistic hand
of Wang Wei[7] to paint for us. As I stand gazing on this beautiful
scene, I suddenly hear the voices of two maidens.

(*Enter Pai Shih and Hsiao Ch'ing.*)

HSIAO CH'ING

Oh, Mistress, see how beautiful the West Lake is!

HSÜ HSIEN

Now I see the two young maidens, so beautiful and modest there
are none lovelier in the world. First they separate, now they come
nearer, now they pause, and look at me from a distance with stead-
fast gazes.

PAI SHIH

Hsiao Ch'ing,[8] who may that charming youth be, so handsome and
so well built? My beauty puts the flowers to shame, and the moon,
even, must veil itself in my presence; but one could say even more
of him, of his snowy white teeth, his rosy lips and the natural pride
of his appearance. He stands just a degree taller than I! See, how
he gazes at me. I cannot let this happy moment pass away. Hsiao
Ch'ing, you must help me with a cool wind and a fine rain.

HSIAO CH'ING

I only need to murmur a word of enchantment and instantly cool
wind and fine rain are here.

(*Enter wind and rain clouds on the right.*)

PAI SHIH

O, what a heavy rain! Where can we hide?

HSIAO CH'ING

Look, Mistress, how would it be if we tried that kiosk?

PAI SHIH

You surely do not have your eyes open. Don't you see there is a
young man standing there?

HSIAO CH'ING

"If the foot remains straight, then one need not fear a crooked shoe."[9] Come! (*They both walk to the kiosk.*)

HSÜ HSIEN

What is your honorable name? You surely do not come from far. What are you doing here, if I may ask?

HSIAO CH'ING

(*Turning to Pai Shih, who is behind her*) When someone asks you a question, you should answer.

PAI SHIH

It would be better for you to talk to him.

HSIAO CH'ING

Since the lady will not speak, I will address you. Please do not think me forward, Sir. Our home is not far from here. It is on Mount O-Mei.[10] I am Hsiao Ch'ing, who has served as lady's maid from my youth.

HSÜ HSIEN

How is the other lady related to you?

HSIAO CH'ING

She is my young mistress.

HSÜ HSIEN

What position does your master hold?

HSIAO CH'ING

My master was a general, but unfortunately he died many years ago. The honorable wife did not lead a pious life and, for that reason, she destroyed her lineage and brought no sons into the world. The house fell into decay, and the daughter was the only one of the family left. Then there came, five years ago, a fire brand from Heaven, and the entire house was swept away in one blow. After that, we had to rent a small house. With her skillful hands, my mistress made clothes for others, and from the scanty profits, we bought rice and firewood. Such days of hunger are hard to endure! This is the first day she has left the house to burn an offering of money on her father's grave, and just at this moment the heavens had to send down rain. There was nothing left to do but flee to this kiosk. You may well take us for a common sort.

HSÜ HSIEN

That is impossible. What are you thinking about?

HSIAO CH'ING

(*Turning to her mistress*) Mistress, the rain does not stop. What shall we do?

PAI SHIH

If only we could borrow an umbrella!

HSÜ HSIEN

How would it be if I were to lend you my umbrella!

PAI SHIH

You are very kind, Sir.

HSIAO CH'ING

(*Taking the umbrella he has been carrying on his arm*) Yes, truly. May I ask your worthy name? How far is your house from here, that I may return the umbrella?

HSÜ HSIEN

If you come over the General's Bridge, and immediately to the east, it is the first house in the Black Pearl Alley.

HSIAO CH'ING

May I ask your name?

HSÜ HSIEN

My family name is Hsü, my name Hsien. I am just seventeen years old, born at noon on the Fifth Day of the Fifth Moon. I am also not married.

(*Clouds exeunt.*)

PAI SHIH

But, Hsiao Ch'ing, you are no fortune teller. Why should you ask him his name and horoscope?[11] See the rain is stopping. Let us go. (*Hsiao Ch'ing and Pai Shih turn and start to walk off.*)

HSIAO CH'ING

(*Looking back*) I only hope the young man will not escape us!

(*Hsiao Ch'ing and Pai Shih exeunt.*)

HSÜ HSIEN

How perfect! Just see how they both followed me with their glances as they left. I am as merry as a cricket! When she returns the umbrella, I will get the servant to arrange the marriage. That's wonderful! (*He exits gleefully.*)

(*Kiosk is removed. Pai Shih and Hsiao Ch'ing reenter.*)

PAI SHIH

The plum blossoms are the spring flowers. The most hidden motives become manifest through them. Their fragrance makes the cicadas fly.[12] (*Chair is set up and Pai Shih sits down.*) I am Pai Shih. You must look your best, Hsiao Ch'ing and bring him to our cave, so that we may become man and wife. Thus you will fulfill my fondest wish. As I think of his beauty, my future seems to be full of happiness. What do I care about becoming a Genius or reaching the Tao?[13] If I could only share the joys of men! What in your opinion would be the best way to assure our arriving at the lovely peach trees?[14]

HSIAO CH'ING

Tomorrow morning before I return the umbrella, I will memorize the words I must speak as go-between.

PAI SHIH

What will you say?

HSIAO CH'ING

Wind and rain[15] are given us to conjure. I will proceed according to the circumstance.

PAI SHIH

I only fear you will say too much, and then he will see your horse's hoof[16] and conclude that we are demons.

HSIAO CH'ING

Calm yourself, Mistress, and take on no unnecessary cares. When I return the umbrella, I will take care of everything. There is nothing to fear that he will become wise to our trick.

PAI SHIH

Wonderful, wonderful! I only want you to express everything very cleverly. Then I will rest assured that all is well.

HSIAO CH'ING

Do not admonish me, Mistress. Only go quietly to our cave and wait there for the good news from me that a trap has been set to catch the hare in the moon![17]

PAI SHIH

Whoever would catch an alligator must set a fragrant bait! (*Exit. Chair is removed.*)

HSÜ HSIEN

(*Enters.*) Immeasurable good fortune comes to me from Heaven! Since I met the beautiful Hsiao Pai[18] on the shore of the West Lake, she has entangled my heart and mind. How can I help being in love with her? Her beauty is like that of a fairy maiden, her sweet and sorrowful voice like the softest music. The servant intimated that it might be possible to arrange a marriage!

HSIAO CH'ING

(*Behind the scene*) Are you there? May I come in?

HSÜ HSIEN

Ah, who is there?

HSIAO CH'ING

It is I!

HSÜ HSIEN

O, please come in.

HSIAO CH'ING

(*Enters.*) Do I disturb you?

HSÜ HSIEN

No, indeed. Please be seated.

(*Table and two chairs are set up and they both sit down.*)

HSIAO CH'ING

It was very kind of you to lend us the umbrella. My mistress sent me here first to return the umbrella and secondly to thank you.

HSÜ HSIEN

It was not worth mentioning. I have something on my heart, but it is hard to speak it out.

HSIAO CH'ING

If you have something to say, speak it please.

HSÜ HSIEN

Very well. There was a reason for my meeting the two maidens yesterday at the West Lake.

HSIAO CH'ING

What kind of reason?

HSÜ HSIEN

After I heard you picture what bitter things your mistress had gone through, I had to sigh when I came home that such a fate had befallen her.

HSIAO CH'ING

It is very kind of the gentleman to think so.

HSÜ HSIEN

How pitiable it is that she is without father or mother or any relatives, that two such beautiful young ladies are left alone, that you have been exposed to misery without rice and fuel. If your master were living, he would surely have found a husband for her.

HSIAO CH'ING

If she only had a husband, it would certainly be wonderful! My mistress has a sad fate. No brothers and both her parents dead. How beautiful she is! The honorable gentleman has already seen it. This Spring she was just sixteen years old. When the master was living, he loved her tenderly and always had it in mind to choose a handsome husband for her. So, to this day, she is still without a husband!

HSÜ HSIEN

Since she has no parents, she should look around for a master.

HSIAO CH'ING

Just because she is so talented and beautiful, she is determined to choose only a handsome husband.

HSÜ HSIEN

What kind of man would be best for her?

HSIAO CH'ING

He must first be handsome, and then talented. The go-betweens have already approached her, but she would not listen and their talking was fruitless.

HSÜ HSIEN

Oh, it is too painful for me to speak!

HSIAO CH'ING

Since she met you yesterday, she has been singing the honorable
gentleman's praises day and night.

HSÜ HSIEN

Does she really have that feeling for me? That can only come from
heaven, no other place! Tomorrow I will send an ambassador to
woo her. I depend strongly upon you to assure a favorable answer.

HSIAO CH'ING

To woo through a go-between would, in my opinion, be wrong.

HSÜ HSIEN

How would it be wrong?

HSIAO CH'ING

Marriage was originally determined in an earlier life. Why, then,
should others be needed to act as go-betweens? From of old it is said
that what the go-betweens say is not worth claiming.

HSÜ HSIEN

How would it be then to proceed without a go-between?

HSIAO CH'ING

That is the only thing to do! I am already prepared in my mind to
play the man [under] the moon for you.[19] You may save your gold
and wine that the go-between demands.

HSÜ HSIEN

But if the lady should not consent!

HSIAO CH'ING

Since she met you at the West Lake, she sings your praises waking
and dreaming. Even if she did not speak a syllable, I could divine
how she feels.

HSÜ HSIEN

Will you have the kindness to speak to her and set the day when the engagement gift may be presented?

HSIAO CH'ING

What kind of present is necessary? If a go-between should hear of this, then there would be idle gossip.

HSÜ HSIEN

How do you think then it would be best to manage it?

HSIAO CH'ING

I think the more in secret the better. (*Rises*.) You play the role of the Chang Ch'un-jui [Chang Chün-jui], and the lady will play Ts'ui Yang-yang [Ying-ying]; I, however, want to play the role of the Hung-niang.[20] Wait this evening on the West Terrace until the moon wanes. I will lead the lady then to the place where you will be waiting and there you will be married according to the customs of the gods of Wu-shan.[21]

HSÜ HSIEN

I only fear the lady will not come.

HSIAO CH'ING

The proverb says that the maiden who stands alone longs for her own home.

HSÜ HSIEN

Nevertheless, a favorable day must be chosen.

HSIAO CH'ING

Today is the Star of Heavenly Virtue. That means good luck! If the day is allowed to elapse, then evil spirits will intervene.

HSÜ HSIEN

I leave everything to you.

HSIAO CH'ING

Leave it to my cleverness and I promise you, I will win the lady for you. This evening after the second watch, I will bring her here. For the time being, I will excuse myself. Meet us on the Terrace, Yang T'ai![22]

HSÜ HSIEN

I will accompany you. (*Stands up.*)

HSIAO CH'ING

Please do not trouble. (*Exit.*)

HSÜ HSIEN

Who in all the world has such luck? (*Table and chairs are removed.*) It is a god-sent fortune, truly wonderful! This marriage costs me not a single present for the bride, and here on the "Terrace of Romance" I will be married to this beautiful young lady. I find no rest, sitting or standing. The sun still lights the firmament. Now the sun is just beginning to bow toward the west. Where are the moon and the stars? Why does the sun not withdraw more quickly to her palace behind the mountain? (*First watch sounds.*) The first watch has at last gone by. (*Incense table is set up, incense lighted, so that the smoke is visible to the audience.*) I have prepared the incense and paper horse[s].[23] Everything is ready now and twilight is past. The moon is just coming up and floods the terrace. You come so early today, O Moon! Your light shines more brightly than usual. Will you not send down the Goddess Chang-O[24] who dwells in you? (*Second watch*) Now I hear the second watch beat. This is just the time when the sublime scholar slumbers on the mountain and the beautiful young lady must be coming through the moonlit forest. What if the servant could have spoken an untruth to me? Could the maid have told tales and made merciless fun of me, a bookworm? Is she late on account of washing, combing and dressing, or arranging her affairs? She should surely be here by this time, if she is coming at all. (*Third watch*) Now, I hear the third watch. (*Cough off-stage*) Do I hear someone cough?

HSIAO CH'ING

(*Off-stage*) May we enter?

HSÜ HSIEN

Have you come, Miss Hsiao Ch'ing?

HSIAO CH'ING

Yes, indeed, the lady is here.

HSÜ HSIEN

Please, come in. (*Hsiao Ch'ing and Pai Shih enter.*) I, only a poor scholar, through some accident have been the recipient of your love. You have honored me with a visit and I did not come to meet you. Please, forgive me.

PAI SHIH

In meeting for this secret rendezvous, I commit a blunder against all that is proper for a young lady. Please do not think me a coquette for coming this way.

HSIAO CH'ING

All was planned in an earlier existence. Why so much talking? Mr. Bridegroom, have you prepared an altar?

HSÜ HSIEN

Everything has been ready for a long time.

HSIAO CH'ING

Then I will help you. First the bride and groom must pray before Heaven and Earth. (*Hsü Hsien and Pai Shih bow three times to each other, then kneel and bow three times at the altar.*) See how the moon lights the firmament. Now the marriage has taken place. Before all Heaven and Earth, it is so decreed.

HSÜ HSIEN

Among men, it will be recorded that two beautiful beings have met in a golden chamber,[25] and in Heaven, two stars have walked over the Silver Stream.[26]

(End of First Episode)

SECOND EPISODE
"The Temple of the Golden Mountain"
One year later

FA HAI

(Enters and sits on the "floor.") After receiving my ordination, I
fasted in the mountain wilderness. Day and night, I pray to Buddha
and read the holy text. If I cannot become a god in Heaven, I have
at least become immortal. I am Fa Hai[27] and serve in the Temple of
the Golden Mountain for the conversion of the multitude. I sit cross-
legged lost in meditation. Suddenly, there arises my heart's blood.[28]
I shall fathom the cause by magic. Today, since the Demon, Pai Shih
has exercised her magic power, Hsü Hsien is coming to the Temple
for protection.

BONZE

(Enters and bows to Priest.) I notify the honorable High Priest that
Hsü Hsien has come to the Temple to bring an offering of incense.

FA HAI

Bid him enter.

BONZE

(Exits and speaks off-stage.) The Master bids you enter.

HSÜ HSIEN

(Enters.) Most worthy Master, I bow before thee.

FA HAI

I return the greeting. Allow me the question, Almsgiver. Why do you
come to the Temple?

HSÜ HSIEN

I implore thee, Master, save me. I will give up all earthly things and in the loneliness of the cloister strive for moral perfection. Please, Master, keep me with you!

FA HAI

I have known the purpose of your coming for a long time, but the time of your earthly relation with the Demon is not yet fulfilled. She carries a "Chuang Yuan"[29] under her heart. As soon as the child is a month old, then and only then will you be separated.

HSÜ HSIEN

I have fled to thee, Master, for protection. Pray, keep me here. I do not wish to go down again from the Mountain.

FA HAI

So let it be, but it remains to be seen how the lady will behave. Go now, and take the tea into the Hall of Spiritual Contemplation.

HSÜ HSIEN

Yes, Master. (*Exit.*)

FA HAI

It proves aright. Infatuated human beings never come to their senses. They are always the victims of demons. (*Exit.*)

PAI SHIH

(*Enters.*) I am Pai Shih, the White Snake, and am married to Hsü Hsien. When I became drunk at the Midsummer Festival,[30] my true form appeared. My frightened husband received such a shock that it killed him instantly. Then I stole the life-giving herb from the South Sea and revived him. Since I feared he would still be suspicious, I made a snake out of a white cloth and cut its head off with my sword to deceive him. He still thought, however, that I was the White Snake and insisted upon going to the Temple of the Golden Mountain to fulfill a vow. All my efforts to prevent him were fruitless. I cannot rest and have sent Hsiao Ch'ing to make inquiries.

HSIAO CH'ING

(*Enters, running*) Mistress, I have followed the master to the Temple and found out that he is staying there as a monk and will not come again from the Mountain.

PAI SHIH

Oh, the undutiful villain! By the love which I brought to him, who would have thought that he had such a cruel heart? The wretched Fa Hai holds him back. There is nothing for me to do but bring him down again from that Mountain. Hsiao Ch'ing!

HSIAO CH'ING

Yes, Mistress.

PAI SHIH

Come with me. We will set ourselves on a light breeze and get him! (*Exeunt. The Temple on a high cliff is pinned to one side of the screen and "water" is placed along the lower edge. The two Snakes reenter in a boat, Pai Shih standing in the front and Hsiao Ch'ing paddling in the rear. They get out of the boat after they cross the screen, and exeunt. Water and Temple are removed and a Temple gate is set up. The two Snakes reenter and knock on the gate.*)

BONZE

(*Enters through gate.*) Who is making so much noise? Oh, look, it is two ladies visiting the Temple. I suppose to burn incense?

HSIAO CH'ING

No!

BONZE

Then to fulfill a vow?

HSIAO CH'ING

Also, no!

BONZE

Neither to burn incense or to fulfill a vow? Then what exactly do
you want?

PAI SHIH

(*Stepping in front of Hsiao Ch'ing*) I want my husband!

BONZE

Oh, a soldier?

PAI SHIH

No!

BONZE

Then an usher?

PAI SHIH

No!

BONZE

A bailiff?

PAI SHIH

No!

BONZE

Neither one nor the other? What do you want then with the priests?

PAI SHIH

I am looking for Mr. Hsü.

BONZE

Oh, Mr. Hsü?

PAI SHIH

Quite right.

BONZE

The master said he could not go down from the Mountain.

PAI SHIH

Why not?

BONZE

He says two demons have appeared, one the White Snake and the other the Black Snake. For that reason, he will not let Hsü Hsien go down from the Mountain.

PAI SHIH

Go to Fa Hai immediately and tell him he must release my husband!

BONZE

And if he should not?

PAI SHIH

I'll not leave one of you priests alive in this Temple! (*Slaps him and knocks him down. The two Snakes stand arms akimbo.*)

BONZE

Oh dear, that's a lot to say at once. Wait, I will inform the master. (*Gets up, goes inside the gate and slams the door. The two Snakes turn around and exeunt. Gate is removed. Bonze and Priest enter.*) You are asked for, Master.

FA HAI

What is all this excitement?

BONZE

I announce that two demons have come to the Temple and carry on an excessively large conversation.

FA HAI

I will go to them; bring my ecclesiastical seal of office. (*Priest and Bonze exeunt. Temple on cliff is set up again. The Priest enters on the Cliff and the two demons below.*)

FA HAI

Oh, you accursed Demon! Begone from this holy Temple; otherwise
it will go badly for you.

PAI SHIH

Oh, Priest, please give me back my husband. I am without guilt or
fault. That evil should come to be is heartless. I am a laywoman,
but you a priest. The priest should always foster love and kindness.
I honor my husband as I honor the heavens and I love him!

FA HAI

If you know the rules of Heaven, why do you bring such suffering
to men?

PAI SHIH

I have done my husband no harm. What you say is not true!

FA HAI

That is only the talk of demons by which they lead men astray.
Have you not gone yet?

PAI SHIH

If you will not grant my friendly request, then hear how I shall revile
you. What is the reason you will not release my husband? Since I
cannot obtain his release with kindness, my wrath and anger grow!
I lift the magic sword. So that you will not escape me, I will seize
you too! (*Both Snakes draw two swords, one in each hand.*)

FA HAI

Where is the Defender of the Faith?

WEI T'O

(*Enters with spear, standing near entrance.*) I am here. What is your
command?

FA HAI

Guard the Temple and watch the two demons.

WEI T'O

I obey your commands.

PAI SHIH

Fa Hai, give me back my husband at once!

FA HAI

Your husband is becoming a monk. How can he return to the world?

PAI SHIH

Is that true?

FA HAI

Yes!

PAI SHIH

That makes me angry. Set him free!

FA HAI

What will you do if I do not release him?

PAI SHIH

I will leave no one alive in this Temple!

FA HAI

Hm, hm!

HSIAO CH'ING

Mistress, perhaps it would be better if you were to ask him politely. Then he might be more likely to set your husband free.

PAI SHIH

Very well! For all I care I will beseech him. (*Kneels.*) Dear Priest, the disciples of Buddha have sympathetic hearts filled with love for mankind. Kindhearted Priest, please release my husband, for we cherish deep love and great understanding for one another. I beg of you to lift up your hand and grant us the privilege of seeing each other again. To do good is fitting to the disciples of the monastery. They should show love and do good works. I am also, as you know,

not of common clay. I have struggled bitterly for one thousand years
in the Way of Perception. I have never sinned against conscience
nor done any wrong to man. It is little wonder that I am tenderly
attached to my husband, for this is not the first time we have met.
In an earlier existence, we were known to each other.[31] Oh, Priest,
do a deed of love! I will then thank the blue sky above with clouds
of incense.

FA HAI

Pooh! Not worth a copper! You bring only confusion to the world
of men. Your husband has been chosen as a Disciple of Buddha and
will become a Genius. Why should I bring this end of Destiny to
naught because of you? Begone from this holy Temple or I'll show
you your true form!

PAI SHIH

Stop! If you will not release my husband, you or I must perish!

HSIAO CH'ING

Now, Mistress, we will prove who is the stronger.

FA HAI

She dares to use force. Where is the Keeper of the Faith?

WEI T'O

Here!

FA HAI

Seize the demons! (*Exit.*)

WEI T'O

I obey your command! (*The battle begins. First the two demons turn
somersaults across the stage and exhibit their skillful sword play and
exeunt. Then Wei T'o with a spear and another Temple warrior with
a knife display their skill. The demons reenter and they do battle,
each one fighting against a temple warrior. When the demons appear*

to be victorious, Fa Hai enters and hurls a dragon staff at them. Pai Shih catches it, whereupon it turns into a dragon. As she fights the dragon the White Snake figure is changed to one with "disheveled hair." As she sways back and forth, the dragon seizes her in its mouth and shakes her in the air. Then she turns into a snake and wraps herself around the dragon. She changes back to human form, as the dragon retreats.)

PAI SHIH

Oh, the brave Fa Hai! He truly orders manifold magic powers. It does not look so possible to me now to overcome him. What am I to do? I have it! Hsiao Ch'ing, order the demons that live in the sea to unfold their powers and set the waters in motion so that they may flood the Golden Mountain.

HSIAO CH'ING

Ay, ay, Water Troops!

(Water is set up and the water demons enter, turning somersaults, water is moved away from the screen so that waves appear to get higher. Wind and rain clouds enter.)

BONZE

(Off-stage) Oh, Master, it is terrible! See how the great water floods the mountain!

FA HAI

(Off-stage) I will fetch my magic alms bowl. Then the waters will flow back. (*Enters and throws his fairy robe, a red cloth, on the cliff causing the waters to recede. Then he throws his magic alms bowl on the White Snake's head, but the God of Literature appears over her head, thus rescuing her. The two demons exeunt.*) I announce that the magic alms bowl has been caught up by the Star Wen-chang[32] and the demons have fled.

HSÜ HSIEN

(*Enters.*) Master, I am scared to death! I am scared to death! Have you subdued the demon?

FA HAI

She has a charmed life and I cannot overcome her.

HSÜ HSIEN

Where has she gone?

FA HAI

She has gone to Hangchow to the House of your brother-in-law.

HSÜ HSIEN

O, worthy Priest, she will give me no peace.

FA HAI

Do not worry. The time of her earthly existence is not yet fulfilled and she has no intention to harm you. When she reaches Hangchow, she will bear a child. After that I will give you further advice.

HSÜ HSIEN

Thank you a thousand times.

FA HAI

Tonight I will take you to Hangchow and there you two will be reunited.

HSÜ HSIEN

When I depart from the refuge of the Golden Mountain, I have no need to fear, because sacred magic protects me.

(*End of Second Episode*)

THIRD EPISODE
"The Broken Bridge at Hangchow"
The following day

(*Enter the two demons.*)

PAI SHIH

In the magic battle of the Golden Mountain, I almost lost my life.
I am the White Snake.

HSIAO CH'ING

I am the Black Snake.

PAI SHIH

When we fought with Fa Hai, he had what no one would have
expected, Celestial Troops, and with their aid almost ruined me.
We were fortunate to succeed in escaping.

HSIAO CH'ING

Oh, Mistress, do you not regret that it has gone this far? You should
never have drunk the wine of the sulphur blossoms at the Festival of
the Fifth Month. When your husband sank lifeless to the ground, it
was your own plan to steal the life-giving herb. In the heated strife
before the Temple, Fa Hai showed his enmity to us and we both
nearly lost our lives. I warn you, Mistress, to make a stroke of the
pen through the little word "Love." Return with me to our mountain to avoid further adversity, for your husband is your enemy!

PAI SHIH

Dear little sister, since I have soiled myself with earthly pleasure,
the Western Mother[33] would not take me back again. I carry an
offspring of the House of Hsü under my heart. Let the little one be
born first and then we will talk further. For fear of those Celestial
Troops, the child nearly lost its life; from the blow of the heavenly
pestle,[34] I am more dead than alive. Facing toward Heaven, I sigh
deeply and call out, "Oh, worthy of hatred you are, my husband.

You, faithless one, think nothing of your duty to your wife. The little word, 'Love,' you have completely set aside." (*Weeps.*)

HSIAO CH'ING

Do not weep, Mistress! Here before us is the kiosk. Let us rest here. (*Kiosk is set up and they enter.*)

PAI SHIH

Oh, my husband, you have done me a deadly wrong. As I enter the kiosk, my tears flow endlessly.

HSÜ HSIEN

(*Enters.*) The words which the Father speaks fill me with sadness. He gave me a Buddhistic charm which will take me home and I will know the rest later. I suddenly raise my head and see my wife standing before me. In fear the perspiration flows from my every pore. (*Kneels.*) Oh, exercise indulgence, dear wife, and bear no enmity toward me.

HSIAO CH'ING

(*Rushes toward him with her sword and grabs him by the collar.*) Ah, here you are, you cowardly person. Take care for my sword!

HSÜ HSIEN

Oh, my wife, save me!

PAI SHIH

Black One, stay your anger.

HSIAO CH'ING

Mistress, make no mistake. I will take vengeance on him for us both, while I split him in two with my sword.

HSÜ HSIEN

(*Trembling*) Please save me!

PAI SHIH

Oh, my husband! What wrong have I done you that you should
have believed in the stray gossip of monks? You should not have
believed Fa Hai when he told you I was a demon. Have I not eaten
three meals a day with you? Have I not shared your bed every night?
If I were really a demon, why did I not devour you? Come to me, my
husband, for I have something to tell you. When you went to the
Temple to fulfill a vow, I waited throughout the day for your return.
I could not reconcile myself to being separated from you. Why do
you say nothing? You vex me! You imagine me to be a demon! You
with heart of steel! Since you went to the Temple with incense, there
was not a night that I did not lie awake to watch the moon rise. I ate
nothing. All this, longing for you. All my waiting did not bring you
back again. I went then before the Temple to wait for you there. The
Priest Fa Hai came threateningly in my way. He ordered celestial
armies so that I almost lost my life. Fortunately, Kwei-Hsing[35] saved
me, and I escaped with my servant.

HSIAO CH'ING

(*Threatening with her sword again*) Mistress, you must not think of
the past. It is best for me to split him in two with my sword and so
take him in vengeance for the Temple of the Golden Mountain.

HSÜ HSIEN

Save my life!

PAI SHIH

Not so, Black One.

HSÜ HSIEN

Oh, my wife, after I came to the Temple to fulfill a vow, the Priest
took me into the musty inner shrine and would not let me go. That
is why I stayed so long. Today is the first time he released me to
come home. I beg you to think no more of earlier wrongs and grant
me pardon.

HSIAO CH'ING

Don't believe him, Mistress. The best thing is to kill him!

PAI SHIH

Oh, Black Sister! I throw myself down on both knees. My face is covered with tears. Let the past be buried. For my sake, let him go, and speak no more of these things. As I speak, dizziness seizes me and great pain wracks my body. I think the little one pushes to the light of day. Where can we find refuge?

HSÜ HSIEN

My wife, do not worry. In the house of my brother-in-law, there are many rooms. Let us go there.

PAI SHIH

Very well, then help me up, my husband. Oh, you have done me a dreadful wrong.

HSÜ HSIEN

You must not speak so, my wife. When you are giving life to a little one, we will endeavor to requite the favor to heaven above.

(*End of Third Episode*)

FOURTH EPISODE
"The Magic Alms Bowl"
One month later

FA HAI

(*Enters.*) Blue sea waves as far as the eye can see between heaven and Earth. Good and Bad appear in a continuous cycle. Through contemplation, I have arrived at this decision. I am Fa Hai and in the Temple of the Golden Mountain have devoted myself to the care of Truth and Self Perfection. Formerly, the White Snake with the

Black one brought on a terrible state of affairs and fought against
me. They gathered together the waters of the five lakes and the four
seas and threatened to flood the Temple. Thanks to the secret art of
my magic, the mountain raised itself up in the same proportion as
the water rose. Then the two snakes could do no more and so with-
drew. The White Snake had married Hsü Hsien and while she carried a little one under her heart, I dared not harm her. I have waited
until the child was a month old before working her downfall.
Dressed as a begging monk, I have made my way with my alms bowl
as if to collect charitable gifts. Now I am before her house and will
beat upon my dish drum.

HSÜ HSIEN

(*Enters.*) What priest is this who begs charity? Oh, it is the Priest Fa
Hai. What charity do you beg, worthy Father?

FA HAI

I wish to ask the Benefactor for an alms bowl full of rice.

HSÜ HSIEN

Wait, let me consult my wife. (*Calls.*) There is a priest here who asks
for an alms bowl full of rice.

PAI SHIH

(*Enters.*) Ah, that is bad! He does not beg for rice. He has come to
demand the life of your wife.

HSÜ HSIEN

Wait then if that is true, I will destroy the alms bowl. (*Light streams
from bowl as he touches it.*) What is that?

PAI SHIH

Oh, my husband! (*Throws herself down on her knees.*) Alas, my
Master! I do not wonder that you cherished suspicion against me.
After the water flooded the Temple of the Golden Mountain and
destroyed tens of millions of people, I have known that retribution
would come. I have thought of fleeing far away, of lifting myself into
the air. I just wanted to wait until our little son had ended his first

month before withdrawing to my cave to live there in concealment. Now, there is no more chance to escape. Life or death is uncertain. Entrust our little son to his aunt,[36] that she may care for him as her own child. As foster mother, she will not deny him love. I have already put his little clothes in order. They are in a pair of leather trunks and will suffice until he is ten years old. My husband, bring the unhappy child to me that I may hold him in my arms once more. (*Exit Hsü Hsien, who returns with the child in his arms.*) Oh, my child, do not cry. Your mother must leave her little son though it grieves her greatly. Dear child, just one month old. How would a mother's heart not grieve for you? You will never see your mother's face again. How can I bring myself to leave you, dear little child? When you have grown up, you must bring honor to the illustrious ancestors. In another moment your mother must leave you. Just see how he looks at his mother as if he understood and sympathized with her. The sadness of his little face tears my heart in two. I want to cry out, "Oh, you of my own flesh and blood! You are so small and yet your little heart seems to understand everything!" Oh, it is hard to tear myself away. My husband, take the unhappy child.

HSÜ HSIEN

Yes, at this sight, my heart softens, and as I take the child, my tears flow endlessly. Oh, my wife, I have brought this misfortune to you. I gave thoughts to the Priest who conjured up this calamity. Never again will I drink the spicy wine with you, never enjoy the splendor of the peony.[37] It proves that married couples must always remain true to one another. Who would have thought that today the end would come? The wild goose[38] has flown, the fish[39] has disappeared in the deep seas, news interrupted, the moon gone, the clouds scattered, the flowers bloom no more. (*Exit with baby.*)

FA HAI

You monster! Have you not yet crawled into the alms bowl? When will you obey my command? (*Pai Shih falls on her knees and swaying back and forth changes into a white snake. She crawls into the alms bowl and disappears.*)

HSÜ HSIEN

(*Enters.*) Oh, worthy Priest, where has the wind carried my wife?

FA HAI

Look into the alms bowl!

HSÜ HSIEN

Let me see! Oh! A snake! I see in the alms bowl a very small white snake. From her eyes, tears flow as if she would say the separation is hard. I hope, worthy Priest, you will tell me if I will ever see my wife again.

FA HAI

It is a firmly set destiny that must be fulfilled. It proves that Truth is hard to separate from Falsehood. Go to the Pagoda⁴⁰ at the West Lake. There you will understand.

(*End of Fourth Episode*)

FIFTH EPISODE
"The Sacrifice at the Pagoda"
Many years later

(*The scene opens with a long procession celebrating the arrival of Hsü Meng-chiao, the son of Hsü Hsien and Pai Shih, who has just passed his examinations. There are musicians, men bearing banners, and soldiers. The latter figures are quite modern, arranged from four to eight men on one control, with wire attached to the knees which can be pushed up and down making the figures march in a goose-step. The Pagoda is set up on one side of the screen. Two servants enter carrying an altar which they place in front of the Pagoda.*)

HSÜ MENG-CHIAO

(*Enters.*) By command of the Emperor, I return home crowned with fame. It is fitting that the son should place filial piety above all else.

I am Hsü Meng-chiao and come from the Black Pearl Alley. My
mother has met the sad fate to be exorcised in the Pagoda, Lei
Feng-t'a [Lei-feng t'a]. I have sought permission from the throne to
destroy the pagoda and set my mother free. Since the Emperor did
not give his consent, there was nothing to do but bring here a royal
sacrifice. I have arrived at the Pagoda, Lei Feng-t'a, to bring my
offering and thereby fulfill my filial duties. (*Lights incense and
kneels before the altar.*)

SPIRIT CHIEH-TI

(*Appears in front of the Pagoda and reads from a scroll.*) My
strength is so inexhaustible that I can carry the lotus throne on my
head. If my magic power were not so great, how could I hold the
Demon Pai Shih bound in the Pagoda. I am the Spirit Chieh-ti.
Today Hsü Meng-chiao has come to bring a sacrifice to his mother
and I have received an order from Buddha to allow a meeting
between them.

HSÜ MENG-CHIAO

I have spread out the sacrificial gifts. Mother, O Mother, your
irreverent son has come to bring you a sacrifice. Oh, my unhappy
Mother, where are you? For years I have not looked into the faces
of my parents. How I hate that rogue Fa Hai who bound my mother
here. I shed endless tears, for I know that we cannot be reunited.

CHIEH-TI

Genius Pai, come forth!

PAI SHIH

(*Behind the scenes*) Here I am! While I was thinking of my son,
I heard the voices of the gods. I belong to the deities. Why have
you called me?

CHIEH-TI

You do not know yet, Genius Pai, that your son has attained the
rank of "Chuang-Yuan," and has come today, at the royal command, to bring a sacrifice. I have received the order from Buddha
to arrange the meeting between you.

PAI SHIH

Accept thanks for your care, O Deity! (*Lights go out for an instant. When they come on again, the top of the Pagoda has been removed and may be seen, held by the cloud spirits on one side. The White Snake appears out of the top of the lower part of the pagoda which is left standing, the upper part of her body in human form, and her snake tail hanging down through the Pagoda.*) I hear that my son has come and great joy is mine! There I see my son slumbering. My son, wake up!

HSÜ MENG-CHIAO

Oh, my Mother, while I am still lost in dreams I hear a human voice. Speak! Who are you? Tell me everything!

PAI SHIH

When I tell you my name, do not be afraid. Believe me, I am your Mother, who has been imprisoned in this Pagoda for many years.

HSÜ MENG-CHIAO

You say you are my Mother?

PAI SHIH

Yes, truly!

HSÜ MENG-CHIAO

Oh, my Mother, who has borne such great suffering.

PAI SHIH

My son!

HSÜ MENG-CHIAO

What a pity that such misfortune has befallen you. Would that I might destroy the Pagoda and set you free.

PAI SHIH

It is also my order that it be so.

HSÜ MENG-CHIAO

How has it happened that such a calamity befell you?

PAI SHIH

Oh, my son! On the O-Mei Mountain, I practiced the Way of Perception for one thousand years. The gods had warned me that I should
not, for any price, befool myself with earthly appetites. I longed,
however, for love. A borrowed umbrella served as a motive. I had
hoped for the happiness of a lasting marriage. How could I foresee
that my husband would prove to be ungrateful? When he went to the
Temple to fulfill a vow, Fa Hai told him everything. After he discovered my origin, he wanted to capture me with his magic. Thus I
fought with the bald-headed priests. When I directed floods to the
Golden Mountain, Fa Hai quarreled with me in hatred and enmity,
but I was saved through the help of Buddha and the gods.

   Your father, apparently good, was bad at heart. He believed the
words of that priest, Fa Hai, and cared no longer for me. One day,
he came home bringing secret magic by which he bound me inside
this Pagoda. I have gone through sorrows here, my son, one thousand fold. Who knows when I am destined to be set free? I have
thought of fleeing by means of magic but feared to oppose the command of the gods and so bring on a guilt that would be hard to
expiate. Seeing you again is, indeed, sweet pleasure, and yet to part
again is doubly painful.

CHIEH-TI

Perceive your destiny, Genius Pai. The hour has struck. Return to the
Pagoda! Return! Return! Return to the Pagoda!

PAI SHIH

Yes, I am coming! Oh, my child!

HSÜ MENG-CHIAO

I am here!

PAI SHIH

Hsü Meng-chiao!

HSÜ MENG-CHIAO

Yes, Mother, I am here!

PAI SHIH

Oh, my son. (*Disappears.*)

HSÜ MENG-CHIAO

Oh, Mother! Just see how my Mother has gone, just as a breath of
wind would carry her off. This separation cuts my heart like countless swords. (*Throws himself down before the Pagoda.*) Oh, my
Mother! Oh, my Mother! (*The Pagoda disappears and Pai Shih
floats across the screen on a cloud.*)

ACKNOWLEDGMENTS

This book could not have been written without the scholarship, guidance, and generosity of the following people, and I thank them sincerely:

Nicole Allensworth (San Francisco State University), Ryan Bean (YMCA Archives), Dr John Bell (Ballard Institute and Museum of Puppetry at the University of Connecticut; Harvard University), Emmett Brennan, Edward Burger (director, *A Life In Shadows*), Dr Dorothy Chansky (Texas Tech University), Dr Fan Pen Li Chen (State University of New York, Albany), Carl Reeves Close, Alan Cook, Cui Yongping, Cathy Yue Cui, Richard Dee, Dr Kirk A. Denton (Ohio State University), Kuang-Yu Fong (Chinese Theatre Works), Timothy Gosley, Dr Guo Jinhai (Institute for the History of Natural Sciences, Beijing), Peter E. Hanff (University of California, Berkeley), Charles A. Hanson (Archivist, Lou Harrison Papers, University of California, Santa Cruz), Hao Sheng (Museum of Fine Arts, Boston), Laurent Hénin, Kathryn Hodson (University of Iowa), David Hogge (Freer/Sackler Gallery of Art, the Smithsonian Institution), Dr Ryan Howard (biographer of Paul McPharlin), Pattice Hughes, Dr Agnes Hsu (the China Institute in America), Jo Humphrey, Grace Ji, Professor Jiang Yuxiang (Sichuan University), Jacky Johnson (Miami University), Jeremy Josephs, Dr Gerd Kaminski (Ludwig Boltzmann-Institut für China-und Südostasien-forschung), Stephen Kaplin (Chinese Theatre Works), Marina Karam, Stéphane Lam (Compagnie Asphodèles), Carlotta Lemieux, Rose McLendon (Harrison Memorial Library, Carmel, CA), Leta Miller (University of California, Santa Cruz), Conrad Minnich, Maureen McGuire, Rev. Steven Naylor (Congregational Church of San Mateo, CA), Jeffrey Pearson (University of Michigan), Cathy Praeger (Compagnie Asphodèles), Annie Katsura Rollins, Alan K. Rome (Library Director of the Saint Mary Seminary Library, Diocese of Cleveland, OH), Curtis Roosevelt, Marco Ropke, Ellie Seagraves, Eddie Song, Ellen Takata (Museum of Fine Arts, Boston), Gilberto Thomas, Daniel Tschudi (University of Hawaii), Alycia J. Vivona (Franklin D. Roosevelt Presidential Library),Wang Shuqin, Wan-go Weng, Elizabeth Wichmann-Walczak (University of Hawaii), Warren Woods (The Historic New Orleans Collection), and Willow Zheng (Northwest China Council, Portland, OR).

Thanks, too, to my parents, for encouraging me to embrace the theatre of life. And thanks to my grandmother, who first served me the legend of the willow plate, along with a slice of chocolate pie, and made me love it almost as much.

I extend a special gratefulness to Jacqueline Mason of McGill-Queen's University Press for her belief in this book and what it has to say.

NOTES

CCSP   Chinese Colored Shadow Plays
FDRPL   Franklin Delano Roosevelt Presidential Library
MMA   Minneapolis Museum of Art
PBC   Pauline Benton Collection, Chinese Theatre Works

FOREWORD

1 Lou Harrison Archive, Special Collections, University of California, Santa Cruz.
2 Dandelet, "Shadow Woman," 51.
3 Lou Harrison Archive, Special Collections, University of California, Santa Cruz; Dandelet, "Shadow Woman," 51.
4 "New and Interesting Show Depicts Chinese Traditions," *Times and Daily News Leader* (San Mateo, CA), 13 October 1939.
5 Lin Yutang, *The Importance of Living*, 80.
6 Among modern-day carriers of the shadow theatre torch in America are Chinese Theatre Works in Queens, New York, www.chinese theatreworks.org (accessed 17 January 2013); ShadowLight Productions in San Francisco, CA, http://www.shadowlight.org/slp (accessed 17 January 2013); Oregon Shadow Theatre in Portland, Oregon; http://www.oregonshadowtheatre.com (accessed 17 January 2013) and one-woman force Annie Katsura Rollins, http://www.anniekat-surarollins.com (accessed 17 January 2013). In November 2011, UNESCO recognized Chinese shadow theatre by adding it to its intangible cultural heritage list of cultural traditions in need of protection ("UNESCO Identifies Endangered Cultural Traditions," *Guardian*, 29 November 2011).

CHAPTER ONE

1   Pauline Benton claims in her unpublished manuscript, "China's Colored Shadow Plays" (Pauline Benton Collection, Chinese Theatre
Works), that she was in China as early as April 1921. In this version –
one of many, each slightly different – of her first experience of shadow
theatre, Pauline says that in 1920 Berthold Laufer, the famous anthropologist, "had put his collection of Chinese shadow figures on exhibition at the Field Museum in Chicago." However, Laufer's exhibition
at the Field Museum did not occur until 1923 – his guide to the exhibition, *Oriental Theatricals*, was published that year. For whatever
reason, Pauline offered reporters who interviewed her several, and
often conflicting, years and situations for her introduction to shadow
theatre. There is no ship's manifest supporting her passage from the
United States to Asia earlier than 1922 (and no evidence to support
her claim that she made more than two trips to China, in 1923 and in
1936). There is a manifest for the ss *Niagara* from 22 July 1922, indicating that Pauline, Mary Benton, and Helen Benton had embarked at
Honolulu for Vancouver, British Columbia. I assume they were returning from the Philippines and that the trip to China occurred during a
second stay in Manila a year later.
2   Hamm, *Manila and the Philippines*, 22–8.
3   Pauline Benton travel diary, 1909–10, Pauline Benton Collection
(hereafter PBC).
4   Kates, *The Years That Were Fat*, 24.
5   Pauline Benton, *Christian Science Monitor*, 22 September 1942.
6   "Culture of China Theme of Exhibit," *New York Times*, 25 September
1942
7   Saint Paul Art Center program for the Konantz-Benton-Minnich
Collection (1966), 5.
8   Conrad Minnich, Minnich Family Collection.
9   PBC; letter from Pauline and Helen Benton to relatives, included with
Mary Benton's funeral program, dated 22 August 1947, Alan K.
Rome, Family Archives.
10 Tchen, *New York before Chinatown*, xxiii.
11 Miller, *Interesting Manila*, 169–71.
12 Filipinos had a form of shadow theatre called *carrillo* which used
cardboard figures as silhouettes in plays put on at harvest time, but
it is doubtful that Pauline, the university president's daughter, would
have ever been in the rural settings where this art form could be
found. See Banham, *Cambridge Guide to Theatre*, 85.
13 Wimsatt, *Chinese Shadow Shows*, xvi and 33.
14 "Because Miss Pauline Benton's father was a former president of

Upper Iowa University," *Fredericksburg News*, 18 April 1935, in
which it is stated that while Pauline was living in Manila with her parents, she first became interested in Chinese shadow theatre, a fact
repeated nowhere else.

15 Ryan Howard, *Paul McPharlin and the Puppet Theatre*, 7-10. Pauline
and Paul McPharlin even died of the same disease. Stephen Kaplin
email to author, 14 August 2011

16 Warde, *Fifty Years of Make-Believe*, 228–30.

17 William Shakespeare, *A Midsummer Night's Dream*, act 3, scene 2.

18 Latourette, *Biographical Memoir of Berthold Laufer*, 43. Another
German fascinated by Chinese shadow theatre in childhood was Lotte
Reiniger (1899–1981), who went on to pioneer animated silhouette
films featuring fairy tale subjects. Her brilliant 1926 film *Die Aben-
teuer des Prinzen Achmed* is the oldest surviving animated feature.

19 Ibid., 45.

20 Laufer, *Oriental Theatricals*, 6.

21 Sandy Rookaird, "Shimmering Shadows Capture Mystery of the
East," *Monterey Peninsula Herald*, 3 March 1973.

CHAPTER TWO

1 Berthold Laufer's *Oriental Theatricals* came out in 1923 (no month
given). He went on an expedition in 1923 but came back in August, so
conceivably would have started in the spring and thus been in Chicago
earlier that year.

2 Helmer-Stalberg, *China's Puppets*, 89–90.

3 Dr Fan Pen Li Chen has videotaped shadow theatre performances as
well as the creating of shadow figures. I thank her for sharing with me
three of her videos: *Shadow Puppet Making & Performance* (1998),
The Temple of Guanyin (filmed in Bidu Village, Xiaoyi County,
Shanxi Province in 1996), and *Nanyue Shadows* (2008).

4 Wimsatt, *Chinese Shadow Shows*, 20.

5 Helmer-Stalberg, *China's Puppets*, 90.

6 Ibid., 89–90.

7 Kuang-Yu Fong and Kaplin, "Indelible Spirits," 3; Laufer, *Oriental
Theatricals*, 37; Minneapolis Museum of Art (hereafter MMA) program, 22 October 1970.

8 Crossley, *Orphan Warriors*, 77.

9 Wimsatt, *Chinese Shadow Shows*, 32.

10 Li, Dray-Novey, and Kong, *Beijing*, 95.

11 PBC, "China's Colored Shadow Plays" (hereafter CCSP), 12.

12 Ibid., 48.

13 PBC, CCSP, 17. Jo Humphrey wrote me on 20 December 2011: "The

Peking West City style does indeed reflect influence from the Shaanxi style. However, the figures were a unique design that was developed by a troupe (or troupes) that performed in the West-city of Peking (Bejing). The East City style is the same as those that are still made in Tangshan and other parts of Eastern Hebei Province."

14 There were two other types of figures from outside Beijing that Pauline was to collect and study: those used in shadow theatre performed in Chengde in Sichuan province, with cowhide figures 18–20 inches tall, and the calfskin figures of Xi'an, in Shaanxi province, a foot tall and not as translucent as the East Side figures but just as prized by collectors. (see MMA program, 8).

15 Cohen, "Documentation Relating to the Origins of the Chinese Shadow-Puppet-Theater," 84–5.

16 See reproductions of figures showing engraved images on bronze mirror in Congmin Ge, "Photography, Shadow Play, Beijing Opera and the First Chinese Film."

17 MMA program, 7.

18 Cohen, "Documentation Relating to the Origins of the Chinese Shadow-Puppet-Theater," 84–108, and Cohen email to author, 11 March 2010.

19 MMA program, 7.

20 PBC, CCSP, 4.

21 PBC, Red Gate program, Beijing, 1940.

22 Pauline Benton, "Old Peking in Shadow Play," *Christian Science Monitor*, 12 February 1944. According to Sandy Rookaird's 1973 interview with Pauline in Carmel, California, Pauline's *Women's Wear Daily* friends persuaded her to go to China to see shadow figures – a very different version of this story and one illustrative of the difficulties of researching Pauline's life. See Rookaird, "Shimmering Shadows Capture Mystery of the East."

23 Wimsatt, *Chinese Shadow Shows*, xvii

CHAPTER THREE

1 Blofeld, *The Wheel of Life*, 93, 103.

2 Ibid., 93.

3 Aisin-Gioro, Puyi, *From Emperor to Citizen*, 81.

4 Strand, *Rickshaw Beijing*, 7.

5 Ibid.

6 Seton, *Chinese Lanterns*, 7.

7 La Motte, *Peking Dust*, 17–18, 20, and 50.

8 Pauline Benton, "Old Peking in Shadow Play." *Christian Science Monitor*, 12 February 1944.

9   PBC, CCSP, iii.
10 Benton, "Old Peking in Shadow Play." "Mei hua'rh, lai, mei hua'rh!" means "Beautiful flowers!" rather than "Come buy"; "mai hua'rh" would convey the meaning Pauline gives it in this article, in which vowels may have been mixed up by the *Monitor*'s typesetter.
11 Benton, "Old Peking in Shadow Play."
12 US Census records, 1870–1910. John and Rosa Konantz had nine children altogether. Besides Emma and Mary were Harry, George, Walter, John, Cora, and Augusta, (Source: Alan K. Rome, a descendant of Harry Konantz).
13 US Government Archives, passport application for Emma Louise Konantz, 18 December 1922.
14 Pauline Ch'en, "In Memory of Miss Emma Louise Konantz," *Ta Kung Bao (Dagong Bao)*, 13 January 1936. *Dagong Bao* is the oldest Chinese-language newspaper in circulation in China.
15 Chen Caixin was born in 1879 and died in 1945. He was director of the mathematics department at Yenching University, 1920–37. I thank Dr Guo Jinhai for this information, and thank Bob Felsing, University of Oregon, for making available to me Emma's article about the book, "The Precious Mirror of the Four Elements: An Expression of Chinese Genius," which appeared in the *China Journal of Science and the Arts*, July 1924.
16 Ch'en, "In Memory of Miss Emma Louise Konantz," 2.
17 Ibid., 3.
18 PBC, CCSP, Introduction, i–ii.
19 Wimsatt, *Chinese Shadow Shows*, xv.
20 PBC, CCSP, Introduction, i–ii.
21 Pauline Benton, "Turning a Gay Hobby into a Full-Time Job," *Christian Science Monitor*, 2 September 1941.
22 Ch'en, "In Memory of Miss Emma Louise Konantz," 3.
23 Benton, "Turning a Gay Hobby into a Full-Time Job."
24 Wimsatt, *Chinese Shadow Shows*, 4.
25 Benton, "Turning a Gay Hobby into a Full-Time Job."
26 Ibid.
27 PBC, Red Gate program, Beijing, 1940.
28 Pauline Benton, "Turning a Gay Hobby into a Full-Time Job."
29 Ibid. and PBC, CCSP, ii.
30 Wimsatt, *Chinese Shadow Shows*, 33.
31 Benton, "Turning a Gay Hobby into a Full-Time Job"; PBC, CCSP, 69.
32 Wimsatt, *Chinese Shadow Shows*, 39. Jo Humphrey suggested to me that the troupe that came to perform in Emma Konantz's garden was possibly that of Li Tuochen himself. It is certainly possible, but given that Li spoke fluent English and that Li's red silk stage was far more

elaborate than the one set up in Emma's courtyard, it seems more likely that it was another company that performed for her that evening.

33 Jo Humphrey interview with author, 16 January 2010.
34 Benton, "Turning a Gay Hobby into a Full-Time Job."

CHAPTER FOUR

1 Schisgall, "International House: Bulwark against War," 24–6, 54–6.
2 Ibid.
3 Tchen, *New York before Chinatown*, 74.
4 Ibid., 58–9.
5 Yoshihara, *Embracing the East*, 65.
6 "Sightseers See Chinatown Murder," *New York Times*, 22 November 1920.
7 Schisgall, "International House: Bulwark against War," 24–6, 54–6.
8 Ibid.
9 "Dr. Guy Potter Benton," *Hamilton Daily News*, 29 June 1927; *Hamilton Evening Journal*, 12 June 1926; "Guy Potter Benton, Educator, Is Dead," *New York Times*, 30 June 1927.
10 While the 1930 United States Census shows Mary Benton living in Minneapolis and employed as clerk in a furnishings business, Pauline is nowhere to be found. There is no record known to me of Pauline working anywhere but at International House, 1927–33, and in the early 1960s as clerk in a Carmel tourist shop. In between these years she was touring her shadow theatre company around North America and donating most or all of her earnings from many performances to the Chinese relief effort. This begs the question of how she supplemented her performance income. My assumption is that after her father's death, Pauline stopped working at International House and was able to found Red Gate and tour without need of a day job because she was living off an inheritance from him. As a single woman who had no obligations other than to her fellow Red Gate members, and was living in a small apartment that was more a storage space for her figures and sets than a residence for herself, Pauline's expenses were likely reasonable, making it more possible to live off an annuity. But we do not know for sure.
11 "Chinese Exhibit," *Hamilton Daily News*, 14 December 1923.
12 Schisgall, "International House: Bulwark against War," 25–6.
13 Benton, "Turning a Gay Hobby into a Full-Time Job."
14 Ibid. See also Roberts, "Where Shadows Come to Life," in which Roberts says that Pauline organized her first shadow play performance

in 1930 at International House and Harry Harris, "More Than a Thousand Years before Donald Duck and Bugs Bunny," relating how Pauline said to Harris, "When I was on the activities staff at International House in New York, I showed the puppets to a Chinese friend. She immediately suggested we put on a play."

15 There are no colour photographs known to me of Pauline with her stage; only Wan-go Weng's 1947 colour film, which shows Pauline with it in performance. For a photograph of Li Tuochen's stage, see Wimsatt, *Chinese Shadow Shows*, 7.

16 Benton, "Turning a Gay Hobby into a Full-Time Job." By "interpreter," Pauline means "go-between"; Li spoke English.

17 Wimsatt, *Chinese Shadow Shows*, 32.

18 Power, *The Puppet Emperor*, 48.

19 PBC, CCSP, 19.

20 Pauline's notes (archived in PBC) describe Li telling her that he had performed for the Guangxu emperor (Zaitian), who died in 1908, "in Tientsin," which does not seem likely. It is possible that Pauline misheard "Xuantong emperor" – that is, Puyi – who did live in Tianjin after he and his court were ejected from the Forbidden City in 1924.

21 Chen, *Chinese Shadow Theatre*, 50–4, 56. In CCSP, 7–8, Pauline later admitted to doubting the Huang Suzhi legend.

22 Chen, *Chinese Shadow Theatre*, iii.

23 Ibid., 2.

24 Wimsatt, *Chinese Shadow Shows*, 33. See Gissenwehrer and Kaminski, *In der Hand der Höllenfürsten sind wir alle Puppen*, 40, where Professor Hao Suming notes that Dong Fuxiang, the Muslim general whose troops were involved in the Boxer Uprising in the summer of 1900, brought shadow players to entertain the Empress Dowager Cixi for her birthday. However, Li Tuochen reported to Genevieve Wimsatt that Cixi was not as fond of shadow theatre as most other members of the Manchu court. The dowager is known to have had a consuming interest in opera, to the degree that she staged photographs of herself in settings and costumes referencing operatic staples such as *The Peony Pavilion* and *The White Snake*. See Hogge, "Piety and Power."

25 Wimsatt, *Chinese Shadow Shows*, 29. Pauline Benton's notes from 1936 (in PBC) describe Li Tuochen's "Christmas Play" as follows:
Enter Wise Man on horse. Star appears in sky. Follow star.
Enter other 2 [Wise Men].
Enter 3 shepherds.
Enter Joseph and Mary.
Exeunt.
Enter Wise Men, following star.
Set up dragon screen.

Enter 4 guards.
Enter wicked governor.
Three Wise Men come looking for child. Exeunt.
Enter 3 walking, following star. Exeunt and reenter. Exeunt.
Sheep and shepherd enter.
Angel appears on cloud. All exeunt.
Enter Mary and Joseph and exeunt.
Innkeeper. They come to him. Tells no place but can go to barn.
Enter Joseph and Mary in barn. Mary exits. Enter heavenly hosts on
   cloud. Mary enters with baby and puts in crib.
Three Wise Men enter. Kneel before baby. Present gifts. Exeunt.
Angel enters on cloud. Gives warning to leave and they flee, Mary
   and baby riding on a donkey.

26 PBC, CCSP, iv.
27 Letter from Lee Ruttle to Paul McPharlin, 2 March 1932, and from
    from McPharlin to Ruttle, 9 March 1932 (Detroit Institute of Arts);
    and Howard, *Paul McPharlin and the Puppet Theatre*, 114. The Benton-
    McPharlin correspondence illustrates where Paul and Pauline were
    similar and where they were not. A letter Pauline wrote to McPharlin
    on 1 August 1935 (Detroit Institute of Arts) made it clear that she
    worked with shadow *figures*, not *puppets*, and would not appear in
    McPharlin's *Puppetry* yearbook in 1936. This is an early example of
    Pauline's effort to stabilize the imagery and terminology for shadow
    theatre in America and, above all, mark it off from puppetry.
28 Scott, *Mei Lan-Fang, Leader of the Pear Garden*, 29.
29 Tchen, *New York before Chinatown*, 86–90.
30 Ibid., 123.
31 Nancy Guy, "Brokering Glory for the Chinese Nation," *Comparative
    Drama*, Fall-Winter 2001–02, 377–92.
32 Scott, *Mei Lan-Fang, Leader of the Pear Garden*, 108. See also Yoshi-
    hara, *Embracing the East*, 30, 59; and Wimsatt, *Chinese Shadow
    Shows*, 31. This appears to be the only time Mei Lanfang actually
    made such comments about shadow theatre and Beijing Opera. In her
    1922 book, *Studies in the Chinese Drama*, Kate Buss writes: "Puppet
    shows are a form of amusement common to many nations and to
    which certain writers attribute the beginning of the Chinese drama"
    (24). And in a 1935 article for *Theatre Arts Monthly*, Sergei Eisenstein
    pointed out: "The Chinese actor has for a long time … retained the
    name of a 'live puppet'" (*Theatre Arts Monthly*, October 1935, 762).
33 Scott, *Mei Lan-Fang*, 7; Forty-Ninth Street Theatre program, matinée
    performance of Mei Lanfang, 17 February 1930 (author's collection).
34 Hayter-Menzies, *Mrs. Ziegfeld: The Public and Private Lives of Billie
    Burke*, 29.

35 Stephen Kaplin email to author, 14 August 2011.

36 Wimsatt, *Chinese Shadow Shows*, 40.

37 Program for "Made In America: The Music of William Russell," Percussive Arts Society International Convention, Philadelphia, PA, 7 November 1990.

38 Ibid.; and William Russell's score for *The White Snake*, circa 1936, in the Pauline Benton Collection, Chinese Theatre Works. The PBC also contains a concert program from 19 May 1935, in which the Helen Parker Ford Studios presents Russell in a concert of "Authentic Confusion Temple Music" – the orthography may be a typo, but it could also describe Russell's light-hearted attitude toward his ability to simulate music of China.

39 MSS 500, William Russell Jazz Collection, 1905–92 , Historic New Orleans Jazz Collection, New Orleans, Louisiana.

40 United States Census 1920.

41 Dr Jeffery Kennedy of Arizona State University, email to author on 20 May 2010, on the history of the Provincetown Players.

42 United States Marine Corps muster rolls, November 1929.

43 On the outbreak of the Second World War, Ruttle was also to distinguish himself as a gunner in the Pacific theatre of battle. He parlayed this experience into a well-received novel with a Second World War setting, *The Private War of Dr. Yamada* (San Francisco Book Company: Stein & Day, 1977). Ruttle was the most flamboyant of Pauline's assistants. Following Ruttle, in order of longevity with Red Gate, were Arvo Wirta, Clarence Jordan, Louis James, Don Summers, and Bill Boyer.

44 The name that was placed over the proscenium of Pauline's red silk stage was "Hong men ying xi" (Red Gate Shadow Show). A New York business licence in the Pauline Benton Collection, dated 4 February 1935, registers the company under the name "The Red Gate Shadow Players." By February 1942 the name was changed to "The Red Gate Players" (documentation in PBC).

CHAPTER FIVE

1 Yoshihara, *Embracing the East*, 78.

2 Princess Der Ling, *Lotos Petals*, 9. See also Grant Hayter-Menzies, *Imperial Masquerade*, 316–19.

3 Yoshihara, *Embracing the East*, 78.

4 Located where MaxMara and Calypso are situated (as of 2011). Mary Konantz Benton died on 15 August 1947 and was buried beside her husband in the Miami University Plot in Oxford, Ohio (Oxford Cemetery records).

5 *Life Magazine*, 10 November 1947.

6 "Seventh Regiment Gives Unique Ball," *New York Times*, 5 November 1933.

7 Ibid.

8 Ibid.

9 "Exotic Pomp Marks Beaux-Arts Ball," *New York Times*, 20 January 1934.

10 Ibid.; *New Yorker*, 23 October 1943. Fully satisfying New Yorkers' taste for style over substance, Kingsley later consulted with decorators to design "Zodiac rooms" for astrologically obsessed clients. Regarding Princess Der Ling, it is interesting to note that she had a connection to the White Snake legend. In 1903, as a newly installed lady-in-waiting to the Empress Dowager Cixi, Der Ling and her sister Rong Ling (Madame Dan Paochao) were photographed along with the dowager on a barge on Zhonghai Lake in Beijing as "Punt Fairies," wearing "the costume dresses of Bai Suzhen, who is the white snake that has taken on human form." The dowager posed as a manifestation of Avalokitesvara, bodhisattva of compassion. See Hogge, "Piety and Power."

11 "Shadow Puppets at Birmingham School," *Tyrone Herald*, 24 February 1934.

12 Howard, *Paul McPharlin*, 44.

13 PBC, Tony Sarg advertisement for *The Chinese Willow Plate Story*.

14 "Shadow Puppets at Birmingham School," *Tyrone Herald*, 24 February 1934.

15 PBC, Reviews listed in Red Gate Shadow Players program circa 1936.

16 Lee Ruttle, "Some Appearances of the Red Gate Shadow Players," 1936, Franklin Delano Roosevelt Presidential Library, Hyde Park, NY. A younger son of Baron Clifford of Chudleigh, Sir Bede Clifford was governor of the Bahamas from 1932 to 1937 and was famed for leading the first British expedition across the Kalihari Desert. He was also renowned for his performance on the tennis court and golf links. His American wife Alice was the daughter of a Midwest banker. See *Montreal Gazette*, 8 May 1937.

17 Tchen, *New York Before Chinatown*, 105–7.

18 Ross Russell, *Door to Door Collecting in the 1930s: The Reminiscences of Ross Russell*, http://research.hrc.utexas.edu:8080/hrcxtf/view?docId=ead/00233.xml accessed 17 January 2013; *Berkeley Daily Gazette*, 7 April 1937.

CHAPTER SIX

1 "Many Ohioans in Chinese Danger Zone," *Portsmouth Daily Times*, 25 March 1927.

2 Welland, *A Thousand Miles of Dreams*, 185.
3 Blofeld, *The Wheel of Life*, 94, 104.
4 Hale, *Indomitably Yours*, 81–2.
5 Lum, *Gangplanks to the East*, 171–4.
6 Holland. *Fascinating Women.*
7 Lum, *Gangplanks to the East*, 171–4.
8 Laurent Hénin email to author, 15 February 2011.
9 Wimsatt, *Chinese Shadow Shows*, xvi.
10 Ibid.
11 Ibid., xvi-xvii.
12 Ibid., 33.
13 "Report of the Death of an American Citizen," form no. 192, American Foreign Service, 8 January 1936, attached to letter from the Mutual Benefit Life Insurance Company of Newark, New Jersey, to the Secretary of State, Washington, DC, from J. Lawrence Boggs, Supervisor of Claims (11 January 1936).
14 Ibid.
15 Ch'en, "In Memory of Miss Emma Louise Konantz," 1.
16 Benton, "Turning a Gay Hobby into a Full-Time Job."
17 Ibid.
18 PBC, CCSP, 22.
19 "Notes from Mr. Lee," 30 May 1936. Pauline mentions that "Mr. Ch'en Hung-shen, assistant librarian at Yenching University took great interest in locating for me any articles in Chinese periodicals which had been recently written on the shadow plays." He also located for her interviews that had been conducted with Li Tuochen. See PBC, CCSP, vii. The seriousness of Pauline's research and her efforts to uphold high standards of scholarship can be seen in the bibliography she added to the manuscript of "China's Colored Shadow Plays." She clearly went to whatever lengths it took to make sure her data was correct. Uncertain of how to provide information in an article on the Luanzhou shadow theatre written by Gu Jiejang (whom she knew as Ku Chieh-kang), Pauline contacted Arthur Hummel, chief of the Orientalia Division at the Library of Congress, who corrected the entry for her (and who had served as one of the references for her White House performance in December 1936). Cecilia S.L. Zung, found at the end of the bibliography, had been a close friend of Pauline's since her college days at Miami University. (The German texts and George Kin Leung's biography/performance program for Mei Lanfang's Broadway performances are still in Chinese Theatre Works' Pauline Benton Collection.)
    BIBLIOGRAPHY – CHINESE SHADOW PLAYS AND DRAMA: Arlington, L.C., *Chinese Drama*, Kelly and Walsh, Shanghai, 1930; Arlington, L.C, and Acton, Harold, *Famous Chinese Plays*, Vetch, Peking,

1937; China Institute in America, Mei Lan-fang, Souvenir Program
of His American Tour, 1929; Chu Chia-chien, *The Chinese Theatre*,
translated from the French by James A. Graham, John Lane, London,
1922; Chu Yu, Series of newspaper interviews with Mr Lee T'uo
Ch'en regarding Chinese shadow plays (in Chinese) in the *World
Daily News*, beginning November 1935; Grübe, Wilhelm, and Krebs,
Emil, *Chinesische Schattenspiele*, herausgegeben und eingeleitet von
Berthold Laufer, Royal Bavaria Academy of Science, Munich, 1915;
Hart, Henry H., *The West Chamber* (translation of a Chinese Drama),
Oxford University Press, New York, 1936; Jacob, Georg, *Die chinesis-
che Schattentheater*, Germany, 1933; Jacob, Georg, *Geschichte des
Schattentheater in Morgen- und Abendland*, Hanover, Germany, 1925;
Kao Yung-ch'ian, "A Survey of the Luanchow Shadow Play" (in Chi-
nese), *Dramatic Magazine* 3, no. 11, Nov. 1934; Ku-Chieh-kang,
"Luanchow Shadow Plays" (in Chinese), *Wen-hsueh Magazine* 2, No.
6, p. 1226 ff. (illustrated); March, Benjamin, *Chinese Shadow-figure
Plays and Their Making*, Puppetry Imprints (Paul L. McPharlin),
Detroit, 1938; Mills, Winifred H., and Dun, Louise M., *Shadow Plays
and How to Produce Them*, Doubleday-Doran, New York, 1938;
T'ang Chi-hung, "A Study of the Luanchow Shadow Plays" (in Chinese), *Monthly Dramatic Magazine* 3, No.11, Nov. 1934; Genevieve
Wimsatt, *Chinese Shadow Shows*, Harvard University Press, Cambridge, 1936; Zucker, A.E., *The Chinese Theatre*, Little Brown,
Boston, 1935; Zung, Cecilia S.L., *Secrets of the Chinese Drama*, Kelly
and Walsh, Shanghai, 1937.
20 PBC, "Notes from Mr. Lee," 30 May 1936.
21 PBC, Pauline Benton notes.
22 Ibid.
23 Kaplin and Kuang-Yu Fong, "A Life in the Shadows," *Puppetry International* 16 (Fall and Winter 2004). The romanization for the Lu family names derives from Kaplin and Fong.
24 Shadow figure collection of Maureen McGuire, daughter of Polly
McGuire, which was shared with the author, August 2010, and exam-
ined by him at Chinese Theatre Works in May 2011.
25 Kaplin and Fong, "A Life in the Shadows"; author interview with
Stephen Kaplin, 14 August 2010.
26 Benton, "Turning a Gay Hobby into a Full-Time Job."
27 PBC, CCSP, 14.
28 Ibid., 14, 16; Benton, "Turning a Gay Hobby into a Full-Time Job."
29 Ibid.
30 PBC, CCSP, 16–17.
31 Ibid.
32 Ibid., 14.

33 Ibid., 45.
34 Ibid., 16.
35 Pauline Benton Collection photographs, Chinese Theatre Works.
36 Idema, *The White Snake and Her Son: A Translation of the Precious Scroll of Thunder Peak*, xv, 9 and 46. Regarding Fa Hai's taking the White Snake away on a cloud, see 82–3. The Thunder Peak pagoda was restored in 2003 and has become a shrine of sorts for the White Snake legend.
37 Ship's manifest.

CHAPTER SEVEN

1   Green, *Te Ata: Chickasaw Storyteller, American Treasure*, xi, 125–6.
2   *White House has a long musical tradition*. See http://today.msnbc. msn.com/id/33384302 (accessed 17 January 2013): and The White House Historical Association, (http://www.whitehousehistory.org/ whha_timelines/timelines_musical-performances.html (accessed 17 January 2013).
3   *American Anthropologist*, new series, 38, no. 1 (1936).
4   Franklin Delano Roosevelt Presidential Library (FDRPL), Lee Ruttle letter, 29 May 1936; Edith Helm letter, 13 June 1936.
5   FDRPL, Red Gate program, 1936, and Lee Ruttle letter, 18 September 1936.
6   FDRPL, Lee Ruttle letter, 12 January 1936.
7   *Time* magazine, 2 October 1933.
8   FDRPL, Red Gate papers.
9   Michael Slatter, "A Portrait of William Russell," *Jazz Journal*, September 1959, 28–9.
10 Russell, *Door to Door Collecting in the 1930s*, http://research.hrc. utexas.edu:8080/hrcxtf/view?docId=ead/00233.xml, accessed 17 January 2013; Raeburn, *New Orleans Style and the Writing of American Jazz History*, 57.
11 The cigarette box is in the William Russell Jazz Collection, Historic New Orleans Jazz Collection, New Orleans, Louisiana.
12 Notes in Pauline Benton Collection; "The White Snake" (play), 89, 114, Chinese Theatre Works.
13 Alan Cook email to author, 24 February 2011.
14 PBC, Red Gate program, Beijing, 1940. Pauline's quote comes from CCSP, 51.
15 Wan-go Weng interview with author, 8 March 2010; Christy, "The Veneration of Ink: An Interview with Wan-go Weng," 73, and "Calmness of the Heart: Music in the Air," 74–83.
16 Wan-go Weng interview with author, 8 March 2010.

17 Ibid.
18 MMA program, 22 October 1970.
19 Ibid. and Idema, *The White Snake and Her Son*, xvi, n 8.
20 Wan-go Weng film, 1947. For Arvo Wirta, see *Honolulu Advertiser*, 4 March 1954.
21 PBC, Red Gate program, Beijing, 1940.
22 Roberts, "Where Shadows Come to Life."
23 Green, *The Triumph of Pierrot*, 16.
24 Stéphane Lam email to author, 21 October 2010.

CHAPTER EIGHT

1   Wong, "Parades, Pickets, Protests," 1.
2   "Chinatown Throng Aids War Refugees," *New York Times*, 18 June 1938.
3   Chang, *The Chinese in America: A Narrative History*, 223–4.
4   Benton, "Turning a Gay Hobby into a Full-Time Job."
5   Advertisement program for King Lan Chew, circa 1935, distributed by the Redpath Bureau, Chicago, IL, University of Iowa Libraries.
6   "Chinese Shadow Plays, Beautiful as Ancient Legend, Now Shown to Public to Aid War Victims of Nation," *New York World-Telegraph*, 15 February 1938.
7   James and Weller, *Treasure Island*, "The Magic City," 1939–1940, 3–15.
8   Ibid., 213.
9   Ibid.
10 Lillian Borghi, "Arts and Artists," *Reno Evening Gazette*, 6 May 1939.
11 Commissioner Jesse B. Cook, former chief of police, "San Francisco's Old Chinatown."
12 In 1940, Red Gate announced performances in a "new theatre" outside the alley at 868 Washington Street (1940 Red Gate performance leaflet, Maureen McGuire Collection).
13 Frankenstein, "Shadow Plays in a Chinatown Alley."
14 Ibid.
15 Ibid.
16 Miller and Lieberman, *Lou Harrison*, 52–3.
17 William Duckworth, *Talking Music*, 99.
18 Foley, "The Lou Harrison Collection," 189–90.
19 Miller and Lieberman, *Lou Harrison*, 53.
20 Cahill, *Fellowship At The Met*, 1953–54.
21 Bulletin of the MMA, 37, no. 2 (1942): 34–5.

22 *Christian Science Monitor*, 21 July 1943.
23 Ibid.
24 Ibid.
25 Jo Humphrey interview with author, 16 January 2010.

CHAPTER NINE

1 Chang, *The Chinese in America*, 242–4.
2 Ibid., 246–8.
3 Ibid., 248–52.
4 Thurston, *Enemies of the People*, 124–31.
5 Meng Zhaozhen interview with author in Beijing, 4 April 2008; Pattice Hughes emails to author, 25 January 2010
6 Ibid.
7 Gissenwehrer and Kaminski, *In der Hand der Höllenfürsten sind wir alle Puppen*, 11.
8 Han Suyin, *Phoenix Harvest*, 53. Not all Red Guards should be classed with the thugs who committed this kind of attack, wrote Han Suyin, who knew some in the 1970s "who risked their lives to protect people. No one talks about them but they are there," 151.
9 Thurston, *Enemies of the People*, 78.
10 Fong and Kaplin, "Indelible Spirits," 5–6.
11 Ibid.
12 Gissenwehrer and Kaminski, *In der Hand der Höllenfürsten sind wir alle Puppen*, 10–11 (author's translation).
13 Fong and Kaplin, "Indelible Spirits," 5–6.
14 Suyin, *Phoenix Harvest*, 41.
15 Program for "Made In America: The Music of William Russell," Percussive Arts Society International Convention, Philadelphia, PA, 7 November 1990.
16 *Honolulu Advertiser*, 4 March 1954.
17 Tchen, *New York Before Chinatown*, 23
18 Stephen Kaplin email to author, 14 August 2011.
19 Alan Cook email to author, 24 February 2011.
20 During the 1960s, Pauline lived in several different cottages in Carmel, one of them not far from Der Ling Lane – yet another connection to the Manchu princess.
21 "Chinese Shadow Play Showing P.G. Feast of Lanterns Feature," *Monterey Peninsula Herald*, 21 July 1958
22 Ibid., 20 December 1959; the sign is part of the Pauline Benton Collection, Chinese Theatre Works. A map of Carmel with data from . the town directories of 1960, 1962–63, and 1964, showing Pauline's

various residences until her death, was kindly furnished to me by Rose McLendon, Local History Librarian, of the Harrison Memorial Library in Carmel.

23 Hutchinson, "Storytellers of the Nation," 19–20.

24 Pauline Benton to Polly McGuire, 28 October 1946, Maureen McGuire Collection.

25 Pauline Benton to Polly McGuire, 16 July 1947, Maureen McGuire Collection.

26 Alan Cook knew of these "kits," so the idea of them had been spread beyond Pauline's immediate circle. (Alan Cook email to author, 24 February 2011).

27 Pauline Benton to Polly McGuire, 16 July 1947, Maureen McGuire Collection.

28 Pauline Benton to Polly McGuire, 8 February and 7 March 1969, Maureen McGuire Collection.

29 Pauline Benton to Polly McGuire, 8, 9, and 13 May 1969, Maureen McGuire Collection.

CHAPTER TEN

1 MMA program 22 October 1970.

2 Ibid.

3 Dandelet, "Shadow Woman," 51.

4 Kaplin and Fong, "A Life in the Shadows."

5 PBC, letter from Jack Walsh of Samuel French to Pauline Benton, 29 May 1941, and Benton to Frank J. Sheil, 22 July 1941. Though I searched the Benton Collection I could not locate a script for *The Chess Game.*

6 Foley, "The Lou Harrison Collection," 189–90.

7 Richard Dee interview with author, 10 April 2010.

8 Ibid.; Lou Harrison Archive, Special Collections, University of California, Santa Cruz.

9 Lou Harrison Archive.

10 PBC, CCSP, 49.

11 Lou Harrison Archive.

12 Richard Dee interview with author, 10 April 2010.

13 "Ojai Festivals Plan Brilliant Performances," *Star-News* (Ojai, CA), 12 May 1971; Twenty-fifth Annual Ojai Festival program for 27 May 1971, Richard Dee collection.

14 Alexander Fried, "White Snake Lady: A Shadow Fairy Tale," *San Francisco Chronicle,* 5 October 1971, 28; PBC, Red Gate Shadow Players' program, 5 October 1971, Richard Dee collection.

15 Alexander Fried, "White Snake Lady: A Shadow Fairy Tale," *San Francisco Chronicle*, 5 October 1971.
16 Lou Harrison Archive.
17 Rookaird, "Shimmering Shadows Capture Mystery of the East."
18 Lou Harrison Archive.
19 Jo Humphrey interview with author, 16 January 2010.
20 Ibid.
21 Ibid.
22 Kaplin and Fong, "Pauline Benton: A Life in Shadows"; letter from Dr John Karam to Jo Humphrey (undated), Jo Humphrey Collection.
23 Jo Humphrey interview with author, 16 January 2010.
24 Ibid.
25 Stephen Kaplin and Kuang-Yu Fong, "Bridge of Wings: Spanning Cultural Difference with Puppet Theatre." Paper presented at the UNIMA Festival in Chengdu, 2012.
26 Ibid.
27 Stephen Kaplin and Kuang-Yu Fong, "Three Women, Many Plays," Chinese Theatre Works, 2004.
28 Ibid.
29 Ibid.

CHAPTER ELEVEN

1 Kaplin, "The Eye of Light."
2 *New York Times*, 10 December 2010. Cui Yongping died on 9 May 2013.
3 Cui Yongping's book on shadow performance techniques, *Zenyang yan piying xi*, was published in 1987.
4 *New York Times*, 10 December 2010.
5 I was assisted at this interview by translator Qian Jiayin, who has my full gratitude for the two hours she spent helping me communicate with Mr Cui and Ms Wang.
6 Rocky Li, *Beijing This Month*, July 2010, 18. Dr Jacques Pimpaneau (b. 1937) is professor of Chinese language and literature at the Institut national des langues et civilisations orientales. In 1971 he founded the Kwok On Museum in Paris, dedicated to the popular arts and culture of Asia, including shadow theatre.
7 Rocky Li, *Beijing This Month*, July 2010, 18.
8 Rollins, *A Year in Shadows*, author biography; Annie K. Rollins email to author, 10 January 2012.
9 Rollins email to author, 10 January 2012.
10 Rollins, *A Year in Shadows*, *Lost and Found*; Rollins email to author, 10 January 2012.

11 Rollins email to author, 10 January 2012.
12 Rollins, *A Year in Shadows*.
13 Rollins email to author, 10 January 2012.
14 Rollins, *A Year in Shadows*, *The End of the Line*, posted 8 March 2011, http://annierollins.wordpress.com/2011/03 (accessed 17 January 2013.
15 Rollins email to author, 10 January 2012.

APPENDIX

1 GHM: Buying and freeing captive animals was a meritorious deed Buddhists were expected to perform regularly.
2 Sometimes called the "Blue Snake" or the "Green Snake," since the Chinese word "Ch'ing" means bluish or greenish black.
3 The Thunder Pagoda.
4 The Red Gate Players.
5 GHM: In "China's Colored Shadow Plays" (hereafter CCSP), Pauline draws similarities between Wei T'o and the King of Heaven (Li Tien-wang): "Generalissimo of the Twenty-six Celestial officers and Grand Marshall of the Skies … The red painted face indicates courageous and upright character" (CCSP, 38).
6 A young man who has passed his examinations (equivalent to PhD) is always referred to as a "Chuang-Yuan"; GHM: *a zhuang yuan* was a scholar who came in first in the imperial exams.
7 A T'ang Dynasty artist and poet (A.D. 699–759), famed for his landscape paintings.
8 Literally, "Little Black One."
9 GHM: Possibly derived from the proverb "If you stand straight, you need not fear a crooked shadow." The original Chinese, "*xin zheng bu pa ying xie*" ("if one's heart is straight then there is no need to fear that one's shadow will be slanted") uses the same character for shadow as *piyingxi*.
10 A sacred mountain in Szechuan Province.
11 GHM: A betrothed couple always had their horoscopes and the characters in their names compared for compatibility.
12 GHM: Cicadas are a symbol of immortality, while plum blossom connotes both virginity and sexual pleasure; the bedspread on a bridal bed was called "Plum Blossom Cover." See Eberhard, *A Dictionary of Chinese Symbols*, 239–40.
13 "The Way," as taught by Lao Tzu, the founder of Taoism.
14 Emblem of marriage.
15 The two Snakes have power over the water elements, including wind and rain.

16 Emblem of perseverance. GHM: The original Chinese refers rather to one who accidentally reveals his true identity.

17 According to the Chinese, the moon is inhabited by a hare, which pounds out the Elixir of Life.

18 GHM: "Little White One."

19 GHM: The Old Man under the Moon fastened a red thread around couples destined for marriage.

20 Characters from the famous Chinese drama, "The Western Chamber." Chang Ch'un-jui was a youth who met a Mrs Ts'ui and her beautiful daughter Ying-ying in a monastery. Mrs Ts'ui promised him her daughter's hand in marriage if he would drive the bandits out of the country. She failed to keep her word, however, at which point, Hung-niang, a vivacious maid-servant, arranged secret trysts between the two lovers.

21 A range of mountains in Szechuan Province, home of the "Fairy of Wu-shan," popular in romantic allusions.

22 Literally "Terrace of Romance." GHM: The night was divided into five watches.

23 Reminiscent of the early times when live horses were sacrificed to the gods. Under the T'ang Emperor, Ming Huang (A.D. 713–756) paper horses were substituted.

24 The Moon Goddess.

25 When the Han Emperor Wu-ti was asked if he would like to marry a certain princess, he replied, "If I could claim her, I would enshrine her in a golden chamber."

26 Refers to the popular romantic legend, "The Cowherd and the Weaving Maid." The story is told that certain stars near the Milky Way are weaving maidens who spend their time weaving and spinning. Every year, it was their custom to visit the earth to wash their silks in the streams. On one such journey, the Seventh Maiden, the most beautiful of them all, became enamoured with a poor cowherd and remained on earth as his wife, where they lived happily until she was found by the Western Mother [GHM: Xi Wangmu, the Queen Mother of the West, one of the most powerful deities of Taoism and dispenser of immortality] and brought back to Heaven. When the cowherd tried to follow her, the Western Mother drew a line across the sky to separate them. This was the Silver River (Milky Way). Once a year, on the 7th of August, it is said that all the magpies in the world come together to form a bridge that the two lovers may meet.

27 A monk's name, meaning "Sea of Learning." GHM: It would be more accurate to read Fa Hai's name as meaning "Sea of the dharma" (Buddhist law).

28 When a supernatural being feels the surging of blood in his heart, he

recognizes a foreboding of evil. By counting on his fingers, he determines the cause.

29 Head of the Literati. GHM: A *zhuang yuan* had received the highest score in the imperial examinations and was thus eligible for appointment to high office by the emperor.

30 The Fifth Day of the Fifth Moon. Also known as the "Dragon Boat Festival."

31 Refers to the time when he rescued her from the market. GHM: In Chinese belief, destiny played a large part in bringing two people together who wished to be married.

32 The Star God of Literature. GHM: Same as Kwei-Hsing.

33 The Queen Mother of the Western Heavens (in Chinese, Hsi Wang Mu), whose abode is believed to be in the K'un Lun Mountains of Chinese Turkestan. The peaches of Immortality, which ripen once every three thousand years, grow in her magic orchard.

34 Meaning Wei T'o.

35 A popular God of Literature, worshipped with Wen Ch'ang, who is the official God of Literature. GHM: Kwei-Hsing (Keuixing) and Wen-chang (Wenchang) are the same god.

36 Hsü Hsien's sister.

37 Emblem of love and affection and symbol of feminine beauty.

38 Emblem of the marital state.

39 Emblem of connubial happiness.

40 Lei Feng-t'a [Lei-feng t'a] (Leifengta, the Thunder Pagoda on West Lake in Hangzhou).

SOURCES

Primary Sources

Pauline Benton Collection, Chinese Theatre Works, Long Island City, NY
    Includes PB's unpublished manuscripts:
    "Chinese Colored Shadow Plays"
    "The White Snake"
Detroit Institute of Arts, Detroit, MI
    Pauline Benton correspondence with Paul McPharlin
Lou Harrison Archive, Special Collections, University of California,
    Santa Cruz
    Lou Harrison Notebooks
Konantz-Benton-Minnich Collection of Oriental Art, Saint Paul Art
    Center, Saint Paul, MN
Maureen McGuire Collection
    Pauline Benton correspondence with Polly McGuire
Minnich Family Collection
Alan K. Rome, Family Archives
Franklin Delano Roosevelt Presidential Library, Hyde Park, NY
    Red Gate papers
United States Government Archives, United States Department of State,
    Washington, DC

Interviews

Alan Cook
Cui Yongping and Wang Shuqin
Richard Dee
Kuang-Yu Fong
Laurent Hénin
Jo Humphrey
Stephen Kaplin

Stéphane Lam
Maureen McGuire
Meng Zhaozhen
Conrad Minnich
Annie Katsura Rollins
Wan-go Weng

Newspapers and Journals

Fredericksburg News (Fredericksburg, IA)
Globe and Mail (Toronto, ON)
Guardian (UK)
Hamilton Daily News (Hamilton, OH)
Hamilton Evening Journal (Hamilton, OH)
Honolulu Advertiser (Honolulu, HI)
Monterey Peninsula Herald (Monterey, CA)
Montreal Gazette (Montreal, QC)
Morning Herald (Hagerstown, MD)
New York Post (New York, NY)
New York Times
Olean Times-Herald (Olean, NY)
St Louis Post-Dispatch (St Louis, MO)
Star-News (Ojai, CA)
Times and Daily News Leader (Burlingame, CA)
Tyrone Daily Herald (Tyrone, PA)
Union Bulletin (Walla Walla, WA)
Westfield Leader (Westfield, NJ)

Film

Chen, Dr Fan Pen Li. Videotapes made in China of shadow carving and
    performances: *Shadow Puppet Making and Performance* (1998), *The
    Temple of Guanyin"* (filmed in Bidu Village, Xiaoyi County, Shanxi
    Province in 1996), and *Nanyue Shadows* (2008)
Chinese Shadow Play [motion picture], China Film Enterprises of Amer-
    ica, Inc., Wan-go Weng, director, 1947 (courtesy of Askwith Media
    Library, University of Michigan)
Thomas, Gustavo. *Wuzhen (II): A Chinese Shadow Shadow Puppet
    experience.* http://gustavothomastheatre.blogspot.com/2007/05/wuzhen-
    ii-chinese-shadow-puppet.html.

Books and Articles

Acton, Harold. *Peonies and Ponies*. London: Chatto & Windus, 1941
Aisin-Gioro, Henry Puyi. *From Emperor to Citizen*. Translated by (W.J.F. Jenner.). Beijing: Foreign Languages Press, 2002
Banham, Martin. *Cambridge Guide to Theatre*. London: Cambridge University Press, 1992
Benton, Pauline. *The Red Gate Players Introduce the Actors and Plays of the Chinese Shadow Theatre*. Beijing: Lotus Court Publications, 1940.
– "Turning a Gay Hobby into a Full-Time Job." *Christian Science Monitor*, 2 September 1941
– "Old Peking in Shadow Play." *Christian Science Monitor*, 12 February 1944
Blofeld, John. *The Wheel of Life*. Boston: Shambala Press, 1978
Bordages, Asa. "Chinese Shadow Plays, Beautiful as Ancient Legend, Now Shown to Public to Aid War Victims of Nation." *New York World-Telegram*, 15 February 1938
Borghi, Lillian. "Art and Artists." *Reno Evening Gazette*, 6 May 1939
Bredon, Juliet. *Peking*. Shanghai: Kelly and Walsh, 1931
Breuer, Hans. *Columbus Was Chinese: Discoveries and Inventions of the Far East*. New York: McGraw-Hill, 1972
Bronson, Bennet. "Berthold Laufer." *Fieldiana* (Chicago). Field Museum of Natural History, new series no. 36, 30 September 2003
Cahill, James. *Fellowship at the Met, 1953–54*. http://jamescahill.info/the-writings-of-james-cahill/responses-a-reminiscences/146-24fellowship-at-the-met-1953-54- (accessed 17 January 2013)
Chang, Iris. *The Chinese in America: A Narrative History*. New York: Penguin, 2004
Chen, Fan Pen Li. *Chinese Shadow Theatre*. Montreal & Kingston: McGill-Queen's University Press, 2007
Chen, Jack, ed. *Folk Arts of New China*. Beijing: Foreign Languages Press, 1954.
Ch'en, Pauline. "In Memory of Miss Emma Louise Konantz," translated by Liu Maoling. *Ta Kung Pao (Dagong Bao)*, 13 January 1936
China Institute in America. *Chinese in America: Stereotyped Past, Changing Present*, ed. Loren W. Fessler. New York: Vantage Press, 1983
Christy, Anita. "The Veneration of Ink: An Interview with Wan-go Weng" and "Calmness of the Heart: Music in the Air – The Flavour of Wan-go Weng." *Orientations*, April 2007
Cohen, Alvin P. "Documentation Relating to the Origins of the Chinese Shadow-Puppet-Theatre." *Asia Major* 13, no.1 (2000): 84–108
Cook, Jesse B. "San Francisco's Old Chinatown," *San Francisco Police*

and Peace Officers' Journal. online at http://www.sfmuseum.org/hist9/
cook.html (accessed 17 January 2013)

Crossley, Pamela Kyle. *Orphan Warriors: Three Manchu Generations and
the End of the Qing World.* Princeton: Princeton University Press, 1991

Dandelet, Lucile Fessenden. "Shadow Woman." *National Retired Teachers
Association Journal,* March–April 1976

Davenport, William. "Chinese Shadow Plays Found Superior to 3D."
Honolulu Advertiser, 19 February 1954

Der Ling, Princess. *Lotos Petals.* New York: Dodd, Mead, 1930

Duckworth, William. *Talking Music: Conversations with John Cage,
Philip Glass, Laurie Anderson, and Five Generations of American Experimental Composers.* Cambridge, MA: Da Capo Press, 1999.

Eberhard, Wolfram. *A Dictionary of Chinese Symbols: Hidden Symbols in
Chinese Life and Thought.* London: Routledge, 1988

Fei Shi (Emil Sigismund Fischer). *Guide to Peking and Its Environs.* Tianjin: Tianjin Press, 1924

Foley, Kathy. "The Lou Harrison Collection: Music and Puppetry East to
West." In *American Puppetry Collections.* Jefferson, NC: McFarland,
2004

Frankenstein, Alfred. "Shadow Plays in a Chinatown Alley." *San Francisco Chronicle,* 16 July 1939

Fried, Alexander. "A Shadow Fairy Tale." *San Francisco Examiner,* 5
October 1971

Ge, Congmin. "Photography, Shadow Play, Beijing Opera, and the First
Chinese Film." *Eras Journal* (Monash University), June 2008.

Gissenwehrer, Michael, and Gerd Kaminski. *In der Hand der Höllenfürsten sind wir alle Puppen: Grenzen und Möglichkeiten des chinesis-
chen Figurentheeaters der Gegenwart.* Munich: Herbert Utz Verlag
GmbH, 2008

Graham, Dorothy. *Through the Moon Door: The Experience of an American Resident in Peking.* London: Williams & Norgate, 1928

Green, Martin. *The Triumph of Pierrot: The Commedia dell'arte and the
Modern Imagination.* University Park, PA: Pennsylvania State University
Press, 1993

Green, Richard. *Te Ata: Chickasaw Storyteller, American Treasure.*
Norman, OK: University of Oklahoma Press, 2002

Hale, Hilda. *Indomitably Yours.* Victoria, BC: Hilda S. Hale, 1998

Hamm, Margherita Arlina. *Manila and the Philippines.* New York: F.T.
Neely, 1898

Han, Suyin (pseud). *Phoenix Harvest.* Chicago: Academy Chicago
Publishers, 1985

Harris, Harry. "More Than a Thousand Years before Donald Duck and
Bugs Bunny." *Philadelphia Evening Bulletin,* 25 October 1946

Hay, John, ed. *Boundaries in China*. London: Reaktion Books, 1997

Hayter-Menzies, Grant. *Imperial Masquerade: The Legend of Princess Der Ling*. Hong Kong: Hong Kong University Press, 2008.

– *Mrs. Ziegfeld: The Public and Private Lives of Billie Burke*. Jefferson, NC: McFarland, 2009

Helmer-Stalberg, Roberta. *China's Puppets*. San Francisco: China Books and Periodicals, 1984

Hoffman, Flora W. "Chinese Design to Be Widely Featured." *Christian Science Monitor*, 22 September 1942

Hogge, David. "Piety and Power: The Theatrical Images of Empress Dowager Cixi." *Trans Asia Photography Review*, Fall 2011

Holland, Evangeline. *Fascinating Women: Dr. Yamei Kiin*. http://beyond victoriana.com/2010/07/18/34-fascinating-women-dr-yamei-kin-guest-blog-by-sandrine-thomas (accessed 4 March 2012).

Howard, Ryan. *Paul McPharlin and the Puppet Theatre*. Jefferson, NC: McFarland, 2006

Humphrey, Jo. "Shadow Theatre in the Land of the Dragon," *Field Museum of Natural History Bulletin*, January 1984

– "A Brief History of the Yueh Lung Shadow Theatre, a.k.a. Gold Mountain Institute for Traditional Shadow Theatre," August 2011

Hutchinson, Louise. "Storytellers of the Nation." *Recreation*, Playground Issue (New York), April 1949

Idema, Wilt L. *The White Snake and Her Son: A Translation of the Precious Scroll of Thunder Peak with Related Texts*. Indianapolis: Hackett, 2009

James, Jack, and Earle Weller. *Treasure Island: 'The Magic City – The Story of the Golden Gate International Exposition*. San Francisco: Pisani Printing & Publishing, 1941

Kaplin, Stephen. "The Eye of Light." Paper presented at Puppetry and Postdramatic Performance: An International Conference on Performing Objects in the Twenty-first Century, University of Connecticut, 1–3 April 2011

Kaplin, Stephen, and Kuang-Yu Fong. "Pauline Benton: A Life in the Shadows." *Puppetry International* 16 (Fall and Winter 2004)

– *Three Women, Many Plays*. New York: Chinese Theatre Works, 2004

– *Bridges and Shadows*. New York: Chinese Theatre Works, 2005

– "Bridge of Wings: Spanning Cultural Differences with Puppet Theatre." Paper presented to the UNIMA festival in Chengdu, 2012

Kates, George N. *The Years That Were Fat: Peking, 1933–1940*. New York: Harper, 1952

Konantz, Dr Emma. "The Precious Mirror of the Four Elements: An Expression of Chinese Genius." *China Journal of Science and Arts*, July 1924

Kuang-Yu Fong and Stephen Kaplin. "Indelible Spirits: The Survival of
    Shadow Theatre in the Twentieth Century." *Puppetry International* 15
    (Spring and Summer 2004)
Lai, T.C., and Robert Mah. *The Jade Flute: The Story of Chinese Music*.
    New York: Schocken Books, 1985
La Motte, Ellen. *Peking Dust*. New York: Century Co., 1919
Latourette, Kenneth S. *Biographical Memoir of Berthold Laufer,
    1874–1934*. Washington: National Academy of Sciences, 1938
Laufer, Dr Berthold. *Oriental Theatricals*, Guide, Part 1. Chicago, Field
    Museum of Natural History, 1923
Li, Lillian M., Alison Dray-Novey, and Haili Kong. *Beijing: From Imperial
    Capital to Olympic City*. New York: Palgrave Macmillan, 2008
Li, Rocky. *Beijing This Month*, July 2010
Lin Yutang, *The Importance of Living*. New York: Reynal & Hitchcock,
    1937
Lum, Bertha. *Gangplanks to the East*. New York: Henkle-Yewdale House,
    1936
McCloskey, Alice Everett. Review of *Japanese Costume and the Makers of
    Its Elegant Tradition* by Helen Benton Minnich and Shojiro Nomura, in
    Journal of the American Oriental Society 86, no.4 (1966)
Mackerras, Colin. *Western Images of China*. Oxford University Press,
    2000
Meyer, Michael. *The Last Days of Old Beijing: Life in the Vanishing
    Backstreets of a City Transformed*. New York: Walker Books, 2008
Miller, George A. *Interesting Manila*. Manila: E.C. McCullough, 1919.
Miller, Leta E., and Frederic Lieberman. *Lou Harrison*. University of Illi-
    nois Press, 2006
Minnich, Helen Benton. "Mementos of an Imperial Palace." *Christian Sci-
    ence Monitor*, 18 December 1963
Power, Brian. "Many Ohioans in Chinese Danger Zone." *Portsmouth
    Daily Times* (Portsmouth, NH), 25 March 1987
– *The Puppet Emperor: The Life of Pu Yi, Last Emperor of China*. New
    York: Universe Publications, 1988
Raeburn, Bruce. *New Orleans Style and the Writing of American Jazz His-
    tory*. Ann Arbor: University of Michigan Press, 2009
Roberts, Bertrand. "Where Shadows Come to Life." *Los Angeles Times*,
    23 May 1937.
Rollins, Annie Katsura. *A Year in Shadows: A Chronicle of My Fulbright
    Fellowship Year Researching Chinese Shadow Puppetry*. http://annie
    rollins.wordpress.com/bio (accessed 17 January 2013).
Rookaird, Sandy. "Shimmering Shadows Capture Mystery of the East."
    Monterey Peninsula Herald, 3 March 1973
Saint Paul Art Center program for the Konantz-Benton-Minnich Collec-
    tion, Saint Paul, MN, 11 May 1967

Schisgall, Oscar. "International House: Bulwark against War." *Rotarian*,
   November 1968
Scott, A.C. *Mei Lan-Fang, Leader of the Pear Garden*. Hong Kong: Hong
   Kong University Press, 1959
Seton, Grace. *Chinese Lanterns*. London: Bodley Head, 1924
Shadow Figures of Asia from the Collection of Pauline Benton. St Paul,
   MN: Minnesota Museum of Art (22 October 1970)
Slatter, Michael. "A Portrait of William Russell." *Jazz Journal*, September
   1959
Strand, David. *Rickshaw Beijing: City, People, and Politics in the 1920s*.
   Berkeley: University of California Press, 1993
Taylor, Millicent. "Gaining Views of Other Lands Essential." *Christian
   Science Monitor*, 21 July 1943
Tchen, John Kuo Wei. *New York before Chinatown: Orientalism and the
   Shaping of American Culture, 1776–1882*. Baltimore: Johns Hopkins
   University Press, 2001
Terrill, Ross. *Madame Mao: The White-Boned Demon*. Palo Alto: Stan-
   ford University Press, 2000
Thurston, Anne F. *Enemies of the People: The Ordeal of the Intellectuals
   in China's Great Cultural Revolution*. Cambridge: Harvard University
   Press, 1988
United States Census. Records of Birth and Death, Customs and Immigra-
   tion. Washington, DC
Walter, Wilhelm P.O. *Das China von heute*. Frankfurt am Main, Societäts-
   Verlag, 1932
Warde, Frederick. *Fifty Years of Make-Believe*. New York: International
   Press Syndicate, 1920
Welland, Sasha Su-Ling. *A Thousand Miles of Dreams: The Journeys of
   Two Chinese Sisters*. Lanham, MD: Rowman & Littlefield, 2006
Wimsatt, Genevieve. *Chinese Shadow Shows*. Cambridge: Harvard
   University Press, 1937
Winchester, Simon. *The Man Who Loved China: The Fantastic Story of
   the Eccentric Scientist Who Unlocked the Mysteries of the Middle King-
   dom*. New York: Harper, 2008
Wines, Michael. "Puppet Masters Try to Bring Art out of the Shadows,"
   New York Times, 10 December 2010
Wong, K. Scott. "Parades, Pickets, Protests." *Humanities*, July/August
   2007
Yao, Weijie. "Artist Finds Audience for Shadow Puppets Abroad." *Beijing
   Today*, August 2011
Yoshihara, Mari. *Embracing the East: White Women and Orientalism*.
   Oxford: Oxford University Press, 2002.

INDEX

Acton, Harold, 70
Afong Moy, 67
American Museum of Natural History, 12, 15, 133, 143–4, 148
Anderson, Marian, 87

Backhouse, Sir Edmund Trelawny, 70
Baker University, 5
Barnum, P.T., 37
Beijing, xv, xviii, 4, 15, 23–6, 47, 69–70, 73, 103, 117, 159
Beijing Opera, xvi, 18, 21, 47, 49, 51, 75, 101, 121, 150
Beijing Shadow Play Troupe, 152, 154
Belmont, Alvina, 59, 63
Benton, Dr Guy Potter, xviii, 3, 10, 38
Benton, Mary Konantz, xviii, 3, 4, 60–1
Benton, Pauline: birth of, xviii, 5; builds shadow stage, 40–1; childhood travels of, 4; and "China's Colored Shadow Plays," 19, 45, 46, 132–3, 137–9, 142; death of, 142; first attempt at shadow performance, 39–40; first experience of shadow theatre, 30–5; founds Red Gate Shadow Players, 57;

love of theatre, 10; "Red Gate Studio," 126
Binondo (Manila's Chinatown), 7–9, 32
Black Snake, 98, 135–6, 137, 168, 169
Blofeld, John, 23, 69
Boettiger, Anna Roosevelt, 90
Boxer Uprising, 13, 17, 58
Broadway, 15, 31, 48–9, 53, 59, 107
Buck, Pearl S., 55, 60, 106
Bunraku (Japanese puppetry), 124
Burning of the Bamboo Grove, The, 32–4, 77–8, 111

Cabrillo Music Festival, 139
Cage, John, 52, 113
Callas, Maria, 47
Carmel-by-the-Sea, California, xv, 74, 126, 129
Carvojal, Carlos, 139
Chang Yen, 80, 82–4
Chaplin, Charlie, 47
Chen Ciaxin, Dr, 28, 80
Ch'en, Pauline, 29–30, 74
Chess Party, The, 133
Chew, King Lan (Caroline), 56–7, 106–7
Chiang Kai-shek, General, and Mme, 79, 87, 117, 122

OKANAGAN REGIONAL LIBRARY
3 3132 03778 5872